STUDIES IN THE EARLY HISTORY OF BRITAIN

General Editor: Nicholas Brooks

Latin and the Vernacular Languages in Early Medieval Britain

Papers delivered to the fifth annual St John's House Symposium

Latin and the Vernacular Languages in Early Medieval Britain

EDITED BY

NICHOLAS BROOKS

LEICESTER UNIVERSITY PRESS

1982

First published in 1982 by Leicester University Press
First published in 1982 in the United States of America
by Humanities Press, Inc., Atlantic Highlands, N.J. 07716
and also distributed by them in North America

Designed by Douglas Martin
Set in 'Monophoto' Ehrhardt
Printed in Great Britain by BAS Printers Limited
Over Wallop, Hampshire
Bound by The Pitman Press, Bath

British Library Cataloguing in Publication Data

Latin and the vernacular languages in early medieval
Britain.—(Studies in the early history of Britain)
1. Latin language, Medieval and Modern—Great Britain.
I. Brooks, Nicholas II. Series
477 PA2896

ISBN 0-7185-1209-X

CONTENTS

ABBREVIATIONS

NOTE Places of publication are given only for works published outside the United Kingdom. Commonly used abbreviations such as *J.* for *Journal*, *Rev.* for *Review*, have been used; other abbreviations are listed below.

ASE	*Anglo-Saxon England*
BGDSL	*Beiträge zur Geschichte der Deutschen Sprache und Literatur*
BICS	*Bulletin of the Institute of Classical Studies*
BT	*An Anglo-Saxon Dictionary*, ed. J. Bosworth and T. N. Toller (1882–98)
BTS	T. N. Toller, *Supplement* to *BT* (1921), revised and enlarged by A. Campbell (1972)
CCSL	*Corpus Christianorum, Series Latina* (Turnhout, in progress)
CIL	*Corpus Inscriptionum Latinarum* (Berlin, in progress)
CLA	E. A. Lowe, *Codices Latini Antiquiores*, 9 vols. and *Supplement* (1934–71)
CPL	R. Cavenaile, *Corpus Papyrorum Latinorum* (Wiesbaden, 1958)
CSEL	*Corpus Scriptorum Ecclesiasticorum Latinorum* (Vienna, in progress)
DNB	*Dictionary of National Biography*
EETS	Early English Text Society
EHR	*English Historical Review*
FEW	W. von Wartburg, *Französisches Wörterbuch* (Paris, 1922—)
Förster, *Flussname Themse*	M. Förster, *Die Flussname Themse und seine Sippe, Sitzungsberichte der Bayerischen Akademie der Wissenschaften*, (phil.-hist.Abt., Jg 1941), Bd i
GPC	*Geiriadur Prifysgol Cymru* (in progress)
JRS	*Journal of Roman Studies*
Lewis, *Elfen Ladin*	H. Lewis, *Yr Elfen Ladin yn yr Iaith Gymraeg* (Cardiff, 1943)
LHEB	K. Jackson, *Language and History in Early Britain* (1953, repr. 1963, 1971)
Loth, *Mots latins*	J. Loth, *Les Mots latins dans les langages brittoniques, gallois, armoricain, cornique* (Paris, 1892)
LSJ	H. G. Liddell and R. Scott, *A Greek-English Lexicon* (revised by H. S. Jones, 1968)
MGH	Monumenta Germaniae Historica
OLD	C. T. Lewis and C. Short, *A Latin Dictionary* (1879)
Pedersen, *VGKS*	H. Pedersen, *Vergleichende Grammatik der Keltischen Sprachen*, 2 Bde (Göttingen, 1909–13)
P Oxy	*Oxyrrhyncus Papyri* (in progress)

PSI	*Papyri greci e Latini* [*Pubblicazioni della società italiana per la ricerca dei papiri greci e latini in Egitto*] (Florence, in progress)
REW	W. Meyer-Lübke, *Romanisches Etymologisches Wörterbuch* (3rd edn, Heidelberg, 1935)
RIB	R. G. Collingwood and R. P. Wright, *Roman Inscriptions of Britain*, I *Inscriptions on Stone* (1965)
RS	Rolls Series
SSCI	*Settimana di studio del centro italiano di studi sull' alto medioevo* (Spoleto, in progress)
TCBS	*Transactions of the Cambridge Bibliographical Society*
Väänänen, *ILV*	V. Väänänen, *Introduction au latin vulgaire* (2nd edn, Paris, 1967)

PLATES

PREFACE

The aim of the series, Studies in the Early History of Britain, is to promote works of the highest scholarship which open up virgin fields of study or surmount the barriers of traditional academic disciplines. As interest in the origins of our society and culture grows whilst scholarship yet becomes ever more specialized, inter-disciplinary studies are needed more urgently, not only by scholars but also by students and by laymen. The series will therefore include both research monographs and works of synthesis, and also collaborative studies of important themes by several scholars whose training and expertise has lain in different fields. Our knowledge of the early middle ages will always be limited and fragmentary, so progress will only be made if the work of the historian embraces that of the philologist, the archaeologist, the geographer, the numismatist, the art historian and the liturgicist – to name only the most obvious. The need to cross and to remove academic frontiers also explains the extension of the geographical range from that of the previous series of Studies in Early English History to include the whole island of Britain. The change would have been welcomed by the editor of the earlier series, the late Professor H. P. R. Finberg, whose pioneering work helped to inspire, or to provoke, the interest of a new generation of early medievalists in the relations of Britons and Saxons. The approach of the new series is therefore deliberately wide-ranging, and will seek to avoid being unduly insular. Early medieval Britain can only be understood in the context of contemporary developments in Ireland and on the continent.

It is true, even in early medieval studies, that historians and linguists have too often gone their separate ways. The Fifth Annual Symposium held at St John's House, the Centre for Advanced Historical Studies in the University of St Andrews, on 12 May 1979, was organised in the twin belief that there were major problems in the relationship of the vernacular languages of early medieval Britain with Latin that were ripe for reassessment, and that a new look would be of importance for historians as for linguists. We were not disappointed. The audience were privileged to hear and discuss four papers, each of which broke new ground, crossed the traditional boundaries of modern academic disciplines and pointed towards new areas of research. It has been my role, as chairman on that occasion, to fulfil the clear wish of the audience that the papers should reach a wider public. Our theme was, of course, a very wide one which could easily have formed the subject of a series of conferences. But one of the intentions of the Studies in the Early History of Britain is to find a place for substantial works that are longer than the traditional article or conference paper, but shorter than a normal monograph. Both the contribution of Dr Gratwick and the joint paper of Dr Lapidge and Dr Page would have fitted ill with the traditional limitations of academic journals. Rather than seek to extend this volume by soliciting other contributions on related themes, it seemed preferable to give them the space to set out their evidence in full.

The history of the Irish church in the early Middle Ages is, of course, so intimately bound up with that of the church in Britain that I welcomed Dr Wendy Davies's suggestion that she should approach the problems of church and state in early Ireland via semantics and from the viewpoint of an historian. Though, as she has taught us, we have to be cautious how we generalize about the 'Celtic church' in Britain, there can be no doubt that the changing concepts that she reveals had their influence on this side of the Irish Sea too. Above all her paper provides a contrasting example of the rich seams that can still be worked by scholars who will venture into the field of early medieval language with their eyes open.

This series does not seek controversy for its own sake, but revolutionary conclusions are apt to arise when a scholarly tradition built up from one side of an academic frontier is reassessed by a scholar trained in the other discipline. Adrian Gratwick approaches the linguistic problems of Roman and Dark Age Britain as a Latinist rather than as a Celticist. His interpretation of the evidence for the reception of Latin into the language of the Britons is therefore set firmly against the background of the linguistic development of the late Empire as a whole; he turns our received opinions on their head and in so doing provides a much more plausible interpretation of the social relations of Romans and Britons over some six centuries. Historians brought up on Professor K. Jackson's pioneering *Language and History in Early Britain* will need time to readjust their assumptions, but we must be grateful to Dr Gratwick for opening with scholarly vigour and with a graceful wit an area of study that has been neglected for too long. He has also drawn attention to the mass of fundamental work that still needs to be done. Research students take note.

Equally radical, if perhaps less revolutionary, is the approach to the glossed manuscripts of late-Saxon England pioneered here by Michael Lapidge and Raymond Page. Many historians of Anglo-Saxon England have, I suspect, hitherto avoided articles on glosses, since the focus of earlier work was often narrowly lexicographical. But in the hands of Lapidge and Page the glosses become a key to the intellectual heritage and attainments of the Anglo-Saxon monastic world. Both scholars draw attention to the many pitfalls in studying, editing and understanding the glossed manuscripts before they can be used to reconstruct the teaching or learning methods of English monasteries in the tenth and eleventh centuries. But they too have opened up a huge new field for study and have given us a foretaste of the conclusions that may be expected and some hints of the problems that will need to be resolved.

Finally the thanks of both editor and contributors are due to St Andrews University for providing hospitality and an ideal venue at St John's House for our gathering; also to Professor D. A. Bullough, the director of the House, who first suggested the theme for our deliberations and who was a source of much practical guidance and enthusiastic support at all times.

St Salvator's College, St Andrews, 20 August 1980 N. P. BROOKS

Latinitas Britannica: Was British Latin Archaic?

A. S. GRATWICK

Preliminary note on spelling and pronunciation

Where troublesome ambiguity would not arise, foreign words have been given simply in their proper spelling. But explicit distinction must often be made between the spelling of a word and its pronunciation, or between the symbol of a phoneme and its particular pronunciation(s). *Phonemes* are marked thus: /s/; the symbol so enclosed is generic, not phonetic. For while a phoneme may have a unique phonetic value, as Classical Latin /s/, always pronounced voicelessly, it may have allophones; so intervocalic Latin /w/, which over a long period some people pronounced as in English 'away' and others as in Spanish 'caballo'. Diamond brackets denote *spellings*, e.g. Welsh ⟨Emrys⟩. When specific reference is made to a Latin spelling, it is given in small capitals, e.g. ⟨QVINTVS⟩. Square brackets enclose a modified phonetic script representing approximate *pronunciations*. For the alphabet, see below. An asterisk emphasizes the hypothetical character of a form.

The modified phonetic alphabet here used is as follows:

Vowels: [a] [e] [i] [o] [u] short, roughly as in *putt pet pit pot put*.
[a:] [i:] [u:] long, roughly as in *farce peace tool*.
[e:] [o:] long, roughly as in French *gai, beau*.

In the cases of the long and short vowels [e(:)], [o(:)] a subscript dot means a closer and a cedilla a more open pronunciation: [lǫ:n] 'lawn', [gẹ:m] 'game' as pronounced in Yorkshire.

Stress-accents are noted when relevant with an acute accent: [ásinus].

Longum (¯) and *breve* (˘) are used to mark not the lengths of vowels but the weights of syllables, heavy and light.

Other vocalic signs: [ə] second vowel in *Arthur*, [å] affected pronunciation of *Bath*, [æ] as in *hat*, [ü] as in Fr. *tu*, all long if accompanied by a colon.

Semivowels: [w] as in *want, away*, [j] as in *yet*.

Consonants: [v] as in *vain*, [β] as in Sp. *caballo*, [f] as in *foot* or (both lips) as in *phew!*; [l] as in *less*, [m] as in *more*, [n] as in *no*, [ŋ] as in *sing*, [h] as in *he*, [χ] as in Ger. *nicht*, [s] as in *sing*, [z] as in *roses*, [ž] as in *pleasure*, [p] [t] [c] as in *plastics*, [b] [d] [g] as in *bulldogs*, [qᵘ] halfway between *keen* and *queen*, [l'], [n'] as in Sp. *caballo, España*.

Example: 'the Latin word written ⟨VITRVM⟩ and pronounced [witru(m)], later [βitru], still later [βẹdrọ] was borrowed into British as *[witron] whence Welsh ⟨gwydr⟩ 'glass' pronounced approximately [gwədr]'.

For the conventions of Welsh spelling the reader is referred to any Welsh grammar, e.g. J. Morris-Jones *A Welsh Grammar, Historical and Comparative* (1913).

I. INTRODUCTION: 'BRITISH LATIN' AS A CONCEPT

In his *Language and History in Early Britain* (Edinburgh, 1953, reprinted 1963, 1971) Professor K. H. Jackson drew on and combined evidence from many tricky fields in what has come to be seen as an authoritative work. These included not only his own special expertise, the ancient Celtic languages and the development in particular of British into Welsh, Cornish, and Breton, but also, for example, the study of Celtic, English, and Latin place-names, the epigraphical material from Roman and sub-Roman Britain, and current opinions about the character of continental spoken Latin, its relation to the Classical language, and the dating of its sound-changes. When first published the book was received with enthusiasm by historians, Celticists, and other students of language.[1] However, it all but escaped notice in journals dealing with Latin studies and Romance philology.[2] No-one, it seems, felt able to review a work of such ambitious synthesis and intricate argument and which offers little quarter to those who know no Celtic. This was a pity. The author's subject impinges on matters Roman and questions of Latinity throughout, and at many points it is the evidence of Latin loanwords in British which determines one's view of the development and separation of the descendant languages. In particular, the third chapter, 'Britons and Romans under the Empire' (*LHEB*, 76–121), together with the detailed discussions in the second half of the book, amounts to a substantial study in itself. Here Jackson repeated and amplified views previously expressed by him in his paper 'On the Vulgar Latin of Roman Britain', published in 1948,[3] and which he briefly restated in 1973 in a contribution, 'The British languages and their evolution', to a standard work of reference.[4]

In brief, Jackson reckons that the Latin spoken during and for some time after the Roman Occupation by the native British was peculiarly old-fashioned and correct, an opinion which has found what seems to the present writer uncritical acceptance.[5] And in general the book seems in danger of suffering the fate to which works of ambitious synthesis are specially liable, that is, to be held by the profane as primary and definitive accounts in their own right. Indeed, in such a subject, which of us is not in some respect profane? It is primarily as a Latinist that I even dare to approach it; for, though I learnt the rudiments of Welsh from my mother, never having lived in Welsh-speaking Wales, I am a failed bilingual, and my authority as a Celtic scholar as such is nil. But in comparative philology it is not the mantle of authority, but first-hand evidence, quantification, and the quality of one's argumentation that counts. To paraphrase Jackson's remarks (*LHEB*, iv) about Max Förster's important work *Der Flussname Themse und seine Sippe: Studien zur Anglisierung keltischer Eigennamen und zur Lautchronologie des Altbritischen*,[6] 'if I have had to differ from the opinion of the great Celticist rather often, this is because as a Latinist I believe the evidence demands it and because his arguments in these cases simply cannot be passed over in silence'.

Jackson's thesis that the loanwords surviving in the British languages show that the Latin spoken by Britons was old-fashioned in its phonology is accompanied by an explanation which has a very specific character and *scenario* with interesting historical and social implications. 'The spoken Latin of Britain', says he, 'differed completely from that of the Western Empire in general and of Gaul in particular . . .' (*LHEB*, 86); '. . . to the ordinary speaker of Vulgar Latin from the continent the language from which the loanwords was derived must have seemed stilted and pedantic or perhaps upper-class and "haw-haw"' (*LHEB*, 109). He ascribes this to the influence of the *grammatici* from whom the sons of well-off landowners in the Lowland Zone are to be supposed to have learnt their Latin, and he has in mind, it appears, the time of Agricola and his successors. 'As Tacitus tells us',[7] these well-to-do Britons 'sent their sons to Latin schools, where they would doubtless be taught, and insist on having, the best Latin available' (*LHEB*, 109). According to Jackson, it was these key persons of native British society who, as decurions and the like, came most regularly into contact and business with the Roman administration; it was from such grandees, rather than from direct and intimate contact with actual Romans, that retainers, farmhands, and servants would have picked up and spread Latin expressions among their monoglot British acquaintance, most of whom, says Jackson, would never meet a Roman:[8] for contact between Romans and the peasantry at large in the Lowland area must have been minimal, and virtually non-existent in the Highland Zone. In the absence of evidence, Jackson had to speculate from what seemed rational probabilities and plausible analogies, which he adduced in fair number and of which the most pervasive though not necessarily persuasive was comparison with the British Raj in India; in fact, French imperial policy would have provided a less prejudicial basis for speculation.

At any rate, bilingualism in Britain can never have been as extensive as it was in Gaul. There the closely related p-Celtic dialects died out to leave only ghostly traces in French (*quatre vingts*, which reflects the Celtic style of counting in 20s). It was rather the monoglot rural peasantry in Britain who were the 'true storehouse of the British language',[9] a language which was evidently already profoundly influenced by Latin before the diaspora caused by the Anglo-Saxon invasions. For, generally speaking, what implies that a Welsh word borrowed from Latin entered British during the Occupation period and not later is that its phonetic characteristics should be incompatible with early medieval development of the same word in French or Spanish and/or that similarly idiosyncratic forms should be attested for Breton and/or Cornish.[10]

In his most recent treatment of the matter (see n. 4 below), Jackson observed that at the time of the Anglo-Saxon onslaught 'refugees must have flooded into the safer hill-country, bringing with them a more Roman civilization and a greater knowledge of Latin; Latin loanwords that had not yet found their way into the dialects of the Highland Zone may have come there now' – i.e., c. A.D. 450–500 – 'the Latin in question being the "educated" speech of the old provincial upper classes'.

Jackson's use of the term 'British Latin' requires clarification, because in practice it has proved ambiguous. It is not simply what might be (and has been) supposed from the simple definition given in p. 5 of *LHEB*, 'the variety of Vulgar Latin spoken in Britain during and for some time after the Roman Occupation'. This has been mistaken as meaning *all* the

Latin of the British provinces – of country, town, and camp; and naturally enough, because of Jackson's definite article. And indeed Jackson will sometimes have it that there is a significant contrast between 'Continental Vulgar Latin' conceived of as *una res*, and 'British Latin' or 'the Latin of Roman Britain' in just this sense. So for example in his discussion of the fate in Britain of the Classical Latin phonemes /b/ and /w/ (*LHEB*, 89f., 374f.),[11] for it is proposed by him that it is significant that there are no spelling-confusions in the Latin inscriptions of Britain. Besides, there is occasional lack of clarity in his book, whether we are to understand that a peculiar form postulated is the borrowed form as might occur in a British *sentence*, or as the form which a Briton would use in speaking *Latin*, which is another thing; so, for example, in discussion of the British fate of *puteus* and *oleum* (*LHEB*, 87, 366).

But we anticipate. In general, Jackson means specifically the brand of Latin spoken by the putative British 'squirearchy' and their heirs in the Lowland Zone from the time of Agricola to the time of Vortigern. At first it would have sounded correct and hardly quaint to a visitor; but, we are invited to believe, it still existed much later, relatively unaffected by the lingo of the now departed legions and traders and the now evanescent townsfolk. For elsewhere Jackson allows that the Latin of the merchant, the soldier, and the artisan will for the most part have been subject to the same processes of change as elsewhere in the Empire; and indeed anyone with a first-hand acquaintance with the epigraphic material or the coinage of Roman Britain could not possibly maintain anything else. So by the early fifth century such Latin as Patrick learnt as a boy in Cumbria, if that is where he lived, would sound distinctly weird not only to a visiting continental but also to a Londoner.

The outstanding peculiarity would have been that the phonemic opposition of five long and five short vowels was maintained in this Latin; everywhere else, the older vowel-arrangement and its complex variety of syllabic structure ([sa:ncto:s], [ma:ter] [pater] [pia:s]; [sa:turni:] [cana:lis] [ado:rno:] [de:cre:sce:(n)s]) had been or was being changed radically so that these words, each of which shows a different pattern of syllabic weight, would be reduced to one of two simple patterns: ¯˘ or ˘¯˘. In the various brands of Latin spoken elsewhere, the length of vowels became a function of the word-accent and was merely allophonic, and there were concomitant changes in vowel quality, so that [wenit] 'comes' and [we:nit] 'came', words formerly distinguished primarily by the feature /± long/, were now distinguished qualitatively as [wę:nit] and [wẹ:nit]. The relative length of both new vowels was adventitious, due to the accent.

If by some miracle of history the Saxons had been repelled, if the prestige of 'British Latin' had prevailed over native British, and if our islands had remained independent of Merovingian Gaul, we should now be speaking a brand of Romance quite unlike that of France, or indeed anywhere else, including places like Sardinia, which is sometimes loosely said to have the dialects most similar to Classical Latin. But even in Sardinia what is to be reconstructed from the extant dialects is a language in which there is no trace of phonemic quantity. From the phonological point of view, it is this change and the concomitant changes of quality and of syllable-weight, that mark off earlier and later Latin more decisively and pervasively than anything else. Of course it is not suggested that the imaginary Romance language of Britain would maintain quantitative distinctions to this day – not that this is inconceivable – but that it would necessarily differ markedly from all other Romance languages in principle, because its starting point would have been a markedly different kind of Latin.

II. TECHNIQUE

1. JACKSON'S APPROACH

Jackson's claim as linguistic fact that 'British Latin' was archaic is nowadays treated as established truth, at least in the English-speaking world.[12] His explanation has also achieved a good measure of acceptance, though some writers have thought to 'strengthen' his case by invoking the general reflection that remote areas are linguistically conservative, and implying to their readers that 'British Latin' means 'all the Latin spoken in Britain'. But, as pointed out above, this line of thought is crushingly refuted by the language of the Roman inscriptions of Britain; and, as Jackson himself rightly says in explicitly rejecting this idea (*LHEB*, 107), the general reflection is hardly applicable to Roman Britain. It is valid for isolated communities whose members enjoy a long peace, never receive visitors, and never go anywhere, but it is a basic mistake to think of Britain in the Roman Empire as that sort of place.

It is the supposed fact which requires attention, for, unless it is true, the question of the explanation does not even arise, and the major part of this paper is devoted to examination of the main claim.

Jackson arrives at his conclusion as follows. First he enumerates various traits in the phonology of British loanwords which point to various widespread Vulgar Latin developments (*LHEB*, 82–6). These are all minor and marginal and, taken in sum, rather seriously understate the 'vulgar' features observable in the loanwords in general, especially as regards morphology and lexis (see below, p. 65). Against these he sets a dozen arguments which take the typical form '*x* is characteristic of Vulgar Latin phonology, widespread by such-and-such a date well within the Imperial period; it is not to be observed in the loanwords in British; *ergo*, British Latin was not vulgar'.

These arguments are presented paratactically and in a curiously inconsequential order, and one is given no help in estimating their relative potency. Four factors are involved: the intrinsic clarity of the vulgar feature not observed in the loanwords; the certainty of its dating in the development of Vulgar Latin; the certainty of its generality throughout the Empire; and the number of loanwords in which one fails to observe it.

The potential strength of Jackson's arguments in fact varies very widely. His items (1) and (4) (*LHEB*, 86 and 88), though oddly separated by two others of quite different character, together constitute a possibly very powerful argument, the absence in British of evidence for the loss of phonemic quantity and the concomitant change of quality in Western Romance of [i] and [u], since this can be checked against a large number of examples (see pp. 47ff.).

On the other hand, argument (6) (*LHEB*, 88) is intrinsically feeble. He finds it significant that British borrowings of Latin words beginning *sc- sp- st-* show no signs of a parasitic vowel developing to support the sibilant: one has Cornish and Breton *scol* from [schola] rather than from [(i)schola]. The parasitic vowel which is regular in the equivalent words in Welsh did not become established until the eleventh century (*ysgol* 'school', etc.). Jackson, following Grandgent[13] here, says 'this is found from the second century on (e.g. *iscolasticus* in a second-century inscription), and was common by the third and later'. This rather twists Grandgent's words: 'the earliest Latin example is probably *iscolasticus* written in Barcelona in the second century; it is found repeatedly, though not frequently, in the third; in the fourth and fifth it is very common'. Now, while it may be observed that the phenomenon deserves a closer and less impressionistic investigation than lies behind Grandgent's statement, it is certain that 'impure *s*' was still a fugitive and inorganic feature in Latin of a very late date; it was determined by sandhiconsiderations, as it still is in Italian, for example (*la scuola*, but *in iscuola*). Why should it be supposed that the British would definitely make an organic vowel of this parasitic sound anyway? Out of a sample of some 540 loanwords listed below (pp. 36–40) there are fewer than two dozen candidates; and among these few, several are borrowed from Latin forms clearly late on other grounds, which quite possibly had a parasitic vowel in their Latin pronunciation, which, however, has been ignored in the Cornish and Breton renderings (*spiritus, strigula, stragulum*). This is all quite without significance.

Jackson's arguments are intended to be cumulative in weight; by numbering them and presenting them as he does he implies that they are of at least roughly equal importance, and the unfortunate reader is not in a position to judge easily whether what purports to be a collection of twelve golden sovereigns does not in fact include a number of new pennies wrapped in foil. The absolute chronology, the spread, and the social nuance of later Latin sound-changes in so far as they *can* be established, are clearly crucial in argumentation of this kind, as well as one's understanding of the notoriously crude terms 'Classical' and 'Vulgar' Latin.[14] These make a very rough-and-ready contrast long since recognized as quite inadequate to the purpose. Here Jackson's authority is entirely vicarious, since he depends, somewhat uncritically, on the outdated handbooks of Grandgent, Sturtevant, and Richter,[15] all of whom were far too prone to facile generalization on the basis of inadequately analysed primary evidence.

As a simple example of Jackson's method, one may take his arguments (11) and (12) as typical:

> (11). Latin *li*, *ni* became palatized *l'*, *n'* (*l, n mouillé*) in the third to the fifth centuries. They evidently did not do so in Britain. See sections 91, 102. (12). Latin *l* plus consonant gave *u* plus consonant about the same time, in Gallo-Latin; e.g. *siluaticus* > *sauvaticus*. It did not do so in Britain. See section 91 (*LHEB*, 94).

Suppose for the sake of illustration that Jackson's oracular pronouncements about the dating, which he takes from Richter, were certainly right. In (11) he has in mind the phenomenon of internal *i*-affection in the development of the British languages (*LHEB*, 579–618; seventh–eighth century on his dating). By this a short vowel in British is subject to qualitative modification if it is followed by a consonant + *yod*. In the genus there is the species involving [l] and [n] as the consonant; and these would naturally include some Latin borrowings. But since the sub-species is so highly determined, it is hardly surprising that there are hardly any examples; perhaps half a dozen Latin words.[16] He uses two of these, *solea* (confused, one must suppose, with *solum*: *REW* 8064) and *cuneus*, which, as Jackson rightly says, must have entered British in the mildly improper forms [solja], [cunjus] (cf. ⟨OSTRIA⟩ for ⟨OSTREA⟩ in the Vindolanda letters, c. A.D. 105) to account for Welsh *seil*, *sail* 'foundation', *cyn* 'wedge'. For if these had been heard as pure disyllables with 'Spanish' consonants as [sol'a], [cun'us], we should expect, says Jackson, sound-substitution of ordinary British [l] and [n] unpalatized; from which one ought to get in Welsh ⟨sol⟩, ⟨cwn⟩, since ⟨o⟩ and ⟨w⟩ are the normal representatives of Latin /o/ and /u/ in other circumstances. One might equally expect the ancient British to do what many of us do in pronouncing e.g. Spanish *mañana* – that is, to re-introduce a *yod* of our own; but never mind that. In (12) Jackson alludes to a feature which is peculiar to French (*aube aumône paume sauvage*; contrast e.g. Spanish and Italian). This does not even stand up as a criterion diagnostic of Western Vulgar Latin. But how desperately limited is the scope of the argument anyway. Apart from the case of Welsh *elusen*, *alusen*, *alwysen* 'charity, alms', which involves a remarkable *[almọ:sina] and worse[17] for [elee:mosüna], there is only *palf* from [palma] 'palm, paw' and *palfod* from [palma:ta] 'slap'.[18] So these arguments would be of minuscule significance, even if there were several cases, and even if they were in principle sound.

2. THE BEHAVIOUR OF LOANWORDS

Both arguments are, however, fundamentally wrong. Jackson proceeds as if the only time at which they tiny haul of words in question in arguments (11) and (12) could have entered British was after A.D. 250, and there is a gross blunder of method here which vitiates the whole of his argumentation. It does not even seem to occur to Jackson that the reason why the Latin words in question do not show the 'expected' vulgar traits might be that they were borrowed into British *before* these changes in spoken Latin were accomplished, whenever that was; for in fact the evidence on this point offered by Richter is quite inadequate.[19]

This undermines the whole of Jackson's argumentation, including those points where one is dealing with something important and at least fairly frequently exemplified. For example in point (9), the feature in question is the voicing of intervocalic [p] [t] [c] in later Latin. Now this is certainly a late development; and Jackson seizes on the broad category '4th to 6th century' into which Richter puts it, as hers is the only categorization which he could find that would explicitly allow for a significant overlap between the Roman occupation of Britain and this development as a dominant trait of spoken Latin at large. One could cavil here at what precisely Jackson took Richter to mean by including '4th century' in her rubric – how much of it? How generally? Where precisely? One would also like to know proportionally how frequent examples of spellings such as ⟨B⟩ for ⟨P⟩, etc., actually are in the material, but it is no use expecting anything so subtle as analytic quantification from Richter, to whom it was all one whether a feature is widely and frequently attested in contemporary documents or extremely sporadic and localized, or in a manuscript or on a stone; if someone tells her that he knows a man who says he has seen a swallow, she believes him, tells us, and declares that it is summer, in spite of the blizzard. But again, let us grant what is unproven, that lots of Latin-speakers everywhere were unambiguously voicing intervocalic [p] [t] [c] by, say, A.D. 350. Jackson's argument about the absence of evidence for this in the British loanwords would only even begin to acquire weight if it could be safely assumed that most of the loanwords were borrowed *later* than A.D. 350. But the reverse is the case. On any view, we must suppose that by A.D. 350 a large number of the surviving loanwords had *already* been definitively borrowed. Besides, there is the point that this kind of change is very slow and gradual. To an English ear, American intervocal [t] resembles a [d], but is not simply the same as an English intervocal [d] ('Sadurday', etc.). How can we hope, then, to tell confidently at what point it would seem natural to British speakers borrowing terms over a long period to render the gradually changing Latin sounds with British /d/ etc.? Since this was certainly not unambiguously clear to Latin speakers themselves until long after the Roman occupation of Britain, the case will not stand up.

Similar considerations apply to argument (8) about the absence of evidence for the palatization of [tj dj cj] (etc.) in the loanwords. As Campanile has pointed out in an important paper,[20] British had no means of representing the intermediate stages between e.g. [diurna:ta] 'day' as an unambiguous quadrisyllable and [žorna:da] as a clear trisyllable; therefore there would be a period during which any borrowings made would render an incipiently palatized [djurna:ta], etc., with British [di-], thus making the loan *look* as though it came from an earlier Latin form than was in fact the case. This consideration is also relevant to the British representation of certain Latin vowels (see pp. 41, 62).

Jackson repeatedly fails to allow adequately for an elementary characteristic of loanwords orally transmitted, so attached is he to the theory that the principal means by which loanwords entered British was through the mouths of well-off bilingual British speakers, who, thanks to Agricola's dominies and their successors over nine or ten generations, spoke a *katharévusa* ever more divergent from contemporary continental *dhimotikí*. A loanword, having once established itself by undergoing the necessary adjustments of phonology and morphology, and maybe also suffering the indignities of popular etymology, *is* a native word. Its users forget that it is an alien at all, especially when bilingualism is rare, as it certainly was in the countryside of Britain. Their children will not know or care; as for the bilingual person, he would notice many similarities between his own language and Latin in vocabulary but, if he understood the question, he would be as hard put to it as we to decide whether, e.g., the words now represented in Welsh by *cach* 'excrete', *caeth* 'slave' were borrowings of Latin *caco captus* or simply cognate with them, and he might wrongly think that the British stems of Welsh *caru* 'love' and *credu* 'trust' were borrowings of Latin [ca:r-], [cre:d-], when in fact these (and many other items) were common inheritance from late Indo-European.

Loanwords, once established, share the phonological developments which native words undergo. Meanwhile, in the language from which the immigrants came, different changes may occur which take the loanwords' parents in divergent phonological directions.

The whole process is of course a psychologically very important aspect of cultural penetration, for 'we', who began by using 'their' word for, e.g., an intoxicating drink made from grapes (British *[wi:non]), a translucent blue-green substance used for bottles (British *[witron]), a warship (British *[lunga:]), a kind of breast-plate (British *[lü:ri:ca:]),[21] etc., come to think of the thing as 'ours' too. It is only in highly literate societies which sport stylists, academies, and philologists that old loanwords are recognized (by some) for what they are. 'Faith' has the same bluff Saxon appearance as, say, 'truth' or 'sloth', but is of course a borrowing from Norman French, which it still much more closely resembles than its legitimate French representative *foi*. Even today, when the creolization of demotic Welsh has, because of radio, television, etc., gone further than ever before, it does not occur to Welsh speakers to use the word for 'house' (pronounced [ti:]) when they mean the beverage [te:], or, conversely, when speaking English, to say [te:] as the English name of the drink [ti:]. Yet the Welsh form represents a pronunciation of the word still current in Ireland, and once current in the English of England:

Here thou, great Anna! Whom three realms obey,
Dost sometimes *Counsel* take, and sometimes *Tea*
(Alexander Pope, *The Rape of the Lock*, iii. 7–8)

Borrowings from English into Welsh often preserve features of older English pronunciation as well as words either obsolete or changed in meaning.[22] A few random examples are *crefft* 'skill, trade' (OE *cræft*), *hebog* 'hawk' (OE *hæfoc*, cf. *havoc*); *cneifio* 'shear' (ME *knif*); *ffald* 'enclosure'; *dracht* 'draught' (of ale, etc.); *chwip* 'whip'. The last two preserve sounds long since lost in the dialects of the West Midlands but still to be heard in Aberdeenshire. Among various expressions for 'bedroom', beside the inevitable *bedrwm*, the half-breed *rwm wely*, and *ystafell wely*, which contains the representative of a Vulgar Latin [stabellum],[23] there are *siambar* from French and *llofft* from Old English, which preserves a sense lost by specialization in English. *(H)astio* 'hurry' and related forms are still colloquial; English *haste(n)* is now all but a book-word. A bus conductor is *tocyn-wr*, medicine is *ffisig*, current expressions for 'nice', 'clever' are *braf*, *ffetus*; and the flies of one's trousers are called not only *fflei* but also *copis(h)*, i.e., 'codpiece'.

Any reasonably educated Welshman will be aware of the extent and perspective of the English loan-element in Welsh, and may know that *sicr* and *siwr* are etymological doublets, the one from French *via* English, the other from what tenuously survives in Scots as *siccar* but is obsolete in England. Even a sophisticated bilingual speaker will be unaware of the full extent of the loan-element in Welsh. For instance, it is not obvious that the Welsh for 'idle', *segur*, is cousin to *siwr* and *sicr*; all three represent, by different descents, Latin *securus*. *Segur* is the direct representative of a relatively late borrowing of the post-Classical form [secu:rus] for Classical [se:cu:rus] which would have given Welsh **swygur* (see below, p. 40). Probably not all Welsh speakers realize that 'crown-prince', *edling*, represents OE *ætheling*, or that the ordinary word for 'hint, suggestion', *awgrym*, preserves the form and vowels of ME *augrim(e)* 'arithmetic, Arabic numbers', itself a by-form of *algorism*, *algorithm*, which buries rather than perpetuates the name of the ninth-century Arab mathematician *al-Khwara:zmi*. Such is fame.

It is now hundreds of years since a majority of Welsh speakers were not competently bilingual, and 'up-dating' and re-borrowing of English expressions has been going on all the time, e.g. *ffarm* beside *fferm*; the language is, many would say, excessively accommodating to neologisms which it is to be hoped are merely transient (*seico-analysis*, forsooth).

Nevertheless, it is striking how conservative the spoken language is even today with respect not merely to the more opaque kind of loan (*awgrym*; *agwyddor*, see p. 58), and one will hear in common use expressions which the user, as English speaker, would feel to be archaic, yet which are not so in Welsh, e.g. 'right' as an adverbial modifier in *reit dda* as an answer to the question 'how are you?'.

As to the period of the Roman Occupation, we may surely agree with Jackson that an active mastery of Latin must have been relatively rare among the peasantry. But it does not follow that a shepherd or a ditcher or cowgirl who lived in a remote part of the fifth century and who, in one real sense, 'did not know a word of Latin', did not know what was by then and perhaps had long since been the *British* for 'ass', 'mule', 'fish', 'arm', 'cheek', 'stone-built enclosure', all words of Latin origin; or that a saddlecloth was [strå:tü:rə] (Classical Latin [stra:tu:ra]), or that there was a drink called [wi:non] and another called [bracå:ton] 'bragget', in which the stem is Celtic[24] and the ending is the Latin [-a:tum], frequently used to denote the flavour of a brew, e.g. *picatum*.

Precisely because such humble folk did not meet 'Romans' and could not speak Latin, they must have been unaware that such words were of Latin origin, and some of them may have been in the language a very long time indeed. By the later fifth century Latin speakers in Gaul were probably already calling 'glass' something like [βẹ:dru], 'saddlecloth' [(ə)stradu:ra], and 'breastplate' [lori:ga] – that is, if this word were still current; for it is one of an interesting group of words in the loan-material (some 15 per cent) which have either completely vanished or become very restricted in domain in Romance.[25] These deserve fuller investigation elsewhere.

Loanwords, then, can fossilize, as it were, features of the phonology of the original language and of its vocabulary. Nowadays, every Welsh speaker is also a highly competent English speaker; and yet one is struck by the conservatism even of the demotic language with regard to old loans, opaque and clear.

If this is true now, how much the more must it have been in ancient Britain, where the peasantry was largely ignorant of Latin, and the extent of competent bilingualism certainly much less than it is now. It would be a gross and obvious error for a philologist of the distant future to use the evidence of twentieth-century Welsh texts and tape-recordings to infer that contemporary English must have been strangely archaic in its phonology and lexis because of the quality of the vowel in *teipio* 'to type' or the fact that the word for 'flies' is *copis(h)*. Yet this is in principle what

Jackson is doing in treating the Latin loan-material in British as he does.

For this reason I do not propose to examine in detail all his propositions, for they are all subject to this flaw, and several are of the same minimal power and scope as points (6), (11), and (12) already reviewed: arguments (2) and (3) (intrusive [w] glides; very doubtfully to be regarded as Latin at all); (5) (reflections of round [q^u]). After repeated readings over several years I still do not understand the point or relevance in its context of (10). There are only two arguments which, in terms of the four factors determining potency mentioned above (p. 7), have apparent force. These are arguments (7), about intervocalic /w/ and /b/ of Classical Latin, and, by far the most important, arguments (1) and (4) about the vocalization of the loanwords taken together, for they are essentially related. But before we examine these important matters in detail, there is the prior question of the date-span represented by the loanwords.

3. THE DATING OF THE LOANWORDS

Jackson defines the period of borrowing as 'from the end of the first to the fifth century' (*LHEB*, 77) and avoids emphasizing any particular century; which, from his point of view, seems strange, because even his best arguments would only begin to carry conviction if it could be safely proposed that there were a significant bias in the material towards late and very late dates of borrowing.

In 1892 J. Loth remarked, in what remains a fundamental contribution to the whole subject, *Les Mots latins dans les langues brittoniques* (Paris, 1892), that 'les mots latins passés en brittonique, empruntés, en les prenant en masse, du IIe siècle au commencement du Ve siècle, plus spécialement aux IIIe–IVe siècles, nous présentent toutes les voyelles toniques intactes avec leur quantité et leur qualité diverses, parfaitement distinctes' (p. 64).

We shall return to Loth's important claim here about the vocalization, repeated by Jackson (*LHEB*, 88) when he says by way of generalization 'with one or two possible exceptions, the loanwords show that the Classical quantity system was preserved, even with unstressed vowels, in the Latin of Roman Britain'. But, apart from the important element of Christian terms, there is no *a priori* reason to suppose a bias in the direction of the latter centuries of the Roman Occupation; and for the rest, it is rarely that one can say with any confidence when a word would have been borrowed on purely semantic grounds. For while one can point to a large number of Welsh words which are both likely and able to represent very early borrowings – *Rhufawn* from [ro:ma:nus], *gwin* 'wine' from [wi:non] and so on – one can never show that a particular word *was* borrowed early, and, on the other hand, words which are clearly borrowings of the fourth century or later (*Dunawd* from [do:na:tus], *Ynyr* from [hono:rius], *ffranc* 'foreigner, enemy, mercenary' from [francus]) are proportionally not very many. This whole matter requires further investigation elsewhere. But what is the upper limit for the entry of loanwords into British, and what does one mean by 'early'?

Jackson says that the unsettled state of Britain 'might probably prevent much in the way of linguistic interchange for a generation after the conquest' (*LHEB*, 77). This is wrong. Unsettled conditions and cultural hostility such as is implied by Tac. *Agr.* 21. 2 (see n. 7) for the Boudiccan period are no hindrance in themselves to the borrowing of words from people whom you dislike (blitzkrieg, stormtrooper), and it is a mistake to suppose that loanwords can *only* find their way from one language to another when significant numbers of those speaking the inferior language have acquired a smattering of the superior. Moreover, it is arbitrary to assume without reflection as Jackson does, following Loth, that no Latin terms had found a permanent home in British in the mouths of monolingual speakers perhaps long before this time.

For the beginning of the period during which we must reckon with the possibility of the entry of loanwords from Latin is not Agricola's governorship nor yet A.D. 43 but the time of Tincommius and Commius, which brings us back to the decade of Caesar's Gallic Campaigns. Words borrowed during this time would, in the first instance, be entering the vocabulary of the Belgae of Cantium and the parts nearest Gaul, whence they might be diffused westwards and northwards as *British* words without the mediation of Latin speakers at all.

The old view, that Caesar's expeditions to Britain represent an isolated episode, and that Britain remained completely cut off from Europe until Claudius' invasion in A.D. 43, is modified (and rightly) in recent accounts of Roman Britain.[26] During this whole period Britain stood uncertainly on the edge of the *oecumene*, increasingly exposed to and affected by its material culture and military presence, and debating with herself, as it were, whether to sign the Treaty of Rome. For example, the British coinage of this period is direct evidence of continental influence. While Tasciovanus of the Catuvellauni (*regnabat* c. 20 B.C.–A.D. 5) used the alphabet to set his Celtic title *rigon*(*os*?) on his coinage, other chieftains were recognized by Augustus as *reges* in some sort of client-relationship with Rome, and Eppillus, for example, used the *Latin* title on his coins;

this not only to impress his subjects, but more especially to assert his status in the eyes of those with whom British traders did business on the continent. These were, of course, not only Romans from Italy, but the Britons' own increasingly bilingual and Romanized relatives, the Belgae. At the beginning of the *Gallic War* Caesar describes the continental Belgae as the toughest (*fortissimi*) of all the Gallic peoples, because, he says, they were furthest from the civilized refinement of Gallic Cisalpina (*a cultu atque humanitate prouinciae*) and because they were least often visited by merchants bringing *ea quae ad effeminandos animos pertinent.*

All this changed, and rather rapidly, after the establishment of the new continental province. As for Britain, Strabo refers to gold, silver, iron, cattle, hides, wheat, slaves, and dogs as British exports to the continent c. 20–15 B.C.; among these items, the British later at any rate had borrowings of Latin [awrum] [be:stia], perhaps [capti:wos] [gra:num]. He remarks that he himself saw two huge but unprepossessing British slaves up for sale at Rome, and adds that 'some of their chieftains have obtained τὴν πρὸς Καίσαρα φιλίαν by means of embassies and services'. This means some sort of reception of the chieftains *in fidem* or perhaps even separate *foedera amicitiae causa.* These chieftains had made dedications on the Capitol to Jupiter Optimus Maximus; and respect for the gods of Rome is evident in the fine classicizing coinage of Cunobelinus. Augustus records in the *Res gestae* that among other *reges* who *supplices confugerunt* to him at Rome were the Britons Dumnobellaunus and another. Strabo concludes by observing that the British δυνάσται whom he had in mind 'have virtually made the whole island Roman property', and that the British willingly paid heavy dues levied by the authorities at the ports of Gaul on both their exports and their imports – 'i.e., ivory armlets, amber ornaments, glass vessels, and other such knick-knacks'. Conquest of Britain would be pointless, he says, because this would not only mean direct military expenditure but also the loss of the lucrative and permanent income represented by the trade-levies, which would cease if Britain were incorporated into the Empire.[27] Pre-conquest glass (W. *gwydr*; [witrum]) has been identified at Camulodunum, along with brooches (*addurn*; [ado:rno]) of Roman workmanship and fine quality pottery, Gaulish and even Arretine, and imported examples of bronze furniture (*ysgafn* 'couch, bed'; [scamnum]) and bronze vessels (*callawr* 'cauldron'; [cal'da:rium], *trull* 'goblet'; [tru:lla]), beside huge *amphorae* attesting the large-scale use and consumption of oil and wine by the rich and powerful.

It is not necessary for the establishment and divulgation of loanwords that there should be numerous bilingual speakers among the borrowing population; a word, once borrowed and established as native, can travel far to areas where the original language is not spoken at all; and this will have been true throughout the Occupation. So, in principle, it is quite *possible* that any or all of the ancestors of the Welsh words cited above, or of *llong* 'ship' ([(na:wis) loŋga]); cf. the case of French *fromage* from [(ca:seus) fo:rma:ticus], *pyg* 'pitch' ([picem]), even (to judge from Fishbourne) *rhosyn* 'rose' from [rosa] and *ffydd* 'faith' from [fidem] as a key-term not of religious but social and political relationship *might*, with many another word, have entered British definitively in the period between Julius Caesar and Hadrian. It should be emphasized that it is not being claimed that any of these *must* have entered so early; the point is rather that they could, and we must recognize that, in any given case, one possible reason why a British descendant appears to conform with Classical as opposed to Vulgar Latin phonology will be that maybe the word *was* borrowed from the spoken form current in the Classical period, much earlier than it seems to have occurred to Celtic scholars to look.

In point of fact, the general claim that Classical quantities are perfectly preserved in the loanwords is seriously misleading and prejudicial, because 60 per cent of the material is represented by Latin word- and syllable-types which would appear the same whether they were borrowed in the time of Caesar or Romulus Augustulus (see pp. 51–3, 66).

III. EVIDENCE

1. INTERVOCAL /b/ AND /w/

Jackson considers it significant that:

> neither in the Latin inscriptions of Roman Britain, nor in the later inscriptions of the Dark Ages . . . are there any examples of the confusion of *v* and *b*; [significant, because] one of the best known characteristics of Vulgar Latin is the way in which Classical Latin *v*, pronounced [w], gave way to the bilabial spirant [β], probably in the first century; and intervocalic *b* became the same spirant [β], beginning about the same time and being well-established by the second century [*LHEB*, 88], [and] complete in the third [*LHEB*, 364].
>
> Since the two were now the same sound, they were regularly confused in writing, e.g. *uibus, iuuente*. According to Sturtevant, we

> must assume the pronunciation [β] . . . for both letters by the third century even in standard as distinct from colloquial Latin. None of this is reflected in the loanwords in British where *v* and *b* were kept quite distinct [*LHEB*, 88].

There are 14 Latin words starting [b + vowel] in the list of 540 discussed in the next section (see p. 36ff.), and there are 15 starting [w + vowel]. But these are of no interest. We know anyway that confusion of Latin /b/ and /w/ in initial position was of very limited importance in most parts of the Empire. The Romance languages generally maintain a strong opposition between the initial consonants of the descendants of [westi:re] and [be:stia], [wacca] and [ba(c)ca]. The opposition here was originally between realizations of the phonemes as [b] and [w]; with the passage of [w] to [β] or [v], whenever that was, there remained a clear phonemic contrast between the stop on the one hand and the spirant on the other. Consentius, writing in the fifth century, remarks that 'some people pronounce ⟨VENI⟩ as a kind of trisyllable', a habit which he counts among various *uitia nationum*.[28] This implies that 'some people' maintained the pronunciation of /w/ as [w] at a very late date, but there is no hint who they might be. It is certainly wrong to assume with Jackson (*LHEB*, 364) that these must have been 'the higher levels of society'; and it is clear that Consentius himself contrasted his own [β]-pronunciation with theirs, which he plainly counted as incorrect. As will presently be shown, there is a geographical explanation.

These words appear in Welsh on the one hand with the spelling ⟨b⟩ and on the other with ⟨gw⟩, the normal exponents of British phonemes /b/ and /w/. But this is entirely insignificant in this context. British borrowers would always have reproduced initial Latin [b] with their own /b/, because it was a stop; and because there was no bilabial or dental voiced spirant in British, they would represent with British /w/ the first consonant of such words as Latin [VINVM, VITRVM⟩ whether pronounced [wi:num, witrum] or [βi:num, βitrum]; whence in either case British [wi:non, witron] but e.g. [bucca:] from Latin [bucca].

It is the case of *intervocalic* Latin /b/ and /w/ that is of potential interest, and in our material (see pp. 36–40) we have

> *bubalinus bubalus cubiculum cubitus desubito diabolus faba fibula laborem liber nibulus praebiter probo scribenda scribo sebum stabellum subula tabella tabula tabulatum* (21 words);

and

> *captiuus captiuitas cauella cauus cauitatem ciuitas ciuitatem diluuium*

diuinus diuiso fouea Iouis lixiuium pauonem priuatus saliua uiuerra (17 words).

The former generally have Welsh ⟨f⟩ (pronounced [v]) representing the subsequent development of British /b/ intervocalically; the latter have Welsh ⟨w⟩, or in a couple of cases, nothing, reflecting a third well-known Vulgar Latin treatment of intervocal /w/, which was to drop it.[29]

Jackson's point is this: in his view, it is a well-established fact that most people everywhere were making e.g. [awe:na] and [(h)abe:na], [manda:wit] and [manda:bit] perfectly homophonous by the third century A.D., and making perfect rhymes of the intrinsically vulgar formations [staβella] 'stables' and [caβella] 'enclosure' for [stabella], [cawella]. How comes it, therefore, that the distinction of the intervocalic Latin phonemes is so accurately reflected in the British loanwords? One would expect confusion in British and hence such forms as Welsh **ystawell* 'room' beside *cawell* 'creel, basket, cage' if sound-substitution of /w/ were the norm; or, conversely, if sound-substitution of /b/ had appealed to the British ear, we should have *ystafell* 'room' and *cafell* – which exists, and means 'sanctuary, chamber', and could, *pace* Jackson, therefore date back to the Roman period, though it is certainly more likely to be a medieval borrowing.[30] One notes that in either case one of the resultant forms necessarily takes on the appearance of a borrowing made from the 'correct' Latin form; for *ystafell* is consistent either with [stabellum] or [staβellum], and *cawell* is consistent with either [cawella] or [caβella]. Invoking this consideration, and guessing that some loans are much earlier than others, one might blur the clarity of the distinction of the Latin phonemes as it appears in British borrowings, but the laws of chance are strongly against this as a wholly satisfactory explanation. We must investigate the Latin evidence.

Jackson regards it as significant that there are no *bv* confusions in the Latin inscriptions of Britain.[31] The inference which he invites his reader to make is that *all* the Latin spoken in Britain, not just that of the British upper class, was aberrant here compared with the Latin of the Empire at large and of Gaul in particular. He relies for his claims and dates on Sturtevant,[32] who, himself merely summarizing at second and third hand received opinion on this matter, wrote:

> the confusion of *b* and *v* in inscriptions begins in the first century A.D.; for example, *baliat*, *CIL* iv. 4874, *beni* 5125, *Berus* 4380, *Bibius* 3145 b; *lebare* iii. 7251 (A.D. 49 or 50), *iuvente* = *iubente* xi. 137 (A.D. 1?) [*sic*: he meant first century A.D.], *vene* = *bene* vi. 7582

> (A.D. 187). By the third century the confusion had become so common that *one is inclined to think* that *v* was then a spirant in standard Latin.

Later on he says that

> before there could be confusion between *b* and *v* both must have become spirants, at least in some local or class dialect. We must therefore conclude that, in the first century, certain persons in Italy, especially at Pompeii, pronounced *v* and intervocalic *b* as a bilabial spirant. *Probably this was not for some centuries a widespread pronunciation.*

So the first edition (43, 113);[33] in the second, which Jackson cited, the first judgment here italicized became 'one must assume' (143), and the second 'The usage spread gradually through Vulgar Latin' (174). Apart from the error of logic in his remark about 'confusion of *b* and *v*', Sturtevant's second thoughts were worse than his first, and even they convey a grossly distorted view of the evidence.

When you interpret spelling mistakes, it is relevant to ask how frequent they are and whether they are uniformly distributed throughout the Empire; and when it is a question of the apparent interchangeability of two letters, it is further desirable to know whether the confusion is genuinely promiscuous or biassed in one direction, and, if biassed, by how much. You would think that before one arrived at the level of abstraction and generalization in Sturtevant these elementary matters of quantification would have been satisfactorily settled; but you would be wrong. The great soft belly, received opinion, matured early in the history of Romance philology. Schuchardt is responsible in this case: 'nicht *parum frequentata* sondern ungemein haüfig war die Verwechselung der Buchstaben B und V im dritte Jahrhundert unserer Zeitrechnung'.[34] This impressionistic assertion was rightly criticized by Corssen;[35] nevertheless it soon became standard doctrine, and, translated from spelling to phonemics, was expressed in such formulations as Seelmann's: 'vom dritte Jahrhundert ab /w/ und /b/ vollständig zusammenfallen und *promiscue* geschrieben werden'.[36] The primary evidence which lies behind this kind of assertion was the famous Stratonicea copy of the edict of Diocletian (A.D. 301), on which see below; but it was and remains incautious to draw broad conclusions from a document which was both drafted by a Greek not very well acquainted with Latin and set up with a Greek version in a place where Greek was overwhelmingly the dominant language.

For by the third century A.D. it is fairly clear that Greek had no intervocalic [b] of its own and there would be a tendency for Greeks speaking Latin to use their [β] in pronunciation and, when writing in the Roman alphabet, to write this with ⟨B⟩; this would happen independently of any native Latin developments in the same direction. As for Latin /w/, as long as this was pronounced [w], the best that Greek could do was to substitute syllabic /u:/ written ⟨OY⟩, because in the *koiné* there was no [w]. This in turn could lead to problems of accentuation in borrowed words – how should one pronounce and accent Λιουιος, Λιουια? – and this may have encouraged sound-substitution by Greeks of their /β/ in the representation of Latin words with intervocalic [w] well before the sound became [β] in Latin, to simplify the problem of accent-placing. Indeed, the question may be posed, whether there is not here another case of *Graecia capta ferum uictorem* . . ., for in the first two centuries A.D. we must reckon with very large numbers of not altogether competent Latin-speaking Greeks in the East, in Egypt, and in Italy.[37] In other words, if one asks among whom it is most likely that intervocalic /b/ and /w/ merged wholly as [β], the answer would be, bilingual Greeks who did not speak Latin very competently, and it is in this light that we should interpret such isolated documents as the Stratonicea copy of Diocletian's edict.

However this may be, it was in the latter part of the nineteenth century that the *communis opinio* was formulated that the *general* collapse of intervocalic /b/ and /w/ in Latin happened early; on the basis, it must be said, of quite inadequately analysed material – the indices to *CIL* only began to become available at the end of the century – and of *a priori* assumption as to what was probable. For it was taken as axiomatic that distinctive features of Classical Latin phonology which are irrecoverable from the comparison of the Romance languages must in fact have disappeared from spoken Latin at a specially early date; for example, the coalescence of /a/ and /a:/, and of intervocalic /b/ and /w/ as /β/.[38] But this is not necessarily true. Such losses of distinction could also have taken place separately in different places at different rates and at widely different times, creating in the sequel the false impression of a homogeneity which never existed. It is the contemporary Latin evidence which must decide. While this is, of its nature, unpropitious for /a/ and /a:/ (since only one symbol was available), the use of ⟨B⟩ and ⟨V⟩ *can* be traced, and linguistically significant variation observed through the spelling.

Two other implicit considerations have combined to give specious support to the idea that /b/ and /w/ collapsed specially early and universally. The first is that spelling-confusion of ⟨B⟩ and ⟨V⟩ is common in the manuscripts of the *auctores* in varying degrees. But this should not be allowed to prejudice interpretation. Any *auctor* who has been transmitted to us by the normal means appears in his earliest extant manuscripts as Hector did to Aeneas,

> *Squalentem barbam et concretos sanguine crinis*
> *Vulneraque illa gerens quae circum plurima muros*
> *Accepit patrios,*

and in this befoulment *bv* confusion is notoriously common, because of the medieval transmission. A minute's reflection will show that Petronius, for example, can tell us a good deal about the lexis, syntax, morphology, and word-order of the more colloquial Latin of the first century A.D., but not much about features of its phonology or the 'accent' which might differentiate it from Classical Latin. The fact that his peculiarly wretched *traditio* offers, e.g., *interpellabit* for *-auit* at *Sat.* 39 and *auellanas* at 137, or that Catullus' manuscripts offer *conturbauimus* and *perambulauit* at 5. 11, 29. 7 where sense requires *-bimus*, *-bit*, or that the Palatines of Plautus have the same error, e.g. at *Cas.* 346, 352, tells us nothing about these authors' spelling (or pronunciation): we must prescind from all that.

Secondly, it has always been assumed that the *Appendix Probi* listing 'good' and 'bad' forms represents a work compiled at Rome in the fourth or even, forsooth, the third century A.D. As such, in the absence of any other tracts of even remotely comparable apparent antiquity, the *Appendix Probi* is familiar to everyone as crucial evidence for the absolute dating of various vulgar phenomena as widespread in the common speech of third- and fourth-century Rome – *plebes non pleuis, tabes non tauis, baculus non uaclus, uapulo non baplo, tolerabilis non tolerauilis* – and it is accorded a prominent place in every elementary handbook. But C. A. Robson has shown in a paper of the first importance[39] that the traditional dating of the work is a mere assumption based on nothing whatever, and that the list of proscriptions is in fact a compilation made by a *Scotus* working at Bobbio aimed at written errors common in his own time, the *seventh* century A.D., and that his standard of correctness was not Classical but contemporary Visigothic and African Christian Latin. This does not rob the work of its linguistic interest; we cite it elsewhere in this paper in that spirit. But it cuts away the special status and diagnostic authority traditionally given to it for the specially early dating of

Romance features, and puts it in the same league as, say, Priscian or Isidore. We come back to the essential point: we must examine without prejudice the contemporary documents.

What are we looking for? Sturtevant seems to think that if a man writes, e.g., *D. M. Geminia Fortuna Talauro Proculo coniugi benemerenti fecit qui bixit annis L mensibus undecim diebus biginti nobem* (*CIL* vi. 19009; Rome, undated) he must be using [β] in what he writes as ⟨DIEBUS⟩ as well as in ⟨NOBEM⟩. But there is an obvious fallacy here. While this kind of spelling shows that he did not have intervocal [w], it is perfectly compatible with his having had *either* just intervocalic [β] in these words or with his having had [β] in ⟨NOBEM⟩ but [b] in ⟨DIEBUS⟩ etc. One cannot tell. Proof of the collapse of intervocalic /b/ and /w/ as [β] is only to be had from inscriptions, etc., which show spellings like those quoted above from the *Appendix Probi* in which we have the spelling ⟨V⟩ for ⟨B⟩, as, e.g., in *CIL* vi. 9162 (Rome, A.D. 522): *qui si uiuos conparaberunt siui erediuusque s(uis)*.

And we need proof, because there is a very marked bias in favour of the spelling ⟨B⟩ for ⟨V⟩ and against the spelling ⟨V⟩ for ⟨B⟩ in earlier times. The imbalance was noted long ago,[40] but its extent has never been properly appreciated. Such was the strength of the *a priori* assumption that intervocalic /b/ and /w/ must have collapsed at a specially early date in most people's speech, that W. M. Lindsay in noting the fact that the spelling ⟨V⟩ for ⟨B⟩ is rarer than the reverse nevertheless embraced the then already standard view, and tried to explain away the imbalance in spelling. In was natural, said he, to write ⟨B⟩ rather than ⟨V⟩ for what was now a spirant consonant, because ⟨V⟩ was also the sign for a vowel; therefore people would feel less inclined to use the spelling ⟨V⟩ for the spirant. This idea has been recently revived by J. N. L. Adams,[41] but it will not bear scrutiny. For one thing, the very same writers who used ⟨B⟩ for ⟨V⟩ and ⟨V⟩ for ⟨B⟩ were themselves far more frequently using the symbol ⟨V⟩ for intervocalic /w/, pronounced by them as [β]; if there had seemed to be something intrinsically 'wrong' about representing the sound [β] with the symbol ⟨V⟩, this would not be the case, and the spelling of both phonemes /w/ and /b/ in intervocalic position with the symbol ⟨B⟩ should have become virtually standard, which it never did become, and praiseworthy, because rational and economical. Again, it is easier to cut a ⟨V⟩ than a ⟨B⟩. If Lindsay were right, we should have to suppose that psychological inhibition here triumphed over the principle of minimum effort; which is not what one observes elsewhere in palaeography, language, or life. The *onus probandi*, then, lies with those who allege that the collapse of intervocalic /b/ and /w/ as [β] was complete and general at an early date; for a more exact analysis would recognize three kinds of spelling with respectively one, two, and three possible linguistic interpretations. These are:

1. (rare, late, and localized) the case of those who, by using the spelling ⟨V⟩ for intervocalic /b/ at all, betray that, in their pronunciation, *(h)abena* and *auena*, *amabit* and *amauit* were homophonous, and that they had only intervocalic [β];
2. (less rare, less late) the case of writers who occasionally use the spelling ⟨B⟩ for intervocalic /w/ but not ⟨V⟩ for intervocalic /b/: these people certainly did not pronounce intervocal /w/ as [w] and they might have only intervocal [β]; but it is an illogical error in Sturtevant and others to suppose that this *must* have been so, for it is equally possible in any given case that the writer had [β] for intervocalic /w/, but [b] for intervocalic /b/, so that the words cited above would not be homophonous for him;
3. (far the commonest at all periods) the case of good spellers, who might have just intervocalic [β] for /w/, /b/; *or* [β], [b]; *or* [w], [b] even at a late date – the last being the people to whom Consentius makes allusion, if we may infer that those who had initial [w] for /w/ in his day also kept it intervocalically.

In any part of the Empire where one finds (as at Rome itself) all three types of spelling, that is as close to the linguistic facts as one can get; but if there are places where only (2) and (3) are to be found, that is a rather strong argument against the collapse of /b/ and /w/ as intervocalic [β] and suggests the survival of a phonemic opposition realized by some as [β], [b] and others as [w], [b]; and if there are places, as there are, where only (3) is attested before the fifth century or even later, that implies not only that an opposition was maintained, but that [w], [b] was the dominant realization even at a late date. The greater the quantity of material, the more sure one may be not only that e.g. ⟨AMAVIT⟩, ⟨AMABIT⟩ were not homophonous in those areas, but also that /w/ and /b/ were realized intervocalically as [w] and [b]; for, in view of the manifold vulgarisms of other kinds that the material presents, this 'correctness' cannot possibly be attributed to the excellence of local schooling.

The *suggestio falsi* in Sturtevant which has misled Jackson on a rather important element of his argument is that promiscuous confusion of /b/ and /w/ in intervocalic position must be assumed as widespread, even dominant, in all brands of spoken Latin and in all places not later than

A.D. 300 or so. This is not only not supported by examination of the evidence; it is unequivocally refuted by the fact that there is significant local variation, which can only be explained by our deducing that we have to do with an important isogloss. In short, *bv* confusion of either kind is so exceedingly rare before the later fifth century in any of the Celtic or German parts of the Empire that there can be no question of the simple homophony in these parts of *(h)abena*, *auena*; *amabit*, *amauit*, etc., for ⟨V⟩ for ⟨B⟩ is conspicuously absent, while the remarkable rarity of ⟨B⟩ for ⟨V⟩ even in the most demotic inscriptions suggests that the pronunciation remained dominantly [w], [b]. This means Britain, the Spains, the Gauls, the Germanies, and Cisalpina.

Within Italy itself there is some marked variation; and it is in those parts where the speaking of Greek was particularly important and deeply rooted that we find the intervocalic spellings ⟨B⟩ for ⟨V⟩ (fairly common from the third century) and ⟨V⟩ for ⟨B⟩ (rare before the fourth century). The variation is sufficiently well marked to imply a material difference between Transalpine Latin in general and the Latin of more directly Hellenized parts of the Empire. W. A. Baehrens noted long ago that the spelling ⟨B⟩ for initial ⟨V⟩ was distinctly rarer in the North and West than elsewhere, and our findings for intervocal position are parallel.[42] Together these observations are of material importance, because they point to a dialect difference within Imperial Latin; and, as everyone knows, such differences do not exist: all the handbooks say so. All that means, however, is that compilers of handbooks like to work at a safe distance from primary evidence, especially if it has not been analysed conveniently; and this evidence has not been analysed at all. In summary, the facts as far as the Western Empire are concerned are as follows.

A. *The early evidence*

i. Pompeii

In the first 9,184 inscriptions in *CIL* iv, mainly *graffiti* of the period A.D. 60–79, one finds:

	Initial		Intervocal	
	⟨B⟩ for ⟨V⟩	⟨V⟩ for ⟨B⟩	⟨B⟩ for ⟨V⟩	⟨V⟩ for ⟨B⟩
Names	6	0	0	(2)
Vocabulary	4	9	(1?)	0

The Pompeian material has been carefully discussed by Väänänen in his study of Pompeian Latin, and he rightly draws attention to the extreme rarity of the phenomena in a corpus of this size.[43] The only possible case of intervocal ⟨B⟩ for ⟨V⟩ is the very doubtful interpretation of ⟨HAB⟩ in a list of food-items (iv. 4186) as meaning [aβ(e:na)]; the two cases of intervocal ⟨V⟩ for ⟨B⟩ are spellings of the name *Vibius*, *-ia*, in which, as Väänänen suggests, we have special cases of assimilation. Remembering how large and illiterate this corpus is, we must assign it to type (3) and conclude that relatively few people had [β] at all, and that the phonemes /b/ and /w/ in intervocal position were strongly opposed as [b], [w] and perhaps [b], [β].

ii. Elsewhere

CIL iii. 7251 ⟨LEBARE⟩ for ⟨LEVARE⟩ is from Tegea in Arcadia, and is conspicuous by its isolation. It occurs in a record of words of the Emperor Claudius composed in A.D. 49/50, but it does not follow, as Richter, Sturtevant, and others seem to assume, that this is anything like the right date of the inscription itself.

The earliest relevant papyri and ostraca from Egypt date from the early second century.[44] Rustius Barbarus has ⟨OBLISCERE⟩, ⟨EXIVT⟩, but no *bv* confusion, nor is there in the small amount of the Vindolanda material (c. A.D. 105) so far published.[45] The letters of the half-Greek Claudius Terentianus from Karanis in Egypt (c. A.D. 115), amounting to c. 1000 words of text, show half a dozen cases of initial ⟨B⟩ for ⟨V⟩, and none of initial ⟨V⟩ for ⟨B⟩; there are two cases of ⟨B⟩ for ⟨V⟩ in intervocalic position (⟨NEGABIT⟩, ⟨QVMQVPIBIT⟩) against about two dozen words correctly spelt, and one very doubtful case of ⟨V⟩ for ⟨B⟩ (*P. Mich.* viii. 467. 16, ⟨. . . ETIVIME . . .⟩ in a fragmentary context interpreted as *et ibi me*), against threescore words with intervocalic [-b-] rightly spelt. This shows how rare the phenomena are at Pompeii; but it is not clear from this evidence that Terentianus had only [β] and this material is no basis for generalization anyway. Next there is *CIL* xi. 137:

> *C. Iul. Mygdonius generi Parthus natus ingenuus capt(us) pubis aetate dat(us) in terra Romana qui dum factus ciues R(omanus) iuuente fato collocaui arcam dum esse annoru L peti usque a pubertate senectae meae peruenire nunc recipe me saxe libens tecum cura solutus ero.*

This interesting epitaph comes from Ravenna, and is merely compatible on epigraphical grounds with a first-century date; supposing this is right, *iuuente* is startlingly isolated if it is for *iubente*; but the meaning is peculiar: 'at the behest of fate I set up this sarcophagus'. One suspects that Mygdonius, a Parthian who learnt evidently pretty slipshod Latin as a young man in slavery, perhaps intended 'becoming a Roman citizen with Fate's help', in which case *iuuente* is merely a slip for *iuuante*.

iii. Second- and third-century evidence

Initial position: *CIL* xiv. 2793 ⟨BERECVNDVS⟩ (Latium, A.D. 143), xiv. 169 ⟨BALBIS⟩ (Gabii, A.D. 169), vi. 2093 ⟨BOVEMVS⟩ (Rome, c. 170), vi. 2099 ⟨BITTATIS⟩, ⟨BACCHAM⟩, ⟨BERBECES⟩ (Rome, A.D. 183), vi. 723 ⟨BICTORINO⟩ (Rome, A.D. 184). Conversely, vi. 7582 ⟨VENE VALETIS⟩ (Rome, A.D. 187+).

Intervocal: *CIL* vi. 2120 ⟨IVBENTVTIS⟩ ⟨IVBENTIVS⟩ (beside ⟨NOEMBR⟩) (Rome, A.D. 155), vi. 32398a ⟨IVBENTVTIS⟩ (Rome, A.D. 174).

The earliest datable case of intervocalic ⟨V⟩ for ⟨B⟩ that I can find (apart from ⟨IVVENTE⟩, see above) is *CIL* vi. 32877 ⟨FAVIANO⟩ (Rome, A.D. 201), after which there is vi. 10944 ⟨LIVERTVS⟩ (Rome, A.D. 209 according to Richter, but what ground is there for this?), vi. 2464 ⟨SEVACIA⟩ (said by Richter to be of A.D. 219; evidence?).

Throughout the second and third centuries, datable examples of these confusions are, proportionally, exceedingly scarce at Rome itself, and the reason why one cites no cases from north of the Alps is that there *are* none.

iv. Diocletian's edict, A.D. 301

The Stratonicea-copy of the price-edict is disconcertingly and suddenly rife with all kinds of *bv* confusion as well as correct spelling (*CIL* iii, pp. 824–6): ⟨BIRIDIS BESTIS BEL BICIAE; VABVLONICVS; CLABO DIBERSI VBAE SIBE OBIFERVS OLIBA PABVS FLVBIALIS DESAEBISSE; VAVVLONICVS; SEVVM PRAESTAVITVR LAVORATVM LIVIDO⟩, etc. ⟨B⟩ for ⟨V⟩ dominates here too over ⟨V⟩ for ⟨B⟩. But this is isolated, and cannot be invoked in evidence for spoken Latin *everywhere*: all that it proves is that by the early fourth century Greeks speaking Latin used intervocal [β] for Latin /w/ and /b/, which is only natural. Other eccentric latin inscriptions from Greek contexts are: *CIL* iii. 218 ⟨CIBITATIOVM⟩ (Cyprus, A.D. 198), iii. 14 ⟨FLABIVS EVDAEMON⟩ (Alexandria, A.D. 199); cf. e.g. *PSI* 756 (Oxyrrhynchus, fourth century) ⟨NOBVS⟩, ⟨TRAVE⟩.[46]

v. Fourth-century material

From Diocletian's edict, one might expect wholesale confusion over ⟨B⟩ and ⟨V⟩ in fourth-century material, but this is not the case: the earliest properly Latin inscription to show any mutual confusion is *CIL* v. 281 dating from A.D. 314 and found at Patavium but probably originally at Rome, a very lengthy text which has ⟨COMPROVARE⟩ once and once ⟨OBSERBANDVM⟩. It is, in fact, only in certain well-defined areas that one finds such confusion on any scale, e.g., in Rome, Ostia and Latium, and in the traditionally Greek parts of southern Italy; see e.g. *CIL* vi. 142 *manduca uibe* (*i.e. bibe*) *lude e beni at me; cum uibes* (*i.e. uiues*) *bene fac, hoc tecum feres* (Rome); *CIL* xiv. 3323 (Praeneste); ix. 10 (Nemetum, southern Italy, A.D. 341); x. 478 (Calabria, A.D. 344).[47]

Again note that one cites no dated examples from north of the Alps, because there are none.

B. *The material from Rome*

i. Its general perspective

The confusions of ⟨B⟩ for ⟨V⟩ and ⟨V⟩ for ⟨B⟩ are at least as common at Rome as they are anywhere else; and the recently completed computer-concordances to *CIL* vi,[48] which contains a vast body of material ranging in date from the first to the sixth centuries (c. 39,000 inscriptions of varying lengths), make it possible to see what one means by 'common'. We find:

1. ⟨B⟩ for ⟨V⟩, initial position, e.g.

uale (-as, -te): bale (-as, -te)	88	:	2
Valens, Valent(in)- : Balens, Balent(in)-	351	:	5
Vener- : Bener-	264	:	14
uend- : bend-	91	:	3
uerna : berna	605	:	7
Victor- : Bictor-	869	:	9
uet(e)ran- : bet(e)ran-	192	:	6
uinum : binum	50	:	0
uirgo : birgo	92	:	1
Vitalis : Bitalis	374	:	10
uita : bita	515	:	14
uix- : bix-	8643	:	100
uiu- : biu-	589	:	14
uiu- : bib-		:	37
uoc- : boc-	33	:	0
Voconi- : Boconi-	26	:	1
uol- : bol-	105	:	8
uou- : bou-	125	:	1

2. ⟨V⟩ for ⟨B⟩, initial position

benemerenti : uenemerenti	3905	:	17

There are *no* other cases.

3. ⟨B⟩ for ⟨V⟩, intervocalic position, e.g.

Flaui- : Flabi-	1808	:	28
ciuis : cibis	114	:	3
curauit : curabit (curaut)	103	:	3 (1)
dedicauit : dedicabit (dedicaut)	51	:	2 (0)
deuotus : debotus	63	:	1
Iuuen- : Iuben-	168	:	8
leuis : lebis	75	:	2
militauit : militabit (-aut)	158	:	6 (3)
prouincia : probincia	310	:	2
uiuus : uibus	589	:	119
uiuus : bibus	589	:	37
Seuer- : Seber-	680	:	11
uniuersus : unibersus	29	:	1

4. ⟨V⟩ for ⟨B⟩, intervocalic position, e.g.

Fabius : Fauius	759	:	3
cubicul- : cuuicul-	271	:	0
libens : liuens	60	:	1
labor- : lauor-	17	:	0
debeo : deueo	84	:	1
(h)abeo : (h)aueo (h)abito : (h)auito	268	:	0
sibi : siui	5035	:	10
quibus : quiuus	96	:	2
sebac- : seuac-	50	:	2
incomparabilis : incomparauilis	325	:	12
liber(tus) : liuer(tus)	8771	:	18

These are crude figures, of course, since they are chronologically undifferentiated and make no allowance for the fact that good spellers might be slovenly speakers; they reveal that intervocal ⟨V⟩ for ⟨B⟩ is at least a visible phenomenon (examination shows that the datable are fourth, fifth, or sixth century); and the only conclusion that can be drawn from this is that there is room here for three kinds of pronunciation – traditional [b]/[w], [b]/[β], and [β] in intervocalic position; not that the last is at all widely demonstrable before the fifth and sixth centuries, from which, in fact, most of the ⟨V⟩ for ⟨B⟩ spellings come. We require to tighten our focus on the material.

ii. The dated Christian inscriptions to A.D. 400

This can be done conveniently by examining the dated Christian inscriptions collected by Gi. B. Rossi and supplemented by Gi. Gatti.

A.D.	275–300	301–325	326–350	351–375	376–400	Total
Total no. of inscriptions	25	19	112	285	442	883
Initial ⟨B⟩ for ⟨V⟩	0	1	11	22	31	65
Initial ⟨V⟩ for ⟨B⟩	0	0	0	1	2	3
Intervocal ⟨B⟩ for ⟨V⟩	1	1	7	23	31	63
Intervocal ⟨V⟩ for ⟨B⟩	0	0	0	0	2	2

This is striking. The material is thoroughly vulgar and precisely dated;[49] ⟨B⟩ for ⟨V⟩ is prominent both initially and intervocalically, while ⟨V⟩ for ⟨B⟩ is represented only by three cases of ⟨VENEMERENTI⟩ and two of the name of the consul of A.D. 395 Probinus as ⟨PROVINVS⟩. The implication is quite strong: intervocalic /b/ and /w/ were still distinguished in fourth-century Christian Latin as [b] on the one hand and [β] on the other, for otherwise there ought to be far more cases of intervocalic ⟨V⟩ for ⟨B⟩ among c. 180 cases where we have correct spelling (⟨AMABILIS⟩, ⟨OBIIT⟩, ⟨CVBICVLVM⟩ etc.).

C. *The overall position in Italy and the Western Empire*

The figures given on p. 31 represent in the same order as above the four kinds of *bv* confusion which we here distinguish; in each case, the fifth figure is the round number of inscriptions in the corpus.

	Initial		Intervocal		
	⟨B⟩ for ⟨V⟩	⟨V⟩ for ⟨B⟩	⟨B⟩ for ⟨V⟩	⟨V⟩ for ⟨B⟩	
CIL xiv (Latium, Ostia)	94	18	70	30	5,400
CIL x (Bruttii, Lucania Campania, Sicily, Sardinia)	110	11	84	16	8,400
CIL ix (Apulia, Calabria, Samnium, Sabini, Picenum)	16	2	42	6	9,200
CIL iii (Greece, Illyria, Asia, excluding the islands and Diocletian's edict)	29	2	67	22	15,200

While there is evidently some considerable variation here, all kinds of *bv* confusion are attested before the fifth century, and one's impression is that Rome fits the picture implied for Latium. North and westwards there is a clear contrast:

	Initial		Intervocal		
	⟨B⟩ for ⟨V⟩	⟨V⟩ for ⟨B⟩	⟨B⟩ for ⟨V⟩	⟨V⟩ for ⟨B⟩	
CIL v (Gallia Cisalpina)	12	1	19	4	9,000
CIL xii (Narbonensis)	5	1	8	7	6,000
CIL xiii (Three Gauls + Germaniae)	7	0	(22)	(25)	12,500[50]
CIL ii (Hispaniae)	2	0	4	1	6,300
CIL vii + *RIB* (Britannia)	(2)	0	(1)	(1)	2,300

The higher among these figures are exclusively accounted for by high concentrations of very late Christian inscriptions (so almost all the cases of intervocal confusion in *CIL* xiii; these almost all belong to the sixth and seventh centuries). The possible British examples are *RIB* 1 ⟨. . . HOMINIBVS BAGIS BITAM . . .⟩ on an imported statue; ⟨IVBENIS⟩ on a plate from York (*CIL* vii. 1336. 546), ⟨VIVIVS⟩ (*RIB* 306).[51]

D. *Conclusions on /b/ and /w/*

The conclusions to be drawn from this evidence seem to be as follows.

1. The spelling ⟨B⟩ for ⟨V⟩ is, before the fifth century, proportionally

far rarer than is often implied in handbooks on Vulgar Latin and Romance.

2. There is a significant local variation in its incidence. It is most frequent in those parts where we must reckon with Greek as a major language (especially Rome, Ostia, and environs; south Italy and the islands). In Gallia Cisalpina and in the whole of Transalpine Europe ⟨B⟩ for ⟨V⟩ is markedly rare, and ⟨V⟩ for ⟨B⟩ still rarer, and it is not until the fifth century that examples become 'common'; if we were to discount these, the contrast would be still stronger. At some places, e.g. Trier, one cannot find any cases even in the late sixth century.

3. Britain is so far from being peculiar in showing very few cases of ⟨B⟩ for ⟨V⟩ that it closely matches the Gauls, the Spains, the Germanies, and Cisalpina in this matter, but not more southerly and eastern parts.

4. This local variation was noted by Baehrens[52] for *initial* ⟨B⟩ for ⟨V⟩; the surprising and important thing is that it is also true of intervocal ⟨B⟩ for ⟨V⟩.

5. If ⟨B⟩ for ⟨V⟩ is rare in the Western Empire right through and beyond the Imperial period, the reverse spelling of ⟨V⟩ for ⟨B⟩ is still rarer. South and east, it is at least visible.

6. This striking correctness of spelling in the North and West cannot be attributed to the good education of the writers and engravers, because the same material which manifests it is rife with other kinds of vulgarism.

7. The evidence of spelling from Cisalpina northwards and westwards is only compatible with a Latin in which /w/ and /b/ remained opposed in intervocalic position much later than is assumed by Romance scholars; /b/ evidently remained [b], and /w/ was [w] and/or [β]; the latter less frequently than in the South.

8. The evidence from Rome southwards and eastwards is more complex and is compatible with the co-existence of [b]/[w], [b]/[β], and [β]-speakers, in indeterminable numbers in the fourth century.

9. Since Greek in Imperial times had neither [b] nor [w], only [β], and since Celtic and German for their part had only [b] and [w], not [β], it is pretty clear why there should be this divergence.

10. Since intervocalic /b/ and /w/ remained opposed intervocalically right through the Imperial period not only in the Latin spoken in Britain but in the whole of the Western Empire, it is entirely without significance that the British loanwords reflect this distinction, whether it was realized by most people as [b]/[β, v] or [b]/[w].

2. QUALITY AND QUANTITY IN THE VOWEL-SYSTEMS

A. *J. Loth and the vocalization of the loanwords*

> Short stressed (Latin) [i] and [u] became respectively (close) [e] and [o] in Vulgar Latin. The former . . . was general in ordinary Vulgar Latin by the third century . . . the second . . . was regular at least as early as the fourth century or before [*LHEB*, 86f.; cf. 274, 283]; . . . the Classical Latin system of vowel quantity . . . was replaced in Vulgar Latin . . . so *dīxī*> *dĭxĭ*, *vălēs*> *vālĕs* . . . in stressed syllables it was general by the fourth and fifth centuries . . . there is no certain trace of any of this in British; with one or two possible exceptions, the loanwords show that the Classical quantity system was preserved, even with unstressed vowels, in the Latin of Roman Britain [*LHEB*, 88, cf. 269–71, 289–90, 303–4, 308, 331, 405].

These points about qualitative and quantitative changes in later spoken Latin in the West are intimately related; they are by far the most important. For they can be checked against a large number of examples; if the premisses are true and the results uniform, we have a powerful argument for the unexpectedly conservative character of 'British Latin', loosely and misleadingly identified by Jackson (*LHEB*, 88) with 'the Latin of Roman Britain' at large.

Because of the special importance of these points, it seems ungenerous on Jackson's part that he should fail to mention here or in his other discussions that their author was J. Loth, who made the essential observation in 1892 in the passage quoted above (p. 14). For Loth, having given a basically correct account of the nature of the proto-Romance vowel-changes, then a relatively recently established matter, very rightly remarked that: 'ces phénomènes se sont accomplis par étapes successives, mais beaucoup moins tôt que la plupart des romanistes ne le supposent' [*Mots latins*, 64], an observation as true now as it was then; and he noted the apparent paradox that the loanwords 'nous présentent toutes les voyelles toniques intactes avec leur quantité et leur qualité diverses, parfaitement distinctes.'

Further,

> la voyelle atone aussi, au moins la posttonique latine ([ásinus, péctinem]), quand elle n'est pas déjà tombée ([wír'dem, sól'dus]), ne semble plus atteinte que la tonique: un phénomène particulier d'accentuation en brittonique l'a préservée du sort des atones.

Loth was alluding to the uniformly penultimate placing of the word-accent in British; accentuations such as [asínus] are of course utterly alien to any kind of Latin. He continued:

> Une remarque ici est nécessaire: les mots latins ont dû passer en brittonique, assez souvent, sous une forme plutôt en quelque sorte classique que vulgaire. C'est ainsi qu'aujourd'hui encore, les mots pénètrent, en armoricain, non sous une forme populaire, mais sous une forme exclusivement classique [i.e., Parisian]. Ils pénètrent par l'école, l'armée, par l'intermédiaire de la classe lettrée. Les conditions étaient assurément autres en Bretagne insulaire [quite], mais il y a là, néanmoins, une possibilité dont il faut tenir compte [*Mots latins*, 65].

From the Latin point of view, the interesting thing to which Loth was here drawing attention was that post-tonic unaccented syllables in such words as

[ásinus cálamus mánica péctinem púrpura círcinus]

whence Welsh

⟨asyn⟩ 'ass' ⟨calaf⟩ 'reed(s)' ⟨maneg⟩ 'glove' ⟨peithyn⟩ 'weaver's slay' ⟨porffor⟩ 'purple' ⟨cylchyn⟩ 'circle, circumference'

were evidently preserved in the Latin from which the British forms were originally borrowed. Loth, being French, and writing when he did, was perhaps unduly impressed by this. Gallo-Latin, at a *very* late stage in its emergence as French, went further than other Romance languages in syncopation of such words, so that we have French

âne chaume manche peigne pourpre cerne,

but e.g. Italian

asino calamo/calmo manega pettine porpora cercine.

The milder and older kinds of syncopation involving liquid consonants which one does find implied by the loanwords (e.g. Welsh ⟨gwyrdd⟩ 'green' from [wir'dem]; Welsh ⟨swllt⟩ 'shilling', Breton ⟨saout⟩ 'beast'[53] from *[sol'tum] for [sol'dum], were widespread and early in Latin, while the harsher kinds characteristic of French did not occur at all in most of the Empire (*peigne*, etc.). One notes that Loth was careful to restrict this claim to post-tonic unaccented vowels; as he was evidently aware, the British treatment of pre-tonic unaccented long vowels by no means unambiguously supports the claim that quantity was carefully maintained in the Latin from which the loans were taken (see below, p. 56ff.).

So, according to Loth, the loanwords reflect an unexpectedly 'correct' Latin and he very tentatively suggested that this might be attributed to the influence of the schoolmaster among others. Jackson refers briefly and out of context to Loth's comparison of the linguistic situation in Brittany in the 1890s (*LHEB*, 111). But he does not make it clear to his reader why Loth made his suggestion, or that Loth had linguistic evidence at all. Now earlier in the same chapter Jackson had written (*LHEB*, 80) that 'Celticists have very largely ignored the facts of chronology in the living Latin tongue, and have tended to treat the sources of the loanwords as if they were the Classical language of Caesar's day'; as suggested above, it cannot in fact be excluded that the source of *some* loanwords was exactly that. Jackson's criticism seems to have been aimed in the general direction of H. Lewis and H. Pedersen;[54] but it is particularly unfortunate and unfair to Loth that, in consequence of Jackson's presentation, any reader of his book will come away with the false impression that it was Jackson who first diagnosed a discrepancy between the kind of Latin implied by the vocalization of the loanwords and the 'living Latin tongue'. Hence Jackson has been given exclusive credit for the diagnosis and the explanation in the best handbooks and articles, and the claim, which is properly Loth's, is treated as objective fact. But the general assertion that the Classical quantity system was preserved in the Latin underlying the loanwords is itself highly misleading.

The changes in the vowel-system of later Latin were such as greatly to reduce the possible word-conformations of Classical Latin. Quantity ceased to be phonemic and became a function of accentuation, but the chronology is by no means as clearly definable as Jackson asserts.

In order to weigh the claims of Loth and Jackson we need an inventory of loan-material. Unfortunately none of the available lists can be regarded as adequately well-documented, analytic, comprehensive, or critical. The fresh compilation of a vocabulary with a detailed commentary displaying all these virtues and including and distinguishing material which may or may not be genuinely ancient is greatly to be desired if there is to be further progress in this whole subject.

For the present purpose, however, a sampling technique will be adequate, for we are concerned in the first instance with the relative frequency of word-patterns and the perspective of the material as a whole.[55] The following list is based *in primis* on the inventory compiled by H. Lewis in his *Yr Elfen Ladin yn yr Iaith Gymraeg* (1943). Lewis seems to have restricted himself to words attested in Welsh for which parallel forms could be cited in Breton and/or Cornish. This was a good working criterion, but it is not intrinsically infallible. For there are cases where a borrowing has or may have entered all three Brittonic languages separately from Old French, as certainly the Celtic representatives (rightly omitted by Lewis) of French *brave* (supposed to be from Latin *barbarus*).[56] It is generally stated that Welsh ⟨ffrwyth⟩, Breton ⟨froez⟩, and Cornish ⟨fruit⟩ 'result, offspring, fruit' all represent Late Latin [fructus] for Classical [fru:ctus], and this is probably right, but one wonders whether it is out of the question that any or all of these forms could, in fact, merely represent borrowings of Old French; for in this case, the post-Latin developments would have run roughly *pari passu* in Romance and Celtic and not divergently, as, say, in a word like *fidem* (see p. 40ff.). The explicit examination of such matters would be a useful aspect of the lexicon which one wishes one could consult. On the other hand other words certainly of ancient stock are attested in only one British language, e.g. Breton ⟨estr-enn⟩ 'oyster' from [ostrja],[57] ⟨gwiler⟩ 'place publique' from [wi:lla:re],[58] and Lewis, writing specifically about the Latin loanwords in Welsh, omits these. His material has been supplemented here to a limited extent from the material in Loth's *Mots latins*, which, used carefully, remains indispensable, from Jackson's list (*LHEB*, 78–80), and from Haarmann's study of the semantic categories of the loanwords in Welsh, so that there are 540 in the sample. One need only look at the first two to appreciate that a good many forms are degenerate or adventitious, certainly not 'Classical' Latin; nevertheless, we arrange the material in groups in descending order of frequency according to their syllabic structure and prosody as it was or should have been before the loss of phonemic quantity. The quantities of final syllables are not noted here as they are of no direct relevance. Proper names are indicated by '(p.n.)' following the name.

B. *Inventory of Latin words borrowed arranged by prosodical pattern*

1. [batt(u)o cattus classis flamma majjor majjus massa palla
pannus saccus pecco cella gemma serra siccus grillo cippus
coccum cloccus cloppus fossa bucca] 22

[amplus arca arma barba calcem factus franci (p.n.) francus
lactis palma parco partem planta planto sacso (p.n.)
scamnum tracto tractus[59] centrum certus gentes membrum
pexa plecta serpem sterno templum tempus tendo testis
wersus cista lignum piscis signum simplum wir'dem wirtus

col'pus corpus coctus cocsa doctus hospes longa pondus pontem porta porto portus postis sol'dus spongus torquem tostus cultrum fundo furca furnus gurdus plumbum turbo turma turta] (=*torta*) 64

[fa:gus fa:ma fa:ta (plu.) gra:num pa:cem pa:gus pa:la pa:lus pla:ga pra:tum ra:na sca:la sta:men stra:ta(?) ce:na ce:ra fe:num fre:num ple:bem re:mus re:te se:bum se:des se:rus the:ca -e:(n)ses de:(n)sus pe:(n)sum me:(n)sa fi:nis li:ma li:tem li:num pi:nus pi:pa pri:mus scri:bo tri:co wi:cus wi:num -o:sus ho:ra mo:rum no:na sco:pa so:lis cu:pa du:rum fu:cus fu:nis fu:rem glu:ten glu:tus lu:na mu:lus mu:rus mu:to mu:tus plu:ma pru:de(n)s pu:rus su:cus] 62

[aether caesar (p.n.) praeda *blaes'cus(?) awctor awrum cawlis lawdo lawrus pawlus (p.n.) poena] (*foenum*, v. fe:num) 11

[la:m'na la:rgus la:csus ma:rcus (p.n.) ma:rtis (p.n.) pa:sco sa:nctus tra:(n)strum ste:lla chri:stus (p.n.) fi:rmus tri:stis di:sco o:rdo fo:rma fru:ctus fu:stis pu:nctum tru:lla] 19

Sub-total 178

2. [ammissus (adm-) commendo affectus effectus] 4

[fossa:tum occlu:do pecca:tum summu:to summu:tus matthaeus (p.n.)] 6

[ascella astilla cancelli castellum compello cultellum porcellus sportella] 8

[abstru:sus alpi:nus alta:re astu:tus cande:la capti:wos compe:(n)sus conde:(n)so condi:co docto:rem excu:so festi:no fonta:na lecti:ca pisca:tus tracta:tus concausa] 17

[aeternus (p.n.) aegyptus awgustus co:(n)sol'dus de:fendo de:fectus de:sertum i:(n)ferna praecepta sa:turnus (p.n.) scri:benda] 11

[cu:pella jo:hannes (p.n.) pu:pilla sco:pella scu:tella wi:werra] 6

[co:(n)so:lor di:wi:nus di:wi:so do:na:tus (p.n.) ju:daeus lo:ri:ca me:(n)su:ra o:ra:tor pa:ge:(n)ses pa:wo:nem praesaepe pri:wa:tus ra:di:ca ro:ma:nus se:cu:rus stra:tu:ra wa:gi:na we:si:ca] 18

[de:sti:llo] 1

[scri:ptu:ra ma:rte:lus] 2

Sub-total 73

3. [brassicae occupo syllaba bajjula] 4

[anchora angelus carcerem circinus comparem culcita fornicem martirem organum panticem pectinem pondere purpura splendidus tempore terminus wesperum] 17

[co:(n)secro co:(n)sonus ci:witas gra:icus la:icus li:tera praebiter (*REW* 6740) spi:ritus tri:nitas u:nitas] 10

[de:struo pra:cticus] 2

[bracchium] 1

[prandium] 1

[ostrea sarcio] 2

[awreus] 1

[be:stia le:ctio ma:rtius] 3

[cingula circulus disculus] 3

[bu:balus c(o)a:gulum fi:bula nu:bilus re:gula scru:pulum se:cale su:bula stra:gulum te:gula] 10

[mu:sculus ra:sculum] 2

Sub-total 56

4. [asinus asina calamus cathegra lapido manica placitum medicus scelere pedites tenerum weneris (p.n.) tripedem monachus opera cubitus cupidus numerus] 18

[cuneus fowea oleum puteus solea] 5

[caprio graphium legio maria (p.n.) radius rapio patior spolium spatium wicia witium] 11

[baculus facula macula populus stimulus stipula strigula tabula humilis] 9

Sub-total 43

5. [(caco) cawus draco faba flagrum gradus latro pater parem spado wac(u)us ferus gregem gena petrus (p.n.) fidem liber picem pila pira (plu.) plico striga witrum focus jowis (p.n.) loco locus modus nota probo schola sonus tonus crucem fuga lucrum putrem *stura(cs)] (=*storax*) 38

[creo leo struo] 3

Sub-total 41

6. [cawella flagellum gemellus locellus necesse patella recessus scamellum stabellum sagitta tabella] 11

[acerbus calendae capistrum columba columna fenestra paternus (p.n.) superbus pedestris taberna] 10

[cana:lis caroenum cate:na coq^{u}i:na coro:na dolo:rem habe:na labo:rem moli:na para:tus peda:lis prophe:ta sali:wa wene:num] 14

[crea:tor rui:na] 2

[ado:rno] 1

Sub-total 38

7.	[capti:witas *almọ:sina] (*REW* 2839)	2
	[anto:nius (p.n.) cal'da:rium contra:rius ecstra:neus secsta:rius licsi:wium psalte:rium salsi:cia *sente:rium]	9
	[eccle:sia commu:nio occa:sio presso:rium]	4
	[q^{u}a:rta:rius]	1
	[co:(n)fectio co:(n)fessio co:(n)stantius de:pendeo]	4
	[ja:n(u)a:rius co:(n)fi:nium de:na:rius o:ra:tio sco:pa:rium]	5
	Sub-total	25
8.	[corrigia grammatica]	2
	[ambrosius (p.n.) historia martirium mercurius (p.n.) *permedium pertineo temperies]	7
	[de:subito o:ceanus]	2
	[co:(n)silium de:ficio di:luwium ma:ceries paeniteo pa:pilio *ro:mania]	7
	[articulus]	1
	[fe:niculum]	1
	[di:scipulus]	1
	Sub-total	21
9.	[bu:bali:nus ca:rita:tem ci:wita:tem tri:nita:tem u:nita:tem]	5
	[impera:tor margari:ta postile:na septima:na tertia:na]	5
	[dispara:tio testimo:nium]	2
	[chri:stia:nus]	1
	[co:(n)struenda]	1
	[offerenda]	1
	Sub-total	15
10.	[agricola (p.n.) diabolus parietem]	3
	[batidio (baptizo) initium manibrium memoria patricius (p.n.) reliq^{u}ia wigilia]	7
	[caliculus capitulum cubiculum]	3
	Sub-total	13
11.	[pecca:to:rem fi:rma:mentum testa:mentum ma:tu:ti:nus]	4
	[ecscu:sa:tio na:ta:li:cia]	2
	[co:(n)stanti:nus (p.n.) sa:turni:nus (p.n.)]	2
	[cancella:rius]	1
	[intelle:ctio]	1
	Sub-total	10
12.	[benedi:co cawita:tem *ceria:sa (cerasus; *REW* 1823) maledi:co maria:nus (p.n.) *parade:(n)sus (paradi:sus) peregri:nus tabula:tum]	8

[elementum monumentum] 2

Sub-total 10

13. [dia:conus] 1
[apostolus episcopus] 2
[febr(u)a:rius hono:rius (p.n.) *pape:rius] (papü:rus; *REW* 6218) 3
[peri:culum] 1

Sub-total 7

14. [*ace:da:rium (>acce:da:rium >ab'ce:da:rium >a:be:ce:da:rium) crea:tu:ra dolo:ro:sus quadra:ge:s(ima) sacra:mentum] 5
[pugilla:res diurna:ta] 2

Sub-total 7

15. [beneficium sacrificium] 2

Sub-total 2

16. [interwenio] 1

Sub-total 1

Grand total 540

C. *Vowel-equations*

Vowel quantity was phonemic in British throughout and for some time after the Roman Occupation; during which it was disappearing in Latin, first in final syllables, then in internal unaccented syllables, last in accented syllables; precision as to the progress, extent, and date of completion of this process is unattainable. The British vowel-system subsequently underwent a reformation broadly similar in principle which was complete, according to Jackson, by about 600 A.D. In modern Welsh the normal representatives of short British /a/ /e/ /i/ /o/ /u/ are written

⟨a⟩ ⟨e⟩ ⟨y⟩ ⟨o⟩ ⟨w⟩

and of long /a:/ /e:/ /i:/ /o:/ /u:/ respectively

⟨aw, o⟩ ⟨wy⟩ ⟨i⟩ ⟨u⟩ ⟨u⟩;

so we have e.g. Welsh *cwyn* from Latin *ce:na* and *-us* from *-o:sus*. Final syllables in general were lost in the course of the sixth century. In principle it has been assumed by Celtic scholars, and it is *broadly* confirmed in practice, that British speakers would represent what they heard as long and short Latin vowels with the nearest equivalent long and short British vowels. Early on this was a straightforward matter, but by the end of the third century (Jackson's dating) long British /o:/ closed to coincide with /u:/ so that doubt might subsequently arise for British speakers over what to do with the accented vowel in a Late Latin pronunciation [sǫ:lem, schǫ:lam] replacing [so:lem, scholam] – when and if this happened in Britain. By the mid-fifth century this [u:] had in turn been fronted to [i:]. Meanwhile British /a:/ was increasingly divergent in quality both from British /a/ and from Latin /a:/ in open accented syllables, and in both cases there is some reason to suppose that, sometimes, qualitative similarity was preferred to quantitative (see below pp. 42, 45f.). This matter of principle did not arise in the representation of short unaccented vowels or of short accented vowels in blocked syllables. However, their representation in Welsh is complicated for us by the phenomena of a- and i-affection in British. Short British /a/ and /u/ when followed by a British ending [-a:], subsequently lost, were modified in quality to [e], [o] without change of quantity. British [wid-a:] 'aspect, appearance' gives Welsh ⟨gwedd⟩ (not *⟨gwydd⟩) and [bu-ta:] 'be' gives ⟨bod⟩ (not *⟨bwd⟩).[60] How this applies to the Latin loanwords which had /i/ and /u/ before [-a:] in their borrowed forms is explained below.

The modifications of quality denoted by i-affection are more complex and various, but, from the Latin point of view, the useful handle is that only *short* British vowels could suffer affection of either kind, and when it is observed in a loanword, the implication is that the borrowed form, and (other things being equal) therefore the Latin word itself had a short vowel. Thus in ⟨Emrys⟩, ⟨myfyr⟩ 'contemplation' from [Ambrósius], [memória], both accented vowels suffer i-affection, which seem to show 'correct' Latin forms with short [ó], and not the relatively long open [ǫ́:] which these words would have acquired according to the rules of Late Latin accentuation and prosody. But this is not the only possibility. These words conceivably might have been borrowed in their late forms and betray themselves as such in Welsh without i-affection as *⟨myfur⟩, *⟨Amrus⟩, with long, close British [u] as an attempt at rendering the adventitious length of the open Latin [ǫ:]; but it is at least as likely that the British might solve the problem by representing the Latin sound with their short, open /o/, even at a late date, preferring qualitative approximation to quantitative. Mark the result – a British borrowing which by pure accident would appear to have been taken directly from the older Latin form with short accented /o/, and one could not tell from the borrowed form whether 'correct' Latin was the source or not. The emperor Honorius' name appears in Welsh as ⟨Ynyr⟩, which implies a British starting-point *[onorios], not *[ono:rios, onu:rios] with a long middle vowel, for otherwise the i-affection evident in the Welsh form would not have occurred, and we should have Welsh *⟨Ynur⟩ (for the first vowels in these hypothetical Welsh forms see *LHEB*, 279, 272, 664–6, 591 with Jackson's references). But the *Latin* name was [(h)onó:rius], later [(h)onọ́:rius], and never [(h)onórius] with a short accented vowel. In this case, therefore, which for obvious reasons is pretty late, we perhaps observe British substitution of short [o] for relatively close long Latin [o:], or still closer [ọ:], as also perhaps in ⟨morwydden⟩ 'mulberry' from latin [mo:rum], later [mọ:rum].

In fact, Loth's broad claim, repeated by Jackson, that in general the quantities and qualities of Classical Latin are perfectly maintained in the loanwords, oversimplifies what is really a rather complex matter and prejudices interpretation, because in the majority of cases the vocalization of the loan-material is merely consistent with a 'correct' Latin form, and is equally consistent with later developments in Latin. We turn first to the pyrrhic-iambic and spondaic-trochaic groups, represented above (pp. 37, 38) by (*caco*) *cauus* etc. and *fa:gus fa:ma* etc., as an illustration.

D. *The Latin disyllables*

In our material we have as *possible* ancient borrowings:[61]

1. Short Latin /a/: *cach* 'defecate' *cau* 'hollow' *draig* 'dragon, lord' (i-affection: late British [draci:]) *ffa* 'bean' *fflair* 'fart' *gradd* 'step, rank' *lleidr* 'robber' (i-affection like *draco*) *pader* 'Our Father', 'rosary' *par* 'pair' *ysbaddu* 'spay, castrate' *gwag* 'empty'.

   Long Latin /a:/: *ffa-wydd* 'beechtrees' *ffaw* 'fame' *ffawd* 'fate, prosperity' *grawn* 'grains' *poc* 'kiss' *pau* 'district' *pal* 'spade' *pawl* 'post' *pla* 'plague' Breton *prad*, Cornish *pras* 'meadow' Breton *ran* 'frog' *ysgol* (*yscawl*) 'ladder' *ystof* 'warp' (as opposed to 'weft') *ystrad* 'valley' (?)
2. Short Latin /e/: (?) *ffer* 'stout, valiant, tough' *gre* 'herd (of horses) *gen* 'jaw, chin' *Pedr* 'Peter'

   Long Latin /e:/: *cwyn* 'dinner' *cwyr* 'wax' *ffwyn* 'foin' *ffrwyn* 'bridle' *plwyf* 'parish' *rhwyf* 'oar' *rhwyd* 'net, snare' *swyf* 'scum, froth, yeast' *swydd* 'office, job' *hwyr* 'late', 'evening' *twyg* 'garment' *-wys* 'inhabitants of . . ., (e.g. *Powys* from [pa:ge:(n)se:s]) *dwys* 'grave, solemn, profound' *pwys* 'pound, weight(y)' *mwys* 'hamper, table'
3. Short Latin /i/: *ffydd* 'faith' *llyfr* 'book' *pyg* 'pitch' *pel* 'ball' *per* 'pears' *plygu* 'fold, bend' *ystre* 'long row, boundary' *gwydr* 'glass'.

   Long Latin /i:/: *ffin* 'boundary' *llif* 'saw' *llid* 'wrath, inflammation' *llin* 'flax' *pin* 'pines' *pib* 'pipe' *prif-* 'chief' (in compounds: *prifysgol*, 'university') *ysgrif* 'article, essay' *trig* 'stay, dwelling' Breton *gwic* 'town' *gwin* 'wine'.

4. Short Latin /o/: Middle Welsh and Cornish *foc* 'hearth' *llog* 'interest, hire' *-llog* '-place' *modd* 'way, means' *nod* 'mark' *profi* 'try, test, taste' *ysgol* 'school' *son* 'noise, mention' *ton* 'tune'.
   Long Latin /o:/: *-us* '-ous' *awr* 'hour' *nawn* 'noon' *mor-wydden* 'mulberry' *ysgub* 'broom' *dydd Sul* 'Sunday'.
5. Short Latin /u/: *crog* 'gallows' (*croes, crwys* 'cross') *ffo* 'flight' *llwgr* (?) 'corrupt' *pwdr* 'rotten' *ystor* 'incense'.
   Long Latin /u:/: *cib* 'cup, receptacle, husk' *dur* 'steel' *ffug* 'fictitious' *ffun* 'cord, chaplet' *ffur* 'clever' (!) *glud* 'bird-lime' *glud* 'sticky' *dydd Llun* 'Monday' *mul* 'mule' *mur* 'wall' *mudo* 'flit' *mud* 'dumb' *plu(f)* 'feathers' *prudd* 'wise, true' *pur* 'pure, very' *sug* 'juice'.

In general the British representatives of these Latin words clearly reflect the quantitative distinction of our two word-classes. This is important as a direct proof that one really is dealing, by and large, with antique loanwords. For in Late Latin the pyrrhic-iambic word-class was assimilated *en masse* to the pattern of the spondaic-trochaic in accordance with the rule of later times that accented vowels *in open syllables* should be relatively long, and there were concomitant changes in quality, which, in the Western Empire, were such that the ten opposed Classical vowels of e.g.

[pater/ma:ter/petrus/se:des/fides/fi:nis/focus/wo:cem/crucem/fu:nis]

were regrouped as seven quantitatively undifferentiated vowels, allophonically 'long' in such words because the syllables were open; for in late Latin, all accented syllables were of roughly equal duration and prominence:

[pa:ter-ma:ter/pę:trus/sẹ:des-fẹ:des/fi:nis/fǫ:cus/wọ:cem-crọ:cem/fu:nis][62]

It is important to realize that the later arrangement could not possibly be deduced from Latin inscriptions, etc.; it is only by comparison of French, Spanish, Italian, etc., that one arrives at it. If there were no Classical Latin, we could not possibly discover from comparison of the Romance languages that the disyllables with [a:] represent two previously distinct word-classes,[63] and it would be a mystery why, e.g., Welsh ⟨ffydd⟩ 'faith' (vowel very approximately[ə́]) should not rhyme with ⟨swydd⟩ 'job, office' (vowel approximately [ú:j]). But before one leaps to any conclusions about the character of the Latin spoken in Britain, certain things need to be examined.

Firstly, since loanwords were entering British over a very long period which, as argued above, stretched back into the first century B.C., as long as from today back to Chaucer's time, and since it is the nature of loanwords to fix and preserve traits of the phonology of the language from which they are taken, we should not be surprised, but rather expect, to observe quite clear distinctions of the older word-classes in this material. *Pace* Jackson, it is far from clearly established, or capable of being established from the Latin evidence, when phonemic quantity finally disappeared in accented syllables (unaccented syllables are another matter); and this and the British material as a whole is potentially important primary evidence on this very point.[64] For, depending how early one dates the later arrangement as *fait accompli*, one might expect a larger or smaller element of the loanwords to reflect its vocalization both as to quantity and as to quality. Even if this was as early as A.D. 250, as many people believe, we should still expect strong signs of the earlier quantitative oppositions to be apparent in the material, represented by those words Briticized earlier than that. This would imply nothing as to the somehow specially 'correct' nature of Latin as spoken in Britain. In fact, there is little sign of the later arrangements at all. But we must be careful here. How might they be expected to manifest themselves? This is our second point.

Let us suppose for the sake of the argument that the later arrangement was established c. A.D. 250. It is clear that British borrowers would go on taking words of the types [fi:nis] [se:des] and [fu:nus] with the same long British vowels as before, the vowels which in Welsh become respectively ⟨i⟩ ⟨wy⟩ and ⟨u⟩; to say, therefore, of these words that they *preserve* Classical quality and quantity is seriously misleading, because some no doubt do, but others could be very late, and we cannot tell from phonological evidence which would be which. One might expect that pyrrhic-iambic words like [pater] would in some cases show the same vocalization as [fa:ma], etc., betraying the late date of their adoption. Welsh ⟨ysbawd⟩ 'shoulder(blade)' might be an example representing a late [spa:t(h)a] for [spatha] which should have given *⟨ysbad⟩; but this is doubtful, because it could represent Norman French *espaude* (cf. Scots *spauld*), itself from *[spalta] for *[spa:tla]. The matter is not simplified by the fact that Welsh ⟨ysbodol⟩ 'ladle' also implies a Latin [spa:tla] for [spatula]. Confusion between the classes in fact goes the other way. Celticists agree (more or less) that one has to posit British forms with *short* vowels to explain ⟨ffa-wydd⟩ ⟨pal⟩ ⟨pla⟩ ⟨prad⟩ ⟨pras⟩ ⟨ran⟩,[65] which is five out of the 13 cases of the *fa:gus*-type (p. 37). Since it is out of the question that there should ever have been *Latin* forms [fagus, pala, plaga, pratum, rana] with absolutely short [a], one must recognize that short British /a/ has been pressed into service to represent the quality of the Latin vowel (which was stable) at the expense of quantity, for British /a:/ was in later times moving in the direction of [ǫ:], which it became c. A.D. 600 (Jackson's dating). This granted, it follows that there may well be some words in the pyrrhic-iambic range *caco cauus* . . .(11 words) which were really borrowed from a Latin with allophonic lengthening of older Latin /a/ and which have been accidentally 'corrected' on adoption into British; we cannot tell. Long British /a:/ and as suggested above even short /o/ appear as alternatives to /u/ in the representation of the long close [ọ:] of the group *-o:sus* to *so:lis*, reflecting perhaps the fact that in later British there was a gap here in the vowel-range.

It will be seen that [petrus]- and [focus]-words maintained their separate identity in late Latin with allophonically lengthened unblocked vowels. British borrowings of these words and of others with these vowels in accented open syllables ([weneris, opera; pedite:s, solea, populus, memoria, historia]) regularly show British short /e/ and /o/. Now one obvious reason for this would be that they were borrowed from Latin forms in which phonemic quantity still existed. But it is tacitly supposed by Celticists who have discussed the matter that therefore all such words *must* come from the Classical, not the later forms with lengthening. Wrong. It is not clear that the accented allophone [o:] of open syllables would not have been represented in British as short /o/; and indeed it is hard to see what else a putative fourth-century borrower of, e.g., [schǫ:la] could have done, because, as Jackson says, long British /a:/ did not become sufficiently rounded to represent this sound until c. A.D. 600.

The case of late Latin /e:/ is essentially parallel, but requires closer examination, because the fates of Latin /ae/ and Celtic /ai/ are involved here. Late Latin [pę:trus], [cę:sar] had *long* open vowels; Jackson is mistaken when he asserts *suo Marte* that Classical Latin /ae/ 'became' short open [ę] in the first to second centuries (*LHEB*, 84, 335; 'On the Vulgar Latin of Roman Britain', 86). In fact, the immediate result of the monophthongizing of /ae/ can only have been a long /e:/ which shared quality with the short relatively open Classical /e/ and quantity with the closer long Classical /e:/.[66] When quantity ceased to be phonemic, first in final and then in other unaccented syllables (first–second century) the automatic consequence will have been the disappearance of the new vowel as it will have merged entirely with short /e/. This is possibly reflected in British, where unaccented Latin /ae/ is regularly represented as ⟨e⟩ in Welsh, e.g. in the first syllable of ⟨preseb⟩ 'manger' from [presȩ:pe] from [praesaepe]. When phonemic quantity disappeared in accented syllables, whenever that was, the same will have happened, because, like any other vowel in a blocked accented syllable, it will have been relatively short by the egalitarian accent rule of later Latin which required that all accented syllables should be equal in weight. Thus [praesto] > [prȩ:sto] > [prȩsto].

So far Jackson's assertion is consistent with the facts. But it is wrong of him to suggest that the immediate result of [caelum], [caesar] ever did or could possibly become a Latin pyrrhic-iambic [cḝlum], [cḝsar] instead of trochaic-spondaic [cȩ̄lum], [cȩ̄sar]; for this is a blatant contradiction of the fundamental character and direction of Latin syllabic and accentual development. What in fact happened was that [caesar] gave [cȩ:sar] in the first to second century, which, like any other word of this prosodic shape ([fa:gus ce:na fi:nis no:na plu:ma laurus]) remained a quantitative trochee for the rest of Latinity. When phonemic quantity disappeared in accented syllables, whenever that was, words like [pĕtrus] automatically merged with words like [cȩ:sar] because of the lengthening of their accented vowels. Hence the parallel development in Romance of e.g. *Pierre*, *ciel* from [pȩ:trus], [cȩ:lum]. Jackson (*LHEB*, 335) regards those cases in British where we have British /e/ representing accented free Latin /ae/ as the norm, though there are a couple of cases where British possibly used a long vowel or diphthong. Let us suppose that he is right, and that the words in question are genuinely antique. Examples would be ⟨Cesar⟩ 'Caesar', ⟨preseb⟩ 'manger', British *[predion] crossing *praeda* with *praedium* 'landholding' and giving by i-affection *⟨preidd⟩, Welsh ⟨praidd⟩ 'booty; flock',[67] ⟨Mathew⟩, ⟨Iddew⟩ from British *[mattéwos, ju:déwos] for Latin [matt(h)a͞éus, ju:da͞éus]. We are invited to believe that the use of short British /e/ in these words directly proves that the vowels in the Latin words were short too. For Jackson has a highly speculative theory (*LHEB*, 324–30) about the precise history of Celtic /ai/ in the Roman period, namely that it was already an open [ȩ:] in the first century A.D., and that it had begun to change back to a diphthong by the sixth century, eventually giving Welsh ⟨oe⟩. Since the British did not use this notional British [ȩ:] in these Latin loanwords (*⟨presoeb⟩, *⟨Coesar⟩), the accented Latin vowel cannot have been long. Jackson's evidence for postulating the reduction of Celtic /ai/ so early, and attributing to it the precise character of a long open [ȩ:], is disturbingly thin; and an alternative view is that Pedersen (*VGKS* i, 212) was right to think in terms of British substitution of short British /e/ in these words 'da man im Brit. keinen entsprechenden langen Vokal besass'. Now if this is right, it follows that in any given case of British /e/ representing an accented latin vowel in words like *Petrus*, *Veneris*, it could represent either older [petrus], [weneris], or later [pę:trus], [wę:neris]; so that, once again, the mere fact that British uses a short vowel to represent the stressed Latin vowel in such words is not diagnostic. It goes without saying that the close British /ẹ:/ leading to Welsh ⟨wy⟩ would have been quite inappropriate on grounds of quality for the later sound.

E. *Stressed Latin /i/ and /u/*

The fact that quantitative distinctions between our two word-classes are reflected quite sharply in the Celtic material emerges as less striking than might at first appear. There remains the question of the qualitative changes in /i/ and /u/. It will be seen from the range of the proto-Romance vowels of the West that borrowings made from that kind of 'Latin' would appear in Welsh as e.g. *⟨ffwydd⟩, *⟨pudr⟩ from *[fẹ:dem], *[pọ:trem], not ⟨ffydd⟩ 'faith' and ⟨pwdr⟩ 'rotten' which require the earlier [fidem], [putrem]. On the other hand, we should expect the short allophones of the late vowels in e.g. *[pẹscem], *[plọmbum]; these might be expected to beget Welsh *⟨pesg⟩, *⟨plom⟩. In fact, we have ⟨pysg⟩ 'fish', ⟨plwm⟩ 'lead' from the older forms. Latin words in *-a* are a special case. As explained above, British a-affection would modify preceding short [i], [u], and the results would be the same in Welsh as if the Latin words had entered British in their late forms in those cases (which are the great majority) where the accented Latin syllable was blocked: as Late Latin *[pẹscem] would give Welsh *⟨pesg⟩, so Late 'Latin' *[cẹsta], *[bọcca] would give Welsh ⟨cest⟩ 'belly, receptacle', ⟨boch⟩ 'cheek', which exist; such forms are as well (but not better in any given case) explained by British a-affection in a borrowed British form *[cista:], *[bucca:]. But ⟨pel⟩ 'ball', ⟨ffo⟩ 'flight', which also have reflexes of short British vowels, probably imply a-affection of forms borrowed into British as [pila:], [fuga:], since one might expect Late 'Latin' *[pẹ:la], *[fọ:ga] to become Welsh *⟨pwyl⟩, *⟨ffu⟩ from Briticized forms of these words in which the stem-vowels were long.

It will be seen that the number of words in the material under examination which have /i/, /u/ is proportionally not many; and, since e.g. *picem* and *uitrum*, *crucem* and *fuga* are quite likely to be rather early loans (though of course one cannot know), there is no great significance in their *failing* to behave as late loans. For *crog* is perhaps not to be thought of as having the late Latin [crọ:cem] as its starting point, because thence one might rather expect Welsh ⟨crug⟩ with the exponent of a long British vowel; Lewis and Jackson invent British *[cruc-a:] to explain the short [o]. Then again, the examples of *Honorius* and *morum* (see above) might be invoked to show that [crọ:cem] might indeed be rendered with British [o]; see with what imponderables the whole matter is beset. The most interesting cases are *fidem* and *liber*, both with the older timbre of Latin vocalization; it is noteworthy that [liber] appears in most Romance languages in a bogus 'learned' form, as if it were from Latin [li:ber] – the French for 'book' ought to be *⟨loivre⟩, the Italian, *⟨lebro⟩ – but that the Welsh form reflects the correct Classical quantity.

Jackson regards it as significant that we do not find evidence for the shift of /i/ and /u/. But there *are* possible cases, and their weight is a function of the frequency with which words having these stressed vowels occur at large. The relevant words in our population overall are:[68]

> [fidem liber picem plico tripedem witrum, pila pira striga; *batidio* beneficium co:(n)silium de:ficio initium manibrium martirium *pa:pilio patricius* pertineo witium, *corrigia reliq^{u}ia* wicia *wigilia*; articulus *caliculus capitulum cubiculum di:scipulus fe:niculum stimulus, stipula strigula*; *ammissus* capistrum cippus circinus circulus *disculus episcopus lignum* piscis siccus simplum *signum* wir'dem wirgo wirtus, *astilla* cingula cista *littera* pu:pilla sagitta] (39 + 15 in [-a])

Here we have, firstly, clearly free accented /i/ (to . . . striga), and, lastly, clearly blocked accented /i/ (from *ammissus* . . .). In between there are the two species of word (*beneficium*, *cubic'lum*) which in losing a syllable in mildly vulgar Latin had the /i/ partly blocked before subsequent Romance developments (palatization, re-division, etc.). In each species the words ending in [-a], if any, are given separately. Parallel to this we have for /u/:

> [awgustus *cubitus* crucem cupidus *de:subito humilis* lucrum putrem, fuga; *cuneus* mercurius puteus; cultrum crucs fundo furnos *gurdus* plumbum *sa:turnus* turbo, bucca columba columna furca purpura turma *turta*] (19 + 8 in [-a])

While most of the cases in [-a] have forms which are explicable by a-affection of borrowed /i/ and /u/, this will not do for ⟨gŵyl⟩ 'feast, holiday', from *[we(g)ẹ́:lia] or Middle Welsh ⟨corrui⟩ (modern

⟨carrai⟩) 'thong' from *[corrẹ́:(g)ia]. For the rest, ⟨swyn⟩ 'charm' and ⟨llwyn⟩ 'grove' look to British forms [lẹ:non], [sẹ:non], implying late forms of the Latin ⟨LIGNVM⟩ ⟨SIGNVM⟩ words the history of which in Latin too is problematic. ⟨Caregl⟩ 'chalice' comes from Late Latin [calẹc'lus, carẹc'lus] for [calic'lus] and cannot be explained away by the arbitrary invention of a feminine *[calic'la] (so *GPC* s.v.); for one thing Latin diminutives take their gender from the base form and *calix* is masculine; for another, so is *caregl* in Welsh. ⟨Cufydd⟩ 'cubit' is either bogus or implies *[cọ:bidus] for [cubitus], in which the voicing of the older [-t-] is a simultaneous indication of lateness; and ⟨ufyll⟩ 'humble', if not bogus, implies [ọ:milis] not [humilis], for, as we have seen, Welsh ⟨u⟩ is the proper representative of a long close [ọ:]. *Crwys* implies Latin [crucs], and *croes* may be a variant within Welsh, but it could also represent a late form [crọcs] in Latin. For *crog*, see above.

F. *The character of the loanwords discussed in* E

These two groups of words serve conveniently as sections across the material as a whole, and are typical of it in that one can quite frequently see that the starting-point in British cannot have been 'correct' Classical Latin but something more or less spectacularly different. Sometimes it is the word itself that is a latecomer (*disc'lus gurdus turta astilla* whence ⟨dysgl⟩ 'dish, quoit' ⟨gwrdd⟩ 'fierce, energetic' ⟨torth⟩ 'loaf' ⟨astell⟩ 'shelf'). 'Learned' influence is evident too. ⟨Disgybl⟩ will be a correct formation if Latin ⟨DISCO⟩ had a long /i:/, but if the ⟨I⟩ was short, we should have *⟨dysgybl⟩. ⟨Cabidwl⟩ 'church assembly, côterie' is formed from a bogus Latin [capi:tulum]; the genuine form with short [i] would have given *⟨cebydl⟩; conversely ⟨perygl⟩ 'danger' implies a false form [peric'lum] with short [i]; the genuine [peri:c(u)lum] (long [i:]) should have become ⟨perigl⟩. Sometimes there is evidence of contamination in the British form – prefix-substitution in ⟨diffyg⟩ 'failure' from [de:ficio]; folk-etymology in ⟨cuddygl⟩ 'cell, booth, bed, shelter', which suggests a false Latin form [cu:bic'lum]; cf. Welsh *cudd* 'hiding-place, concealment'. One often cannot tell whether an aberration from 'correct' Latin is due to Latin or to the British development. The dissimilation in ⟨caregl⟩ and the treatment of liquids in ⟨cylch⟩ 'about, around; circle; circum-' (Latin [circ'lus], *[cilcus]? cf. *[spalta] (p. 44)) could be Latin or British, and a vulgar Latin [episcọ́:pus] alongside [epẹ́scopus] is conceivable in this loanword, for most of the oblique cases of this word were exactly so accented in Greek. So it is not necessarily a British accentuation which has given rise to ⟨esgob⟩ 'bishop'. [awgustus] or [agustus] or [awstus] are all possible Latin forms which would given Welsh ⟨Awst⟩ 'August'.

Then, however, there are cases where the peculiarity must be attributed to Latin. Welsh ⟨rhelyw⟩ implies some form of [reliq^{u}ia] in which there was voicing of the [q^{u}]. ⟨Bedyddio⟩ from [batidio] for [baptizo] is grossly vulgar. ⟨Emys⟩ 'stallion' requires [ammissus] not [admissus] (potentially *⟨eddfys⟩) or [amissus] (potentially *⟨cfys⟩). ⟨Swmwl⟩ 'goad' is *[stum(b)'lus] displacing correct [stimulus] (*REW* 8261). ⟨Sofl⟩ 'stubble' is *[stub'la] or *[stọb'la] for *[stup'la] (note the voicing) which replaced correct [stipula] (*REW* 8265). Old Cornish ⟨streil⟩ 'horse-comb' represents vulgar [strig'la] which replaced correct [strigil]. ⟨P̣ebyll⟩ 'tent' must be from [papilio] not Classical [pa:pilio] because otherwise i-affection would not have taken place. ⟨Ffenygl⟩ 'fennel' (not ⟨ffwy-⟩) from [fenic'lum] and ⟨Sadwrn⟩ (not *⟨Sodwrn⟩) 'Satur(day)' from [saturnus] also involve vulgar Latin forms; the correct Latin had long vowels in the unaccented first syllables. This should be a Latin phenomenon, not British; British had no objection in principle to unaccented syllables with long vowels – but later Latin did. Contrast e.g. ⟨pubell⟩ 'pupil of eye' ([pu:pilla]), ⟨cusyl⟩, ⟨cusul⟩ 'advice, cheer' with the correct weight of the first syllable of [co:(n)silium] maintained; normally, and in the form of this word ⟨cysul⟩ and in ⟨cysur⟩ 'comfort, solace' ([co:(n)so:lor]), this prefix is eliminated and native *cy* substituted. ⟨Padrig⟩ is either bogus or late [patri:cius],[69] with lengthening like that in the vulgar forms [par(i)ẹ́:tem] (*REW* 6242), [macẹ́:ria] which lie behind ⟨parwyd⟩ 'partition' and ⟨magwyr⟩ 'enclosure, wall' for Classical [párietem], [ma:céria] (whence the other Welsh form – ⟨moger⟩); or it has, quite improperly from the Classical standpoint, been given the termination [-i:cius] by false analogy with e.g. [salsi:cia] whence, correctly, ⟨selsig⟩ 'black pudding, sausage'. The correct Latin [patricius] should have given *⟨Pedryg⟩ as [manibrium] gives ⟨menyfr⟩ 'handle'.

Thus in eighty-odd words in this sample, which is entirely representative, about one-third positively require a Latin which is markedly 'incorrect' for their incubation and adoption as British, either because of their intrinsic form, their morphology, their phonology, or their lexical character. That the rest appear consistent is either because they *were* taken over before a diagnostic sound-change was widely established, or because we cannot diagnose the Welsh form as late or early, or because the word is in some way bogus, by which I mean either wholly or partly influenced in its Welsh form by the written Latin form well after the Roman period.

Two conclusions can be drawn. First, the reformation of quantity and quality in accented syllables took place later than Jackson thinks. Second, the idea that British Latin was specially 'correct' in its phonology or anything else is evidently mistaken.

G. *Intrinsically 'uninformative' word-patterns*

In general, if we set aside the matter of /i/ and /u/ in accented syllables reviewed above and which cannot be regarded as diagnostic because its absolute dating is in dispute, it is apparent that all Latin words which, in their Classical forms, had short, unblocked vowels in internal unaccented syllables (if any) and either short blocked or long unblocked accented vowels, would naturally maintain this prosodical character in Late Latin; allowance made for various kinds of syncopation of unaccented vowels before and after the accent, which are epiphenomenal. This means in terms of our inventory:

all of (1) ([batt(u)o amplus fa:gus aether]) except the [la:m'na] group	158
most of (3) ([brassicae] etc.)	49
all of (6) ([cawella] etc.) except [ado:rno]	37
most of (9) ([bu:bali:nus] etc.)	13
all of (12) ([benedi:co] etc.)	10
all of (13) ([dia:conus] etc.)	7
	Total 274

In words of these types we normally find in British borrowings long vowels set for long and short for short. This is of course consistent with an origin in 'Classical' Latin; but it is, in these cases, equally consistent with an origin in much later Latin. Even in these 'uninformative' patterns, however, we can often see for other reasons that we certainly are not dealing with a 'correct' Classical Latin as the starting point. The following are variously typical:

[cattus] [coccum] [clocca] [cloppus] [gurdus] [turta] [pi:pa] [praebiter] [disc(u)lus] [septima:na] (Welsh ⟨cath⟩ 'cat' ⟨coch⟩ 'red' ⟨cloch⟩ 'bell' ⟨cloff⟩ 'lame' ⟨gwrdd⟩ 'energetic' ⟨torth⟩ 'loaf' ⟨pib⟩ 'pipe' ⟨pryfder⟩ 'priest' ⟨dysgl⟩ 'dish, quoit' Old Cornish ⟨seithun⟩ 'week') are intrinsically 'unclassical' in lexis;

[cere:num] for [caroenum] 'vat',[70] [carcarem] for [carcerem] (vowel-harmony), [littera] for [li:tera], [batto] for [battuo], [ceria:sa] for [cerasus] (*REW* 1823), [pletta] for [plecta], [febra:rius] for [februa:rius], [pape:r(i)us] for [papü:rus] (*REW* 6218), [parade(n)sus] for [paradi:sus], [pergeri:nus] for [peregri:nus] are variously unclassical in formation (⟨cerwyn⟩ 'vat', ⟨carchar⟩ 'jail', ⟨llythyr⟩ 'letter', ⟨bath⟩ 'mint (coins)' ⟨ceirios⟩ 'cherries', ⟨pleth⟩ 'plait', ⟨Chwefror⟩ 'February', ⟨pabwyr⟩ 'rushes, wick', ⟨paradwys⟩ 'paradise', ⟨pererin⟩ 'pilgrim').

⟨Achub⟩ 'save, make the most of' from [óccupo] not only shows the same odd first syllable as ⟨achos⟩ 'because' from [acca:sio] for [occa:sio] (so Jackson) but also a blatantly false quantity, as if the Latin were [occú:po], which is perhaps *just* conceivable at the time when Latin compound verbs came to be re-composed in some Vulgar Latin. More likely it is just barbarous. ⟨Yspryd⟩ cannot represent [spi:ritus] and its only Latin excuse would be extrapolation from a late pronunciation of the dative in the common prayer *gloria Patri et Filio et Spĭrítui san(c)to amen.* For ⟨perygl⟩ falsely from [peri:culum] see above, p. 49. ⟨Cardod⟩ 'charity' cannot represent [ca:rita:tem] with syncopation in British for that would normally give *⟨cordod⟩; nor can it represent [ca:r'ta:tem], for that should give *⟨corthod⟩.[71] A 'good' Latin [cărĭtā:tēm] as an *ionicus a minore* is most improbable; either there is contamination with native [car-] (cf. Welsh *caru* 'love') or this is one of those cases where a long Latin [a:] in Late Latin has been rendered with short British /a/ (see above, p. 45). So also in ⟨diagon⟩ 'deacon', if it is not bogus; [dia:conus] ought otherwise to appear as *⟨diawgon⟩.

The sub-group of words of the prosodic pattern [bū:bălŭs], in contrast with tribrach-pattern [băcŭlŭs], reveals some extraordinarily scruffy Latin forms as ancestors of British borrowings: [bu:balus]/[bu:bulus] and [scru:pulum] give ⟨bual⟩ 'drinking horn', ⟨ysgrubl⟩ 'beast of draught' (for the semantics, cf. n. 53 on *sol'dus*), which are directly compatible with the 'correct' Latin forms. But then we have Middle Welsh ⟨ceul⟩ 'curd' from 'correct' [c(o)a:g'lum] against ⟨ystraill⟩ 'mat' not from 'correct' [stra:g'lum], but from a form, it seems, with a shortened Latin [a]; ⟨hual⟩ 'fetter' seems to cross [fi:bula, *fu:bila] 'fastening' with [su:bula] 'pointed instrument'; ⟨niwl⟩, ⟨nifwl⟩ 'mist' requires [ni:bulus] (*REW* 5979) for [nu:bilus]; [se:cale] gives Cornish ⟨segal⟩ with a short first vowel; so, apparently, ⟨rheol⟩ 'rule', Breton ⟨teol⟩, for the correct Latin forms were [re:gula] and [te:gula].[72]

We append to these 'uninformative' word-patterns the following:

part of (2) ([ammissus fossa:tum ascella abstru:sus])	35
part of (7) ([capti:witas antonius eccle:sia])	15
Total	50

These words have an initial unaccented Latin syllable containing a blocked short vowel. This regularly appears as a short British vowel; the point of interest is that some of these syllables, in particular those where the juncture with the accented syllable consisted of a geminate group, were lightened in late Vulgar Latin (we English speakers, and singers, are notoriously incapable of rendering, e.g. [pec-ca:tum] correctly).

Since in British the subsequent development of certain geminate groups differs from those of single intervocalic consonants, one can sometimes say something about the borrowed Latin form. Thus ⟨eglwys⟩ 'church' represents a late [e-clẹ:sia] not correct [ec-cle:sia] which would have given *⟨echlwys⟩, cf. ⟨achludd⟩ 'death, grave; sunset' from [oc-clu:do] not [o-clu:do]; ⟨symud⟩ 'alter, move' from either or both of [sum-mu:to] and [sum-mo:tus], not *⟨syfud⟩ from [su-mu:to], (su-mu:to], [su-mo:tus]. But this is not a very powerful criterion, and within this group we have the variously Latin forms [ammissus] [ascella] [astilla] and other diminutives of the type; British [caχti:wos] from Latin (capti:wos] (possibly a very ancient borrowing; the same form is presupposed by French *chétif*); [concausa] [almọ:sina] (*REW* 2839) for [elee:mosüna] (this word in its various forms involves *almus* and [*kyrie*] *eleison*) and, apparently, [sentẹ:rium, -a] (could this be by false analogy with [di:cte:rium] 'wit, witty remark' from Greek δεικτήριον, nothing to do with *dico*?); whence respectively ⟨emys⟩ 'stallion', ⟨asgell⟩ 'wing', ⟨ceithiw⟩ 'enslaved, bound; captivity' ⟨cyngaws⟩ 'lawsuit, advocate', ⟨aluson⟩, ⟨elusen⟩, ⟨alwysen⟩ 'alms, charity', ⟨synnwyr⟩ 'skill, wisdom, sense'.

H. *Short unblocked accented vowels*

These 'uninformative' patterns account for 60 per cent of the material. We turn now to those which, *a priori*, might be expected to show a substantial change of shape as between Classical and Late Latin. First there are the cases where a short vowel is accented in an open syllable:

all of (5) (*cáco*)	41
all of (4) (*ásinus*)	43

all of (8) (*corrígia*)	21
all of (10) (*agrícola*)	13
(15) and (16)	3
Total	121

In these words British regularly has a short vowel. But, as we have seen above in considering in detail the behaviour of pyrrhic-iambic words (group 5) it does *not* follow from this that all of them were taken from specifically Classical Latin: for it is not clear that these British vowels will *not* have seemed appropriate to the representation of the allophonically lengthened versions of these vowels which were to be heard in later Latin pronunciation, with the accidental result that the *borrowed* forms in British take on a uniformly 'correct' appearance as regards quantity. There is also the point that formations of the type [bac(u)lus] would not involve such allophonic lengthening until that very late date when they were re-syllabified as e.g. [ba:-clus] for [bac'-lus].

If classical correctness is our standard, it can only be said that there are some exceedingly ugly customers amongst the Latin forms presenting themselves as sires to loanwords in this category. Eight of the 13 words in group 10 we have already seen to be variously improper: [parię́:tem] [batidio] [patri:cius] [reliq^{u}ia] *uel sim.* (wegę:lia] [calęclus] [capi:tulum] [cu:biculum] (see p. 49f.). Group 8 is no better. For [corrę:(g)ia] [macę:ria] [papilio] [fenic'lum] [di:scip'lus], see p. 48 above. Besides these, we have to postulate *[permedium] as an expression for 'guts' (Welsh ⟨perfedd⟩); [tempę:ria] replacing Classical [temperie:s] with lengthening of the accented vowel is required by ⟨tymhwyro⟩ 'temper' (iron); the compound [de:subito] underlying ⟨disyfyd⟩ 'sudden; unaware' is a typically vulgar formation. Then there is the extraordinary [ocjá:nus] which one must postulate in place of the correct [o:céanus] to explain ⟨eigion⟩ 'ocean'. This involves the now familiar correption of an unaccented long Latin vowel which, borrowed in British as a short vowel, was subject to i-affection; cf. ⟨eidion⟩ 'bullock' from British *[otion-], ⟨Meirion⟩ from Latin [maria:nus]. Evidently the vulgar Latin form had been given the common suffix [-á:nus] in place of the correct but unusual [-éanus]. ⟨Rhufein⟩ implies *[ro:mania]. So at least a third of this group are brutish in various ways.

Among the trisyllables of group 4 we have met [cọ́:bidus] [ọ:milis] [stum(b)lus] [strig'la] [stub'la] [solja] already (p. 48f.), whilst [fac'la] giving ⟨ffagl⟩ 'torch, flame' is a form which is condemned in the *Appendix Probi*. Welsh ⟨nifer⟩ has the exponent of a *long* vowel where

*⟨nwfer⟩ from [numerus], not from false *[nu:merus] or even falser *[ni:merus], was to be expected. Tribrachic and anapaestic words with a middle vowel undefended by a consonant usually appear as Welsh monosyllables with i-affection where appropriate (14 cases out of 16); as one might expect if a colloquial Latin were the origin.

Exceptions to this are ⟨olew⟩ 'oil' and ⟨pydew⟩ 'pit, well' (beside ⟨pyd⟩ 'danger'?). These imply a trisyllabic starting-point in Latin, and, together with the other loanwords in ⟨-ew⟩, deserve a closer examination than is possible here.

Three observations must be made, however, on Jackson's treatment (*LHEB*, 87, 366f.; cf. 323). Firstly one can think of various borrowed forms which a word for 'oil' *might* have taken, and perhaps once did, but which do not lie behind ⟨olew⟩. *[oljon] should have given Welsh *⟨ail⟩; a disyllabic *[ole᷍on] should have become *⟨olau⟩; a trisyllabic *[oléon] *might* have generated ⟨olew⟩ (so Pedersen, *VGKS*, i. 253; Jackson's allusion to Thurneysen, *LHEB*, 367 n. 1, is not to the point); but an objection is that there is no satisfactory native British analogy for a substantive with a stem in [-é] simply exposed before the termination in hiatus. Such a form would sound 'odd', and would be assimilated to some more acceptable native pattern. For example *[oléjon, olíjon, olí:on] would be conformable to native usage, and this might perhaps explain Welsh ⟨eli⟩ 'balm' (but *GPC* refers this to Latin [oli:βum]). Alternatively a British [oléwon] might be formed by analogy with native words which had stems in [-éw-] such as the British ancestors of Welsh ⟨rhew⟩, ⟨tew⟩, and its result would be ⟨olew⟩. This would be a matter of *morphological* adjustment.

So, secondly, it is not true that the [w] of [oléwon] 'cannot be of native origin because it is not found in native words' (*LHEB*, 366), i.e., as an intrusive glide, for that dogma is proposed from too narrowly a phonological point of view and neglects the fact that loanwords on adoption may sometimes undergo morphological adaptation which involves more than changes of inflexion. So it does *not* follow that we must postulate a hiatus-filling [w] in British Latin which is '. . . remarkable because it is entirely opposed to what happened in the Vulgar Latin of the rest of the Empire' (*LHEB*, 366): Welsh ⟨olew⟩, ⟨Iddew⟩, etc. can be referred to *British* forms [oléwon], [jü:déwos], etc. which are taken from *Latin* forms [óleum], [ju:dę́:us], etc.

For, thirdly, Jackson confuses the issue by gratuitously postulating that the spoken *Latin* forms in question must have been [oléwum], [ju:déwos], etc. Now forms such as these are neither Roman fish nor

British fowl and, considered as Latin of any kind, involve the grossest barbarisms of accentuation and quantity, as well as the intrusive [w]. If one is to understand that the British spoke Latin habitually with the paroxytone accentuation of British, that is fair enough, but it is pure assumption, and sits ill with the idea that British Latin was markedly good in quality because of the *grammatici*; and it is surely bizarre to see in or behind such mangled forms of spoken *Latin* as *[oléwum], *[putéwus] evidence of 'the speech of an educated or conservative level of society' (*LHEB*, 87), 'of a higher social level' (*LHEB*, 366f.). The dating of all this is left entirely obscure, and there is confusion of distinct things – a man's pronunciation of a word in British as British, and the same man's pronunciation of a word in Latin as Latin. As we have seen, the mediation of loanwords does not necessarily require any extensive bilingualism, especially not the mediation of words like 'oil' and 'well'. One possibility that at least deserves consideration is that the trisyllabic forms which lie behind Welsh ⟨olew⟩, ⟨pydew⟩, were relatively *early* borrowings; once established as native trisyllables of paroxytone accentuation, that was that. But the whole matter is best left open, for I fear that there is simply not enough evidence to settle *olew*'s business.

1. *Long unaccented vowels*

Groups 2, 7 and 8 include some words with a long vowel in an initial unaccented syllable. The British versions of these words sometimes preserve this length, which is consistent with the older Latin scheme of things, and sometimes they do not, which implies late borrowing. Neglecting indeterminable cases (e.g., ⟨Awst⟩ from [awgustus], [agustus], or [awstus]) we find:

1. ([a:]) *Length preserved*: ⟨Ionawr⟩ (from [ja:n(u)a:rius]); ⟨moger⟩ ([ma:ceria]) 'enclosure'; ⟨morthwyl⟩ (*[ma:rte:lus] for [ma:rtellus], 'hammer'; ⟨Powys⟩ ([pa:ge:(n)ses]); ⟨ystrodur⟩ ([stra:tu:ra]) 'saddle(cloth)' 5

   Length neglected: ⟨lleyg⟩, ⟨llyg⟩ (from [laicus, *leicus]), not *⟨lloeg⟩ from [la:icus], cf. ⟨Groeg⟩, ⟨Efroeg⟩ from *[gra:icus], [(h)ebra:icus] 'lay' (opp. 'clergy'); ⟨magwyr⟩ (vulgar [macẹ:ria]) 'enclosure'; ⟨chwarthawr⟩ ([quarta:rius]; *quartus* and derivatives should probably have long [-a:-], *v.* Walde-Hofmann *s.v.*) 'joint of meat'; ⟨Sadwrn⟩ ([saturnus]); ⟨gwain⟩ (*via* ⟨gwe-in⟩ from late [wagi:na] for correct [wa:gi:na]) 'sheath' 5

Doubtful cases: ⟨llaes⟩ (from a form [lacsus]; it is not certain that the correct form was [la:csus]) ‘loose’; Middle Welsh ⟨pawin⟩, Modern ⟨paun⟩ (the latter from vulgar [pao:nem], the former from correct [pa:wo:nem] or vulgar [pawo:nem] *via* *⟨pawun⟩); Old Cornish ⟨redic⟩ from vulgar [radi:ca] for correct [ra:di:cs]; or from Old English 3

2. ([e:]) *Length preserved*: ⟨diffyn⟩ ([de:fendo]) ‘protection’; similarly with British prefix-substitution (native [di:-]) in borrowings of [de:ficio de:fectus de:sertum de:sti:llo de:subito di:luwium]; Breton and Cornish ⟨diner⟩ ([de:na:rius] with short British [a] for long Latin [a:], no doubt late) ‘coin’; ⟨disgybl⟩, see p. 49; ⟨chwysig-en⟩ ‘bubble, blister, bladder’ ([we:si:ca]) 3

Length neglected: ⟨ffenygl⟩, see p. 50; ⟨mesur⟩ ‘measure, bar, ([me(n)su:ra]); ⟨segur⟩ ‘idle’ ([secu:rus]) (should be [me:(n)s-], [se:-]) 3

3. ([i:]) *Length preserved:* ⟨uffern⟩ ‘hell’ ([i:(n)ferna]); ⟨priod⟩ ‘spouse’ ([pri:(w)a:tus]; the loss of [-w-] in the progression ‘close vowel – open vowel’ is unusual, as it normally occurs in Latin only in the reverse progression (⟨PAONEM⟩, ⟨NOICIVS⟩, etc.)); ⟨ysgrifen⟩ ‘writing’ ([scri:benda]); ⟨gwiwer⟩ ‘squirrel’ ([wi:werra]) 5

Length neglected: ⟨dewin⟩ ‘wizard’ ([dewi:nus] for [di:-]); ⟨dewis⟩ ‘choose, choice’ ([dewi:so] for [di:-]; ⟨ysgrythur⟩ ‘Scripture’ ([scrittu:ra] for [scri:p-]) 3

4. ([o:]) *Length preserved*: ⟨Custeint⟩ ‘Constantius’,[73] ⟨Dunawd⟩ ‘Donatus’; ⟨llurig⟩ ‘breastplate, mail⟩ ([lo:ri:ca]); ⟨Rhufawn⟩ ‘Roman’ ([ro:ma:nus]); ⟨ysgubawr⟩ ‘barn’ ([sco:pa:rium]); ⟨ysgubell⟩ ‘besom’ ([sco:pella]) 6

Length neglected: Ieuan ‘Iohannes’ (should have [jo:h-]); ⟨arawd⟩, ⟨arawdr⟩ ‘speech, speaker’ (*[ara:tio, ara:tor] for [o:ra:-]; ⟨eigion⟩ ‘ocean’, see p. 54 4

5. ([u:]) *Length preserved*: ⟨cibell⟩ ‘skin, hide, shell’ ([cu:pella]); ⟨Iddew⟩ ‘Jew(ish)’ ([ju:dāēus]); ⟨pubell⟩ ‘pupil of eye’ ([pu:pilla]); ⟨ysgudell⟩ ‘dish’ ([scu:tellum]) 4

Words like *praecepta*, *praesaepe* are excluded because though they uniformly show British short /e/ one cannot tell whether this represents a long or short Latin vowel (see above, p. 46). The ‘score’ overall is about 22 to 17 in favour of the preservation of correct quantity (not necessarily quality) in the unaccented syllable. Then there are words of group (14): ⟨creadur⟩ 'creature' ⟨Carawys⟩, ⟨Grawys⟩ 'Lent' ⟨sagrafen⟩ 'sacrament' fail to preserve the correct quantity of the long vowel preceding the accent in [crea:tú:ra] [q^{u}adra:gé:sima] [sacra:méntum] but ⟨dolurus⟩ from [dolo:ró:sus] does keep it; the remarkable ⟨agwyddor⟩ (⟨egwyddor⟩, ⟨gwyddor⟩) 'alphabet, principle' represents a telescoping of [a:be:ce:dá:rium] in which the first two syllables have been correpted but not the third; and even more barbarous *[aceda:rium] might have given *⟨ageddor⟩.

Jackson implies that the different long Latin vowels are subject to shortening before the accent in different degrees and that this somehow proves that the phenomenon has nothing to do with the better-known lightening of unaccented long vowels in disyllabic patterns. But, firstly, the enumeration of the words in question shows that one can hadly come to any very firm view about the ease or otherwise with which such vowels were shortened, because some of the words will have been borrowed earlier than others and because the numbers are so few. It is hardly to be proclaimed significant that there are no cases of the shortening of pretonic [u:] when there are only four words of this species. Secondly, it would in any case be entirely natural that different vowels should show greater or less resistance to correption in the period during which quantity in unaccented syllables was ceasing to be phonemic anyway. As it happens, group 14 words represent a pattern in which there was a strong tendency in Old Latin towards lightening of pre-accentual syllables; in Plautus and Terence words and phrases of this prosodic pattern may be scanned ◡ – – ⏓ or ◡ ◡ – – as one species of so-called iambic shortening, but it is very clear that e.g. [wŏlūptā́tēm] so behaved much more readily than words with a long vowel before the accent like [wĕrē:cū́ndŭs] and that among words of the latter type some long vowels were more readily correpted than others. What one never finds in the dramatists are shortenings of unaccented long vowels in words of the pattern of group 11. But this is standard in the British loan-material; only ⟨esgusawd⟩ 'apology, excuse, essoin' and Middle Welsh ⟨Nodolyc⟩, Old Breton ⟨Notolic⟩ are compatible with Classical forms [ecscu:sa:tio], [na:ta:li:cia]. For the rest we have Modern Welsh ⟨Nadolig⟩, Cornish ⟨Nadelik⟩ 'Christmas'; ⟨pechadur⟩ 'sinner' from [peccato:rem] not [pecca:to:rem]; ⟨ffurfafen⟩ from *[fo:rmamentum] for [firma:mentum]; ⟨testafen⟩ from [testamentum] not [testa:mentum]; Old Cornish ⟨metin⟩, ⟨mettin⟩ 'morning' and perhaps Welsh ⟨meitin⟩ 'a good while since' look to [mat'ti:num] like the Romance words (*REW* 5434) which, *via* [matuti:num], come from correct [ma:tu:ti:num].

The evidence of groups 2, 7, 8, and 14, 11 as to unaccented long vowels before the Latin accent is quite clear: about 25 borrowed forms show preservation of quantity, but about the same number do not, and there is some evidence of double borrowing (*natalícia*, *macéries* for example). This is naturally to be explained as reflecting the fact that the loans were made over a long period, and is absolutely inconsistent with the claim that British Latin was specially correct.

J. *Long blocked vowels ('hidden quantity')*

Lastly there is the matter of 'hidden quantity'. For the purposes of scanning Classical verse one merely has to distinguish between heavy and light syllables (not 'long and short syllables'; vowels are long or short, syllables are heavy or light). But in fact the weights of syllables in Classical Latin (and ancient British) could vary considerably and to an important extent independently of the word-accent. This must have marked the articulation and pace of Classical Latin speech-rhythm as very different from the Esperanto-like simplicity of Late Latin syllabification. The stressed syllables of Classical [sa:nctus a:ctus ma:ter factus] were all decreasingly heavy and of [pater pia] decreasingly light. The weight-balance of isosyllabic words varied greatly: [sa:ncte], [pu:ri], [pia:s]. The whole of e.g. [pia] was lighter than the first syllable of e.g. [sa:nc-te]. By contrast in Late Latin all accented syllables were relatively heavier than unaccented, and might not vary as extra-light or extra-heavy. Thus *pia* by stretching and *sanctus* by squashing came to weigh more or less the same; this involved the simplication of complex groups (hence e.g. *santus*, *sactus*),[74] and, what is most important, the elimination of phonemic quantity. Jackson's account of this matter is unsatisfactory (*LHEB*, 270–1), and, apart from making some mistakes about 'hidden quantity' in individual Classical words,[75] he creates the false impression that the British loan-material is more or less unanimous in preserving it, and that where it does not, the explanation lies in *British* correptions.

1. *Hidden quantity preserved*: Mawrth 'March, Tues(day)' (*Mawrth Ynyd*, 'Shrove Tuesday') ([ma:rtis], [ma:rtius]); trawst 'rafter' ([tra:(n)strum]); Ystwyll 'Epiphany' ([ste:lla]); bwyst 'beast' ([be:stia]); Crist 'Christ' ([chri:stus]); Cristion ([chri:stia:nus]); addurn 'decorate' ([ado:rno]); ffurf 'form ([fo:rma]); urdd 'order, league' ([o:rdo]); Custennin, Custeint ([co:(n)stanti:nus],

[co:(n)stantius]); ffust 'flail' ([fu:stis]); misgl 'mussels' ([mu:sc'lus]); trull 'goblet' ([tru:lla]) 13

2. *Hidden quantity not preserved*: ⟨llafn⟩ 'blade' from [lamna] not *⟨llofn], *⟨llawfn⟩ from [la:m(i)na]; ⟨pasg⟩, 'feeding, well-fed', ⟨pesgi⟩ 'fatten (stock)' from [pasco] not *⟨pawsg⟩ *⟨posgi⟩ from [pa:sco]; ⟨March⟩ from [marcus] not *⟨Mawrch⟩ from [ma:rcus]; ⟨sant⟩ from [santus] and (place name) ⟨Seith Pedr⟩ from [sacti petri] (genitive or rather locative); ⟨chwarthor⟩ 'joint of meat' from [quarta:rius] not [qua:rta:rius]; ⟨rhasgl⟩ 'spokeshave, rasp' from [rasc'lum], not [ra:sc(u)lum]; ⟨cwsg⟩ (noun) ⟨cysgu⟩ (verb) 'rest, sleep' from [quiesco] not [quie:sco]; ⟨llith⟩ 'lesson, article' from [lectio] not [le:ctio] (the i-affection presupposes a British form with short [e]) and ⟨athrylith⟩ 'talent, genius' from [intellectio] not [intelle:ctio], cf. ⟨athrywyn⟩ 'intervene, reconcile' from [interwenio]; ⟨ysgrythur⟩ 'scripture' from [scrittu:ra] not [scri:ptu:ra]; ⟨distyll⟩ from [de:stillo] not [de:sti:llo], cf. [sti:ria] 'drop'; ⟨ffrwyth⟩ 'fruit, result' from [fructus] rather than *⟨ffru-yth⟩ from [fru:ctus]; ⟨pwyth⟩ 'stitch' from [puctum] rather than *⟨pu-yth⟩ from [pu:(n)ctum]. In these last cases Jackson reckons that the shortening is British, not Latin, but does not take this line with ⟨llaes⟩ 'loose' from [lacsus] for [la:csus] (in fact the Classical quantity of this word is not certain); add ⟨praethig⟩ 'practical' from [practicus] not from correct [pra:cticus]; ⟨llary⟩ 'meek, generous', if the Latin was [la:rgus] (so Walde-Hofmann); ⟨ffyrf⟩ (not *⟨ffirf⟩) if the Latin was [fi:rmus]; ⟨dysgu⟩ (not *⟨disgu⟩) 'learn' if the word was [di:sco] (cf. ⟨disgybl⟩ p. 49); ⟨mysgu⟩ is as Jackson says probably Celtic anyway. 18

K. *Conclusion on quality and quantity*

Supposing even that only a dozen of these 18 are in fact to be explained as having their origin in Latin forms in which hidden quantity had been lost before they were borrowed, we find that Jackson's claim that 'one may say, then, that by and large the new quantity system of later vulgar Latin is only very doubtfully represented in Brittonic, if at all' (*LHEB*, 271), is simply false with respect not only to the matter of hidden quantity but also the whole series of matters under examination in this section.

IV. OVERALL CONCLUSIONS AND OUTLOOK

I. THE IMPORTANT ARGUMENTS

A. /b/ *and* /w/

Jackson has only two apparently substantial arguments for asserting the archaic character of 'British Latin'. The first of these, which is of more limited scope than appears in Jackson's account since only about 7 per cent of the material is touched by it, is the question of the treatment of intervocalic Latin /b/ and /w/; their clear distinction in the loan-material, however, is insignificant, because, as we have seen, received opinion that the phonemes collapsed totally in intervocalic position is mistaken (see pp. 17–32).

B. *Vocalization*

The second, potentially much more powerful argument, as the whole vocabulary is involved, is properly Loth's observation, and concerns quality and quantity in the vowel-system. It is true that by and large the vocalization of the loanwords is compatible with an origin in Classical Latin, but since 60 per cent of the material is of such configuration and syllabic structure that we should have the same vowels whether the words were borrowed early or late, this cannot be used as an argument to assert that all these words *were* borrowed from specially 'correct' Latin pronunciation. For the rest, somewhat over a fifth of the material are words which, in their classical forms, had short stressed vowels in open syllables:

Classical	[á]	[é]	[í]	[ó]	[ú]	
◡́ ◡̄	11	6	8	10	6	Group 5 in Inventory
◡́ ◡ ◡̄	18	6	6	7	6	Group 4
◡ ◡́ ◡ ◡̄	1	0	11	1	0	Group 10
…⏓⏓ ◡́ ◡ ◡̄	2	5	12	2	3	Groups 8, 15, 16
	32	17	37	20	15	*Total* 121

These prosodic patterns were eliminated in Later Latin, where all stressed vowels in open syllables were by definition relatively long. British regularly uses its short vowels to represent these Latin ones, though there are exceptions. The implication of this is that a good many of these words were definitively borrowed before the disappearance of phonemic quantity in accented syllables, whever that was; but it may not be assumed that they all were, because we do not know for sure that the British would not continue at a late date to render allophonically lengthened Latin stressed [á:] [ẹ́:] (ọ́:] (69 words) with the short British [a] [e] [o], as the qualitatively closest approximations to those sounds, thus making it appear that they were borrowed from forms older than would be the case; a possibility which must be taken the more seriously into account, as there are a significant number of cases where Latin words which had in Classical Latin a long accented [á:] [áe] [ú:] are rendered with short British [a] [e] [o] against expectation, since these Latin vowels would have remained long in Late Latin, and would have been identical in quality with the allophonically lengthened versions of the old short vowels. As for short unblocked [í] and [ú] (52 words), these are regularly though not exclusively rendered with short British [i] and [u] subject to subsequent modification in Welsh where an [-a] followed; signs of the lengthening and of the change of quality of these vowels to [ẹ́:] and [ọ́:] in open accented syllables do appear in the Welsh material, but only to a limited extent ([wigilia] [corrigia] [caliculus], three offenders in 37; [cubitus] [humilis], two in 15).

C. *Inferences as to dating*

The implication of this is, again, that most of the words were borrowed before that change was characteristic of spoken Latin, whenever that was. But before one assumes that this means that British Latin was unusually 'correct', one must take into account two other diagnostic criteria – the representation in British of hidden quantity, lost in later Latin, and the lightening of unaccented syllables by correption of long vowels in Latin. On both these points the remainder of the material (c. 15 per cent) is very divided, as one would expect if some words were taken before and others after the loss of length in these words. This imposes the conclusion that the change of quality of stressed [i] and [u] was later than the period of the Occupation as a general feature of spoken Latin (fifth–sixth century); that the loss of phonemic quantity in unaccented syllables was appreciably earlier; and that the loss of phonemic quantity in accented syllables came somewhere in between (fourth century).[76]

D. *Pervasive flaws in Jackson's case*

Jackson's argumentation as a whole is weakened by his failure to allow for the fact that loans, once established as native words, fossilize traits of the phonology of the original language. He takes too simple a view of what is 'Classical' and what is 'Vulgar' Latin, of the certainty of the absolute dating of phenomena in the development of the latter, and of their generality throughout the Empire. He assumes wrongly that the earliest loans in British must date from the time of Agricola. In fact we must reckon in principle with the possible entry of some loanwords already before the time of Christ.

2. JACKSON'S EXPLANATION REVIEWED

In sketching his view of the *Apartheid* of 'Roman' and 'Briton' Jackson draws too heavily on analogies drawn from our own Imperial experience and practice, and in doing so implicitly exploits essentially modern notions of cultural identity, race, and nationalism; and he begs the question of what is meant by 'Roman'. In particular he fails to take into account the effect of the peculiar Roman law of manumission. By this a slave, whether captured in war or bought on the market or bred on the farm became himself a *ciuis Romanus libertinus*; a second-class citizen, it is true, subject to the obligations of clientship to his former master, but enjoying the right to own property and to marry; and his children would be full *ciues ingenui*. For this reason an important part of the free citizen population of *uici* and towns will have been of mixed and pure British blood already in the second century. The case of Mygdonius of Ravenna is a good illustration of the principle (see above, p. 26). As for immigrant *ciues Romani* of one sort or another, the chromosomes of Latium will have been as thinly spread in Britain as they were elsewhere, for unlike the Jews or the Athenians the *populus Romanus* never had any highly developed racial self-consciousness; their foundation-myths and the law of manumission precluded that. His interesting theory, then, rather over-simplifies our conception of a society which was in part manorial and rural, in part military and transient, in part commercial, in part tribal yet exposed directly to the *polis*-values of Greco–Roman society, and in which on both sides slavery was an accepted fact of life. As to the extent to which British was to be heard in London or Vindolanda, it was a wise *grammaticus* of Agricola's generation who remarked that *inter uirtutes grammatici habebitur aliqua nescire*.[77]

Jackson greatly over-interprets Tacitus *Agr.* 21. 2 in elaborating Loth's theory that the supposed correctness of British Latin was due to the influence of the schoolmaster. Tacitus, in fact, is referring to the introduction of an education *in eloquentia*, i.e., Greek and Latin rhetoric, for a small élite.[78] It is quite mistaken to infer hence either than once and for all a 'correct' British Latin was established, which for some obscure reason remained uncontaminated for 400 years by the influence of ordinary spoken Latin, or alternatively to suppose that each generation of 'British' villa-owners hired specially 'good' (or pedantic?) schoolmasters to teach their children Latin afresh. When we consider the status of the teaching profession, the general level of its practitioners, and their social position in the Roman Empire, it seems very hard to accept that a self-proclaimed teacher (for anyone could open a school) would enjoy any more prestige in the eyes of a Briton than a cook, a gardener, or a mosaicist – surely less. Is it not probable that the kind of influential Briton whom Jackson has in mind would desire to imitate the bluff language of the centurion, the surveyor, and the company commander as that of an *umbraticulus*? Besides, there is implicit in Jackson's theory the assumption that in the late Empire the grammarians somehow contrived to maintain a correct tradition of *pronunciation*; as if in Modern Greek the phonemic register of the *katharévusa* were in any particular different from that of the *dhimotikí*. In fact, later grammarians could not possibly know what was a correct Ciceronian *pronunciation*; what they could do, more or less competently, was to describe, prescribe, and proscribe for the written language of the *auctores*, a language increasingly divergent in lexis, syntax, word-order and morphology from the spoken. Lastly there is the point that Jackson neglects to consider the role of women in the matter. He treats Latin as if it were entirely a man's affair; are we then to suppose that the *matronae* and their daughters in the villas could *not* speak Latin? If they could, where did they learn it? At the other end of the social spectrum, Jackson also neglects the certain fact that low-class British women in large numbers will have been picking up Latin from the Latin-speaking Batavians, Latins, Gauls, Greeks, and Palmyrenes to whom as concubines they were bearing children. It emerges that Jackson's scenario for the transference of loanwords into British is far too specific and is altogether gratuitous; it attributes quite incredible prestige and influence to the 'Roman' dominie. We may conclude that Loth's original idea has been exaggerated out of all proportion.

3. THE GENERAL CHARACTER OF THE LOAN-MATERIAL

'It is not easy to say why a good number of Latin words should not also have entered British from the normal Vulgar Latin speech of the towns, the army, and the rest', admits Jackson (*LHEB*, 111), having argued himself into this absurd position; and he adds that 'in one or two cases apparently they did so, or may have'. This is a preposterous and amazing understatement. In the course of our examination of the loan-material from other angles, we have come across numerous examples of forms and words which are variously and more or less markedly 'improper'. It is as if by p. 111 of *LHEB* its author had forgotten that on pp. 82–6 he had listed 18 categories of phonological impropriety typical of 'normal Vulgar Latin' and reflected in the loanwords. Most of this evidence, not all, is rightly interpreted by Jackson, but he does not weigh it or count it, and it is not complete. Besides, phonological evidence is not the only available nor the best and simplest and most striking. That is surely the lexical evidence. In Modern Greek everyone knows the formal, correct expressions for 'bread' and 'wine', ἄρτος and οἶνο , but the everyday expressions are quite different – ψωμί and κρασί. At the same time a large part of the vocabulary is common both to pure and to popular Greek, either wholly (φιλόσοφος) or with secondary morphological and phonological differences (ὀκτάπους/χταπόδι 'octopus'). Analogies are never perfect, but the relationship of the correct, classicizing Latin of the classroom and of 'normal Vulgar Latin' was not unlike that of the modern Greek *katharévusa* and *dhimotikí* in this matter of vocabulary. Now if *grammatici* played the decisive role in Britain assigned to them by Jackson, if for their part upper-class Britons set such store by the Latin of Terence, Cicero, Virgil, and Livy, etc., and if direct mediation of expressions into British from 'normal Vulgar Latin' were as minimally important as Jackson makes out at *LHEB*, 111, one must wonder how it is that the British borrowed e.g. [cattus] 'cat' not [fe:lis] and [cloppus] 'lame' not [claudus], to go no further than the first few words in the Inventory given above; for these and a good many other borrowings proclaim their shameless vulgarity not in their phonology but in their very form. This whole matter of lexis is neglected by Jackson, a serious omission. There is a large subject here which deserves proper investigation.

At the same time, there are some loanwords in British which represent Latin terms which must have dropped out of ordinary use in later Latin generally, because they do not beget legitimate offspring in Romance. Jackson also misses this point. Its interpretation, however, is not that these words represent an archaistic aspect of the Latin spoken in Britain, but that some of them were borrowed before the Latin expression dropped out of use, while others may be more or less certainly suspect of coming not from a spoken Latin with a continuous oral pedigree of whatever quality but from books. As noted above (p. 13), there is another whole subject here.

More than half the loan-material consists of terms which existed in Classical Latin and which survived through later colloquial Latin without deformation or changed only in ways which cannot be perceived in the descendants of the borrowed British forms. Such loanwords, therefore, could have been borrowed at any time as far as phonological criteria are concerned. A *prima facie* accusation of correctness or archaism can only properly be levelled at a loanword which is definitely unaffected by some post-Classical change in Latin which we know for certain was dominant well within the Occupation period, and, as we have seen, such criteria are rarer and less powerful than Jackson makes out. In particular, the slur of correctness should not be cast against that whole class of words, which is the majority, whose form is compatible either with an origin in 'good' Latin or in 'bad'. If an old lady has a broom and we see her flying around on it, we know what to call her; but it would be bad logic and worse justice to go round denouncing all the old ladies we have seen sweeping their gardens with brooms, for though some no doubt belong to the coven, others certainly are innocent, and we cannot distinguish them.

It is only occasionally that we can definitely identify a British loanword as coming from a distinctively correct Latin form; it is a good deal easier to say when a loanword does not. The 80-odd words with accented Latin /í/, /ú/ examined above (pp. 47–9) will serve conveniently as a first random sample of the material as a whole. The words italicized in the two lists there given are printed in their correct forms, when there is one; but the loanwords in question are either from intrinsically vulgar Latin expressions, or from vulgar deformations of the correct Latin, or do not represent an authentic Latin pronunciation at all, but rather someone's misinterpretation of the written word. These taken together amount to a third of the sample.

This sample is fairly representative of the whole from the semantic point of view, but it is biased in favour of long words, because accented Latin /í/ is common in long words. If we define a short word as of three or fewer syllables (groups 1 to 6 in the Inventory), the sample has 60 short and 21 long words, while in the rest of the population we have 369 short words and 90 long. Now the odds against drawing a sample of *any* 80 words from the Inventory and getting these proportions of short to long words are about three to one,[79] and the imbalance is a direct function of the definition of the sample. What matters here, however, is rather that the longer a Latin word, the more chance there is of its suffering some post-Classical change and of this being visible in a British borrowed form. For this reason I suspect that one third is a rather unrepresentatively high proportion of identifiably incorrect Latin forms. On the other hand, the overall proportion is hardly less than a fifth to a quarter of the whole. This in any case greatly exceeds the proportion of identifiable cases where one may postulate, without begging the question, a specifically correct Latin form as the source of a British loanword; these are very few. As emphasized above, we must leave out of the reckoning all those words which, upon interrogation, refuse to tell us about their pedigree, and especially avoid the error of supposing that because a word could have its origin in Classical Latin it did, when an origin in much later Latin is equally possible.

There is scope here for a good deal more analytic work, and it is not our intention here to examine more closely the manifold observable improprieties of the loan-material. Our purpose is protreptic, and one example may be cited to show how seriously misleading Jackson's characterization of the loan-material actually is. On p. 119 of *LHEB* he dates the entry of the Christian Latin terms in British between the fourth and sixth centuries, and he says that 'these differ in no essential way from the secular ones' (first to fifth centuries); the Christian terms represent 'the old upper-class language'. But the first of these assertions is hazardous and the second is false. At the beginning of his discussion Jackson gives representative lists of Latin words borrowed into British (*LHEB*, 78–80). These are well chosen and are arranged in broad semantic categories, of which the longest are 'Religion' (57 words) and 'Daily life' (43 words). Jackson cites these in their Classical forms, if they have one, for the sake of simplicity, but this is rather misleading. For if we identify the cases where the British borrowing looks to a Latin form which is incompatible with 'good' Latinity one finds as follows. Most of these words have been impugned above.

Religion: [batisa:ti:], [batidjo], [car'ta:tem], [clocca], [eclẹ:sia], [almọ:sina], [eβaŋgelium], [laicus, leicus] for [la:icus], [manachus], [nata:li:cia], [parade:(n)sus], [pergeri:nus], [prebiterum], [peccato:rem], [salmus], [salte:rium], [quarrage:sima], [sacramentum], [sactus/santus], [scrittu:ra], [spiritui], and possibly [crọcs], [ep'scǫ́:pus], [diaconus], [contra:lius].

In a couple of cases here we also have a British form which is compatible with correct Latin ([monachus]) or demands it ([na:ta:li:cia]), but this does not affect the point that about 25 of the 57 words definitely imply a shoddy Latinity – shoddy either because the source is a bad but genuinely oral Latin, or because the source is a book read by people ignorant of Classical quantities. These words answer our enquiry 'are you of improper lineage?' with a cheerful 'yes!'; most of the remainder simply refuse to reply ([alta:re], [templum], [martirium], etc.); and it is only in a few cases that the answer is 'no – and here is my birth certificate'. But even the birth certificate may be forged. Welsh ⟨pab⟩ 'pope' rather than ⟨*pawb⟩ is consistent with latin [papa] not [pa:pa], but the criterion here invoked is doubtful, as we have seen above (p. 45). ⟨Crist⟩, ⟨Cristion⟩ are Welsh forms consistent with the correct Latin [chri:stus], [chri:stia:nus], not with the incorrect [christus], [christia:nus], which should have given Welsh *⟨Cryst⟩, ⟨Crystion⟩. But it cannot be ruled out that the Welsh ⟨i⟩ has been determined simply by the Latin spelling.

Turning to Jackson's list of words under the rubric 'Daily life' we find relatively few frank vulgarians – [ant(e)ce:nium] [corrẹ:(g)ia] [palma:ta] [sol'tus] [ọ:milis] [starnere] [tabarna], perhaps [di:na:rius] [fragellum] [gemellus] [c'ingula] (palatized; Welsh ⟨tengl⟩?) [mon'mentum]; say eight in 43. But then there are still fewer which can back up a claim to 'correct' ancestry – [stra:tu:ra] has the best case. The great majority here are neutral – [fu:nis] [flamma] [prandium], etc. – either offering no evidence or the kind of evidence which we have seen is not diagnostic.

Now the overall ratio of 'short' to 'long' words in our population is 429:111; in Jackson's sample of religious words it is 28:29, and in his quotidian word-sample it is 37:6. Perusal of groups 1–6, the short words, and 7–16, the long, will show that the latter ratio is somewhat under-representative of secular long words, though not significantly so, and that Jackson's sample of religious terms has proportionally about the right balance of short and long words for religious terms in general. However, it is clear that a ratio of 28:29 is untypical of the loanwords at large. The longer a word, the greater the chance that it will be able to declare positively the quality of its lineage; and this no doubt goes a long way to explaining why such a large proportion of the religious terms can be seen definitely not to come from 'correct' Latin (25; the rest, 32). But it remains a question whether this factor of word-length in itself accounts for the large discrepancy between the proportions for religious terms and for secular (8; the rest, 35), for the chances of these proportions being drawn from a truly homogeneous corpus are very small (about three chances in a hundred).[80] There is scope here for more work. But it is clear that the Latin from which the religious loanwords come was markedly impure and in no way can it be characterized as 'good' as Jackson supposes.

4. CURRENT OPINION

We conclude with a brief doxography to illustrate how Jackson's authority has imprinted itself upon recent historical scholarship.

Two standard and complementary works on Roman Britain appeared in the late 1960s, those of Frere (1967) and Liversidge (1968); the latter quoted Jackson's claim and his explanation with approval,[81] while the former wrote that:

> Jackson has been able to show that the spoken Latin of Roman Britain was of a somewhat archaic kind, different and in some respects of purer quality than the . . . vulgar Latin prevalent in the Western provinces as a whole. In part this may have been the result of insularity but he has suggested that it was also the result of schooling. Britons, in other words, maintained a purer Latin because they did not learn it in the nursery but acquired it at school . . . It is perhaps better to visualize a British type of Latin fostered indeed at first by the schools but kept alive by the insular character of the leading families and for all we know by whatever institutions Britain possessed for higher education.[82]

In the same year that Frere's book appeared, F. Millar referred in an important paper to what he called 'the now classic demonstration by Kenneth Jackson that the vast majority of the words which passed from Latin into the Brittonic language did so with an archaic and conservative phonology distinct from the vulgar Latin of the continent; hence the Latin predominantly spoken in Britain was the correct 'book-Latin' of the schools'.[83] Also in 1968, D. Greene argued for 'massive bilingualism' on the parts of the Britons against the opinion that few of them spoke much Latin, and saw it as beyond doubt that there was a 'distinctive dialect of British Latin', a view which he sought to corroborate, but did not prove, from the semantic developments in Welsh and Irish of certain Latin loans;[84] he accepted Jackson's claim that, whatever the explanation, the sound-system in British Latin was conservative.

J. C. Mann, reviewing the evidence of the inscriptions of Britain for vulgar Latin features, went out of his way to emphasize that he did not dispute the claims made by Jackson, adding, like Frere, that perhaps insularity had something to do with it,[85] and in a speculative and not always clearly expressed paper published in 1975 E. P. Hamp remarked that 'Jackson has quite rightly fastened on certain features of remarkable conservatism and even pedanticism that characterized the Latin spoken in Britain; the value of /w/ and the fate of some loans in Welsh (and even in Breton) are certainly striking . . .'.[86] Shortly after this, J. P. Wild stated as a fact that 'the character of British Latin was conservative as can be seen from its phonology', referring to Greene and Jackson as his authorities, dissenting from Greene as to the extent of bilingualism,[87] pointing out (rightly) that the borrowing of Latin vocabulary could take place without the medium of bilinguals, and directing us to another famous book which appeared in 1953, U. Weinreich's *Languages in Contact* (New York, 1953). Most recently, A. L. F. Rivet and C. Smith have expressed great admiration for Jackson's work, but with reservations about his explanation, which, as they rightly emphasize, can be separated from his fundamental claim: according to them, 'the ultra-correctness of some of the loanwords in the Celtic languages is a fact: the circumstances in which they were taken from Latin is a matter for debate'.[88]

It is the main burden of this paper that this 'fact', this 'now classical demonstration' does not bear scrutiny. There is no ground for the claims that there was a 'British Latin' which was specially archaic or correct in its phonology, still less in its lexis; on the contrary, the evidence, in so far as it can be penetrated, implies that the Latin spoken in the province whether by Britons or by others was like that of Gaul and Spain, and that there is a contrast between Transalpine Latin in general and that of the endemically Greek parts of the Empire on one observable feature of phonology. We have also seen, and it is born out in the passages quoted, that there has been some looseness in the definition of what one might mean anyway by 'British Latin'. T. H. Parry-Williams has pointed out in a review of the English loan-material in Welsh certain recurring themes: that Welsh often has an obsolete English term, that sounds subsequently lost or shifted in English are preserved in Welsh borrowings, as also meanings changed or obsolete in modern English; that sometimes an English word has been borrowed twice or more at different stages in the evolution of English; and that there have been several avenues by which loan-material has entered Welsh from English.[89] Our examination of the Latin loan-material implies the same general observations for the antique British borrowings from Latin which survive and which can be safely distinguished from early medieval or later material. But before there can be real progress in this frustratingly intangible archaeology of the word, it is necessary that a more satisfactory corpus of loan-material be compiled with a specially scrupulous eye given to the *Quellenkritik* and the credentials of words borrowed. This is a task not only for the Celticist, but also for the student of Latin, of Romance, and of Old English. Place-name studies have in our time greatly advanced our knowledge of late Roman and dark age Britain: but as to vocabulary in general, we at least know that there is a rich site and where roughly it is. But we are still merely poking at it with sticks, and we do not even know where are its edges. Without such a study, we cannot hope to subject the material to the quantitative and qualitative analysis which it surely deserves.

NOTES

I should like to record my special thanks to Dr Nicholas Brooks not only for the opportunity to ventilate these opinions but also for his acumen and patience during the gestation and parturition of this study: though neither he nor any of those acknowledged in these notes are to be associated with the controversial viewpoints expressed or the errors of interpretation and of detail committed. I should also like to thank Professors A. L. F. Rivet and C. Smith for reading a late draft and suggesting some modifications: again, *quod peccaui, id totum meum est*.

1. J. N. L. Myres, *EHR*, LXX (1955), 630–3; E. Bachellery, *Etudes Celtiques*, VII (1955), 187–94; O. Szemerenyi, *Modern Languages Review*, L (1955), 205–6; E. V. Graves, *Word*, XI (1955), 630–3; J. Pokorny, *Zeitschrift für celtische Philologie*, XXVII (1958–9), 315–17.
2. I. Ll. Foster, *JRS*, XLVI (1956), 195–8; E. Polomé, *Latomus*, XLII (1954), 257f. Not in *Classical Review*, *Gnomon*, or any of the American journals.
3. *Mediaeval Studies in Honor of J. D. M. Ford*, ed. U. T. Holmes and A . J. Denomy (Cambridge, Mass., 1948), 83–100.
4. *Literature and Western Civilization*, II: *The Mediaeval World*, ed. D. Daiches and A. Thorlby (1973), 113–26.
5. A. L. F. Rivet and C. Smith, *The Place-Names of Roman Britain* (1979), 8–9, refer to the book as a 'national monument', although 'its form and content are inevitably daunting'.
6. Förster's work was only published in April 1942 *durch die Kriegsverhältnisse* instead of the intended July 1941 (Förster, *Flussname Themse*, vii). Jackson explains that he did not come across the work until 1947, when his own researches, begun in 1944, were well advanced (*LHEB*, viii–ix). Förster's work was actually *vorgetragen in der Sitzung* as long before as 1927, and one would like to know precisely what circumstances had led to the eventual publication of this great work in the early *1940s*. It is an ill wind that blows nobody any good.
7. The allusion, obscure in its context, is to Tac. *Agr*. 21. 2, quoted (with a mistaken reference) several pages earlier (*LHEB*, 98). For other interpretations of the passage, see the commentary *ad loc.* of R. M. Ogilvie and Sir Ian Richmond (1967).
8. But what is a 'Roman'? See below, p. 63. Agricola himself was probably of Gallic blood on his mother's side.
9. *LHEB*, 111.

10. Recognition of the Latin loanword element goes back to the Renaissance, to Griffith Roberts in his *Welsh Grammar* (Milan, 1567): see *DNB* s. n. The most important compilation of borrowed words is in Loth, *Mots latins*, which has c. 925 words and draws evidence from all three Brittonic languages and remains absolutely indispensable. This served as the basis for Förster's studies in *Flussname Themse*; H. Pedersen also used it in his *VGKS*, especially Bd i, 189–242, and H. Lewis in *Elfen Ladin*. This useful monograph owed much in turn to both Loth *Mots latins* and Pedersen *VGKS* but deals only with Welsh words (c. 525), deliberately excluding Cornish and Breton evidence, and omitting entirely attestations and credentials; this is a severe drawback, which is partly compensated for by the information given in the articles on individual words in *GPC*. Jackson depends heavily on Loth, Pedersen, and Lewis in the chapter of *LHEB* in question. Lastly there are H. Haarmann's interesting semantic studies *Der lateinische Lehnwortschatz im Kymrischen* (Romanistische Versuche und Vorarbeiten 36: Bonn, 1970) and *Der lateinische Lehnwortschatz im Bretonischen* (Hamburg, 1973), who again, *via* the sources mentioned, is heavily indebted to Loth. Considering these studies as a whole, a Classical scholar feels himself uncomfortably and undesirably far from precise and dated and detailed information about the attestation and status of Celtic forms cited, and notes that, with the exception of the entries in *GPC*, the tendency has been to drift away from rather than towards proper documentation in successive compilations.
11. Here and *passim* /a/ denotes a *phoneme*, [a] a *pronunciation*, ⟨A⟩ a Latin *spelling*, and ⟨a⟩ Welsh *spelling*. Where these distinctions are unimportant, words quoted are simply italicized.
12. For illustration of this, see below, p. 69, 'Current opinion'.
13. C. V. Grandgent, *Introduction to Vulgar Latin* (Boston, 1907), 98.
14. 'In Wirklichkeit wird sich eine logisch unangreifbare und zugleich sachlich befriedigende Abgrenzung des Vulgärlateins nie gelingen' (E. Löfstedt, *Syntactica*, Bd ii [Lund, 1933], 355); 'Du coté des romanistes, on peut constater, que depuis le commencement du siècle, ils n'opposent plus, comme le faisaient les 'néogrammairiens' du siècle dernier, le latin vulgaire et le latin classique en tant que deux idiomes différents' (V. Väänänen, *ILV*, 1f. This is much the best book available on the subject). A major criticism of Grandgent's book (*op. cit.* in n.13), still of immense influence in the English-speaking world, is that it does just that. There are still great virtues in W. Corssen's *Ueber Aussprache, Vokalismus, und Betonung der lateinischen Sprache*, 2 Bde (2nd edn, Leipzig, 1868, 1870), E. Seelmann, *Die Aussprache des Latein nach physiologisch-historischen Grundsätzen* (Heilbronn, 1885), and W. M. Lindsay, *The Latin Language* (1894) which is still the most fully documented account in English. It is rather strange that Jackson did not use it; Lindsay made extensive and intelligent use of the Welsh loan-material. I have his heavily annotated copy of Loth's *Mots latins* in front of me as I write (St Andrews University Library catalogue number sPB 2021 L2 L7).
15. Grandgent, *op. cit.*; E. H. Sturtevant, *The Pronunciation of Greek and Latin* (1st edn, Chicago, 1920; 2nd edn, Philadelphia-Baltimore, 1940); Elise Richter, *Zur Geschichte der Romanismen* i: *Chronologische Phonetik des Französischen bis zum Ende des 8. Jahrhunderts* (Beihefte zur *Zeitschrift für romanische Philologie*, LXXXII, 1934).
16. One finds in Loth's list the following words which fit the very specific conditions: *crotalia* (OW gloss cleteirou), *interuenio* (W. *athrywyn* 'intervene'), **pullicantium*

(W. *plygain*, *pylgain* 'dawn, cock-crow, Midnight Mass'), *millefolium* (Breton *milfer*, Welsh *minfel*), *spolium* (*-are*, *de- -are*) Welsh *ysbail*, (*ysbeilio, disbeilio*), besides the two discussed.

17. See Förster, *Flussname Themse*, 660 n.1; *REW* 2839. It is unfair of Jackson to criticize Romance scholars for neglect of the evidence afforded by British loanwords from Latin, *LHEB*, 76; W. Meyer-Lübke had incorporated the evidence of Welsh, Cornish, and Breton (from Loth) in the third edition of *REW* published in 1935, and it was actively exploited by W. von Wartburg in his monumental *FEW* begun in 1922 and which by 1952 had reached the letter I; presumably he had not come across them, important as they are; nor does he seem to make any use of J. B. Hofmann's revision of A. Walde's *Lateinisches Etymologisches Wörterbuch* (Heidelberg, 1939 *et seqq.*), which I follow on matters of quantity.
18. I do not count *salm* 'psalm', cf. *LHEB*, 128 n.2.
19. See Richter, *op. cit.*, 112, 114.
20. E. Campanile, 'Valutazione del latino di Britannia', *Studi e saggi linguistici*, IX (1969), 87–110. I thank Dr M. Lapidge of Clare Hall, Cambridge, for drawing my attention to this important paper.
21. The phonetic values here assigned are roughly what one might expect for the fourth century on Jackson's account of the changes in the British vowel system.
22. See T. H. Parry-Williams, *The English Element in Welsh* (Cymmrodorion Record Series no. 10, 1923) *passim*; *idem*, 'English-Welsh loanwords' in *Angles and Britons* (O'Donnell Lectures, University of Cardiff, 1963), 43–59; A. S. C. Ross, 'Notes on some English loanwords in Welsh', *Trans. Philological Soc.* (1943), 1–4; R. A. Fowkes, 'On the gender of Early English loanwords in Welsh', *Word*, X (1954), 66–70; A. R. Thomas, *The Linguistic Geography of Wales* (1973), *passim.*
23. The word is not actually recorded, but is a conceivable Vulgar Latin form; *stabulum* is no more a diminutive than e.g. *conciliabulum*, so the analogy of e.g. *porculus/porcellus*, *cistula/cistella* would be false, but would swim with a well-known trend in Vulgar Latin (*fax non facla*, *catulus non catellus*, Appendix Probi; *oreille* from [orẹc'la] for [awricula]): Väänänen, *ILV*, 93.
24. Conversely, the British word appears borrowed into Latin at Vindolanda alongside *ceruesa*: J. N. Adams, 'The Latin of the Vindolanda writing-tablets', *BICS*, XXII (1975), 20–4.
25. See H. Haarmann, *Die Lateinischen Lehnwortschatz im Kymrischen* (Bonn, 1970), 209; his list is not complete.
26. See C. E. Stevens, 'Britain between the Invasions', in *Aspects of Archaeology in Britain and Beyond*, ed. W. F. Grimes (1951), 332ff., and the opening chapters of Joan Liversidge, *Britain in the Roman Empire* (1968), S. Frere, *Britannia* (1967), H. H. Scullard, *Roman Britain: Outpost of the Empire* (1979).
27. Strabo, *Geog.* iv, 5. 2–3.
28. *Grammatici Latini*, ed. Keil, v. 395: '*V quoque litteram aliqui exilius efferunt ut cum dicunt 'ueni' putes trisyllabum incipere*'; W. S. Allen, *Vox Latina* (1965), 41. Consentius probably came from a wealthy family of southern Gaul.
29. W. M. Lindsay, *The Latin Language* (1894), 52; Väänänen *ILV*, 52.
30. *efengyl* with final i-affection from [eβangelium] rather than [ewwangelium] (Allen, *op. cit.* in n. 28, 42) should, on Jackson's dating, be earlier than c. A.D. 600.
31. But see below, p. 31.
32. *The Pronunciation of Greek and Latin* (2nd edn, Philadelphia, 1940), 143, 174.

33. Chicago, 1920.
34. H. Schuchardt, *Der Vokalismus des Vulgärlateins*, Bd 1 (Leipzig, 1866), 131, contradicting Osann.
35. W. Corssen, *Ueber Aussprache Vokalismus und Betonung der lateinischen Sprache*, Bd 1 (2nd edn. Leipzig, 1868), 131–5.
36. E. Seelmann, *op. cit.* in n. 14, 239–41.
37. For statistics on Greek practice in dealing with Latin /w/ in borrowed Latin words, see Th. Eckinger, *Die Orthographie lateinischer Wörter in griechischen Inschriften* (Munich, c. 1890), 82–94. Quintilian *Inst.* i. 1. 13 comments from the Latin point of view: (*a sermone graeco puerum incipere malo . . .*) *non tamen hoc adeo superstitiose fieri uelim ut diue tantum graece loquatur aut discat sicut plerisque moris est* (n.b.). *hoc enim accidunt et oris plurima uitia in peregrinum sonum corrupti et sermonis* (n.b.) *cui cum graecae figurae adsidua consuetudine haeserunt in diuersa quoque loquendi ratione pertinacissime durant*. So in the late first century at Rome to speak Latin with a Greek accent had in certain well-off Roman levels of society the same sort of social and 'heducational' implications as an exaggerated public-school accent; and it is interesting that when ⟨B⟩ for ⟨V⟩ become visible at Rome itself in the second century A.D., it is not so much in vulgar, but in decidedly pretentious public documents (e.g. the almost comic *baccham* for *uaccam* in the Arval Acts, *CIL* vi. 2099, A.D. 183) that it occurs.
38. E. Parodi in a paper of some influence in its day ('Del Passaggio di *V* in *B* e di certe perturbazioni delle legge fonetiche nel latino volgare', *Romania*, XXVII [1898], 177–240) specifically excluded the intervocal cases from consideration because it seemed so obvious that the coalescence of /b/ and /w/ as [β] was general and early.
39. C. A. Robson, 'L'*Appendix Probi* et la philologie latine', *Le Moyen Age*, LXIX (1963), 37–54. See Väänänen, *ILV*, 254.
40. Lindsay, *op. cit.*, 49. The absolute rarity of ⟨B⟩ for ⟨V⟩ in Spain was noted by A. Carnoy, *Le latin d'Espagne d'après les inscriptions* (2nd edn, Brussels, 1906), 135, and for Gaul by J. Pirson, *La langue des inscriptions latines de la Gaule* (Brussels, 1901), 62.
41. J. N. L. Adams, *The Vulgar Latin of the Letters of Claudius Terentianus (P. Mich. VIII 467–72)* (1977), 31, referring to B. Löfstedt, *Studien über die Sprache der langobardischen Gesetze* (Stockholm, 1961), 153f., who in turn merely depends on Lindsay, *loc. cit.*
42. W. A. Baehrens, *Sprachliche Kommentar zur Vulgärlateinischen Appendix Probi* (Halle, 1922), 80: 'sehr haüfig in Rom, ziemlich oft auch in Latium (Süditalien) und auch auf griechischem Gebiete, sehr selten dagegen in Norditalien, Spanien, und Gallien'.
43. V. Väänänen, *Le latin vulgaire des inscriptions pompéiennes* (2nd edn, Berlin, 1959; 3rd edn, 1966), 48–52.
44. R. Cavenaile, *CPL* nos. 303–9 (ostraca of Rustius Barbarus, Wadi Fawakhir), nos. 250–5 (letters of Claudius Terentianus, Oxyrrhynchus; cf. Adams, *op. cit.* in n. 41).
45. See *interim* J. N. L. Adams, 'The Latin of the Vindolanda writing-tablets', *BICS*, XXII (1975), 20–4.
46. Other examples will be found in *P. Paris* 4 and *P. Lond.* ii. 481 (*CPL* nos. 277, 278), fourth-century Greco-Latin glossaries from Egypt written by Greek speakers of great interest for the spoken Greek and Latin of the time: we have e.g.

cibitas polis, labamanos nibson ceras, cabicola clindi, aparai leba in the one, and βέντος ἄνεμος, νᾶβες πλ[οῖο]ν but οὖας σταφύλιν in the other (*uentus, nauis, uua*).

47. These fourth-century Italian examples could be multiplied.
48. *CIL* vi, pars 7, fasc. 1–6 (Rome, 1974–5).
49. Gi. B. Rossi, *Inscriptiones Christianae Vrbis Romae septimo saeculo antiquiores*, I (Rome, 1861); Gi. Gatti, *Inscriptiones Christianae Vrbis Romae, Supplementum* I (Rome, 1905). Cf. H. Zilliacus, *Sylloge Inscriptionum Christianarum veterum Musei Vaticani* (Acta Instituti Romani Finlandiae), I (ii) (Helsinki, 1963), 12, analysing *bv* in 330 inscriptions (51 confusions agreeing well in type and frequency with the 128 in 883 inscriptions here analysed). In E. Diehl's *Inscriptiones Latinae Christianae Veteres* (3 vols, Berlin, 1925–8), which includes the material in Rossi and Gatti, the dated Mauretanian inscriptions break down as follows: third century A.D., 12 inscriptions, no intervocal confusion; A.D. 300–24, 18 inscriptions, no confusion; A.D. 325–49, 20 inscriptions, no confusion; A.D. 350–74, 26 inscriptions, one case of 〈B〉 for 〈V〉 (〈FABENTE〉, A.D. 352, no. 3339a); A.D. 375–400, 20 inscriptions, no confusion. Further analysis would be out of place here.
50. It is noteworthy that the Christian inscriptions of Prima Belgica (Trier, Metz) score 0, 0; 0, 0; 285. Most of these are later than A.D. 400, and this contrasts most strikingly with the spelling of the Christian inscriptions of Rome prior to A.D. 400, which score 65, 3; 63, 2; 883, see above. N. Gauthier, *Recueil des inscriptions chrétiènnes de la Gaule antérieures à la renaissance carolingienne*, t. 1: *Première Belgique* (Paris, 1975) notes the rarity of *bv* confusion in Prima Belgica with some surprise, p. 67; we have initial 〈V〉 in 308 cases, initial 〈B〉 in 24; intervocal 〈V〉 in 52, and intervocal 〈B〉 in 15, all correctly spelt. Compare the situation apparent in C. M. Carlton's *A Linguistic Analysis of a Collection of Late Latin Documents composed in Ravenna between A.D. 445–700* (*Ianua Linguarum* series practica 89, The Hague, 1973), 119–30, especially 123, 127, which indicates that 〈B〉 for 〈V〉 and 〈V〉 for 〈B〉 only even *begin* to be confused in the sixth-century material.
51. I owe these British examples to Miss Jean A. MacDonald who as a fourth-year undergraduate student at St Andrews in 1977–8 wrote a dissertation under my supervision on the statistical variations in various provinces of certain spelling features with a view to the identification of potentially significant variation.
52. See above, n. 42.
53. Compare the semantics of *pecu-nia*, English *fee*, German *Vieh*.
54. Lewis, *Elfen Ladin*; Pedersen, *VGKS*; perhaps also J. Morris Jones, *A Welsh Grammar, Historical and Comparative* (1913).
55. The present writer has not the expertise or knowledge to assess the *Quellenkritik* and relies here on the authority of Lewis and Jackson *in primis*. But error in this matter will be independent of word-pattern and should not seriously distort ratios.
56. *FEW* s.v. The semantic development involved here, and that evident in Welsh *ffur* 'clever' (from *furem*) and perhaps *ffer* 'heroic' from *ferus* (cf. Fr. *fier*), *gwrdd* 'energetic, lively' from *gurdus* provide an interesting commentary on the values of those whom Gildas upbraids.
57. Attested at Vindolanda; cf. Adams, *op cit*. in n. 45.
58. There are some odd absentees among the loanwords: [wi:lla] as such is not attested in any of the British languages, and if it is true that *ystrad* and cognates

(meaning 'valley') have nothing to do with Latin [stra:ta], it too is absent. If the only objection to the identification of *strata* and *ystrad* is the short British vowel, the objection is invalid, since several disyllabic Latin words with [a:] appear in British with [a] (see p. 45).

59. This word and cognates (*tracto*, *tracta:tus*) are wrongly supposed by Jackson to have had a long [a:] in Classical Latin (*LHEB*, 405); if it had, we should not get e.g. *con-trect-are* (Plautus +). For a modern statement of 'Lachmann's Law' describing under what circumstances a verb with a short stem-vowel has a long vowel in its participle and its derivatives, see W. S. Allen, *Vox Latina* (1965), 68–71.
60. See Morris-Jones, *op. cit.* in n. 54, 89–93.
61. This list, while no doubt incomplete, is intentionally more hospitable than our others to words whose credentials are disputable, but not so as seriously to disturb the true ratios of the word-species.
62. The same applies to vowels in blocked syllables: [factus/a:ctus/festa/cre:sce/pisce/ui:lla/cornu/fo:rma/turma/fu:rtum] gives way to [factus/actus/fęsta/cręsce/pęsce/uilla/cǫrnu/fǫrma-tǫrma/furtum]; the only difference being that these latter blocked vowels were all relatively short.
63. Except, of course, to the limited extent that by setting one's proto-Romance in the wider context of Indo-European one would be able to say that at some stage the words 'father' and 'mother', etc., had come to rhyme perfectly.
64. Many of the criticisms of approach which were raised above in connection with the fate of /b/ and /w/ in later Latin apply to the question of short accented Latin /i/ and /u/ (see pp. 47–9); a proper examination of the Latin evidence, which is vast and complex, would go far beyond the scope of this paper. For a start one must distinguish carefully between accented and unaccented syllables, and between unaccented final and internal syllables. As Väänänen says (*ILV*, 37) 'le changement [*ŭ*>ọ], sauf à la finale, est très peu attesté meme à l'époque tardive' (i.e. fifth century); il est sans doute ['probably'] postérieur au changement [ĭ>ẹ]. Carlton, *op. cit.* in n. 50, could only find one doubtful example of the former and seven of the latter (56, 45) and observes (230) that there is 'a curious lack of corroborative evidence for the VL merger of /e:/ and /i/', which, like others, he *assumes* was 'typical of Vulgar Latin as early as the third century' (44, with the usual secondary references). But the kind of evidence which has been advanced for this is highly unsatisfactory as the basis of any *general* conclusion. With monotonous regularity the handbook-compilers quote *CIL* iv. 1216 *ueces* out of context and without informing the reader that it is unique in the Pompeian material, thus creating the false impression that it establishes change of quality and quantity in accented syllables in the first century A.D. But before one assesses the significance of this word, one should need to know how many words of parallel type (*uirum*, *fidem*, *picem*, etc.) occur at Pompeii; and we need to know the inscription, to assess whether it is intrinsically good evidence. But the wit who scrawled *futebatur inquam futuebatur ciuium Romanorum atractis pedibus cunus inqua nule aliae ueces erant nisissei dulcisime et pissimae* in a *lupanar*, if that is the right reading of his drunken scrawl (see Zangemeister's reproduction of the end of *CIL* iv), seems to have been comparing the high-class ladies available in the good old days to the implicit disadvantage of the present practitioners; *dulcisime et pissimae* clearly must denote *persons*, 'the prettiest and nicest *girls*', as they are personal adjectives; therefore *ueces* must denote persons too; and how that is

compatible with its being *uices* is hard to see, unless it stands for *merces*. The handbooks with leaden failure of discrimination (Richter, *op. cit.* in n. 15, 51, is typical; delete *uellam=uillam* Cic. *Att.* 14. 19. 6; she does not realize that the word was [wi:lla] with a long [i:]) go on to mix undated examples of accented and unaccented ⟨E⟩ for [i]. Forms frequently quoted are *nesi* and *sene*; but these no more enjoy an intrinsic word-accent than *si* or *in*, and similarly the frequent *menus* occurs almost always in the formula *plúsmenus*, wherein it is an unaccented form. The *very* occasional type represented by *RIB* 154 *ella* for *illa* will not do either, because this word too is of ambiguous accentual status. This leaves fairly frequent examples of the type *-éssimus* for *-íssimus*, *demēdiam* for *dimidiam*, e.g. *RIB* 988 *felicessimus*, *RIB* 306, 978 *baselicam*; but again one needs the counter-cases, and these form a well-definable group in which dissimilation may be the cause of the change of quality. What is needed are good clear and frequent cases of 'Italian' spellings of e.g. *fides* (*fedes* on a coin of Carinus minted at Rome 275–300; but not a single case of ⟨FEDES⟩ in *CIL* vi against 85 occurrences of *fides* spelt right) and of e.g. *tomolom*. And what is required is not merely a hotch-potch of isolated cases, but an assessment of their weight in the light of the absolute frequency of words of the relevant type. At Rome there is one single example of *lebens* for *libens*, which occurs 60 times. There is no doubt that one can find cases within the Imperial period (e.g. ⟨LEVENS⟩ in the peculiar inscription *CIL* ii. 5728), but assessment of these is a matter of *quantification* and *dating*, and, even if they occurred more frequently than they do, would hardly provide a proper basis for the premature conclusion that this Romance sound-change was actually 'general' in the third century A.D.

65. Jackson accepts a *Latin* [fagus] [plaga] and recognizes a British short vowel for a Latin long in [pa:gus], but does not discuss [pa:la] [pra:tum] [ra:na] [stra:ta] (though cf. *LHEB*, 130, for Irish ⟨srāid⟩). Loth mentions [pra:tum] and [ra:na] only to reject them on the basis of circular argument that they ought to show British [a:]. Welsh *pal* could well be from Old English *pal*, but that possibility is evidently not the only one. Förster (*Flussname Themse*, 699, 813) discusses only *fagus pagus* (*paga*), *pala*. Pedersen faces the problem of W., Br. *pal*, Br. *ran* (*VGKS* I, 204) and accepts both.

66 See R. Coleman, 'The monophthongization of /ae/ and the Vulgar latin vowel system', *Trans. Philological Soc.* (1971–3), 175–91, and (1974), 86–92.

67. Jackson is right to deny that this simply represents Classical [praeda]; that should have given Welsh **proedd*.

68. The italicized forms are those which in fact require a more or less markedly unclassical form as the British starting-point; see below, p. 66.

69. For the correct distinction of [-i:cius] and [-icius] see M. Leumann, 'Die Adjektiva auf *-īcius*', *Glotta*, IX (1918), 129–68.

70. Close [ẹ:], not open [ę:], was the normal development of Latin /oe/ in Vulgar Latin and Welsh ⟨-wy-⟩ is therefore what one would expect. Jackson lists this word among navigational terms (*LHEB*, 80), confusing it with [cari:na] and perpetuating the confusion in Loth, *Mots latins*, 148, 234.

71. Correct Jackson's remarks at *LHEB*, 269, 652 accordingly.

72. This whole group deserves closer examination than is possible here.

73. In Latin, [con-] had a short vowel except when before [f], [s], cf. Cic. *Or.* 159, Allen, *op. cit.* in n. 28, 65f., wherein the vowel was lengthened, *and* the consonant kept (at least in Cicero's pronunciation). This is normally obscured in the

loanwords by prefix-substitution (W. *cy-*).

74. E. P. Hamp, 'Social gradience in British Spoken Latin', *Britannia*, VI (1975), 155, claims that while the form [sant-] which lies behind Welsh and Breton *sant* and which is indirectly attested for Britain by *RIB* 369 *defuntus* for *defunctus*, the [saχt-] which he labels as 'bilingual substandard' and which is implied by the place name *Seith Pedr* (see above) 'would have sounded postively foreign'. Hamp seems unaware that forms such as *defuctus* (*CIL* ii. 4173) *coniucta* (*CIL* xiii. 2417) and *sact-* (*CIL* vi. 2626, 15511, 19495, 25741, 27375, 30432, Rome; *CIL* xiii, 6384, 11976, Gaul; x. 8249, Sardinia; viii. 23181, 483, 10665, 20600, Africa; v. 6580, Cisalpina) are to be found everywhere; whether these indicate a Latin pronunciation [-χt-] or [-ct-] we cannot tell, but they make it perfectly clear that *Seith Pedr* (and the personal name *Seithin*) could easily represent a vulgar Latin [sacti petri, sacti:nus] about which there would be nothing peculiarly *British*.
75. I follow A. Walde and J. B. Hofmann, *Lateinisches Etymologisches Wörterbuch* (Heidelberg, 1938) and Allen, *op. cit* in n. 28, on this matter. Among Jackson's mistakes are his treatment of *sanctus* (406 and n. 2), *tracto* (405) and his mentioning (271) of only six convenient forms: these are dismissed, and the vague argument invoked that hidden quantity was often lost in British too. This conveys a misleading picture.
76. So rightly Förster, *Flussname Themse*, 427; Jackson (*LHEB*, 283 n.1) found this surprising and remarks that 'the examples quoted by Richter and Grandgent are sufficient refutation'. Consult Richter, *op. cit.* in n. 15: '*uea*=*uia* Varro *RR* i. 2. 14 und *CIL* xii. 1477'. But Varro is alluding to the archaic and rustic pronunciation of the Italian countryside, which has nothing necessarily to do with our phenomenon; *CIL* xii. 1477 is far later and from Gaul, and the implication that there is a simple connection is most implausible. 'uellam=uillam Cic. *Att.* 14. 19. 6'. But the word was [wi:llam], rustic [wẹ:llam] (see Allen, *op. cit.* in n. 28, 55 on this 'broad' pronunciation); the intrinsically bad idea that there is meant to be a rhyme in Cicero's expression *uillam et cellam* (*ALL* 1. 357) ignores quantity. '*ueces*=*uices* Pomp. 1261'. But see above, n. 64. '*sene (dolo) CIL* vi. 10464, *nesi*=*nisi* vi. 25184 usw'. But these are *not* examples of the accented syllable. '*Corentus* viii. 9426'. But this is not a Latin word. 'pientessimo xii. 1128'. Yes, but of what date? So much for Richter's evidence. As for Grandgent (*op. cit* in n. 15), all he does is to refer us, at second hand, to material, which for the most part, is of the fifth to seventh centuries, including the Itala sources, Fredegar, Gregory of Tours, and the like. Now a case for the early dating in *some* Latin of the shift in quality of /i/ to [e] can be made out, but this is not it. We insist once more: careful attention to primary evidence and quantification is essential in these matters, not impressionistic assertion at several removes from the evidence.
77. cf. Quintilian *Inst.* i. 8. 21. A. L. F. Rivet and C. Smith deal boldly and well with this matter in the introduction to *The Place-Names of Roman Britain* (1979), a work which appeared too late for me to exploit fully in the preparation of this paper.
78. See R. M. Ogilvie and Sir Ian Richmond on this passage in their *Agricola* commentary (1967).
79. χ^2 with Yates' correction 1.3183, z-score 1. 1482.
80. χ^2 with Yates' correction 4.585, z-score 2. 14.
81. Liversidge, *op. cit* in n. 26, 318.
82. Frere, *op. cit* in n. 26, 313. Frere fails to define 'British Latin' sufficiently precisely

(see above, p. 4f.), and begs a question by appealing to British 'insularity' (see above, p. 6). See most recently Scullard, *op. cit.* in n. 26, 147 (also favourable).

83. F. Millar, 'Local cultures in the Roman Empire', *JRS*, LVIII (1968), 126f. 'Vast majority' and 'predominantly' greatly oversimplify the matter.
84. D. Greene, 'Some linguistic evidence relating to the British Church', in *Christianity in Roman Britain*, ed. M. W. Barley and R. P. C. Hanson (1968), 77.
85. J. C. Mann, 'Spoken Latin in Britain as evidenced by the Inscriptions', *Britannia*, II (1971), 219.
86. Hamp, *op. cit.* in n. 74, 150.
87. J. P. Wild, 'Loanwords and Roman Expansion in North-West Europe', *World Archaeology*, VIII (1976–7), 58.
88. Rivet and Smith, *op. cit.* in n. 5, 17 n. 1.
89. Parry-Williams, *op. cit* in n. 22, 58f.

Clerics as Rulers: Some Implications of the Terminology of Ecclesiastical Authority in Early Medieval Ireland

WENDY DAVIES

A single writer's choice of words is obviously a significant aspect of his individual approach; a generation's choice of words can identify the attitudes of a culture. Indeed, the changing meaning of words can be a pointer to changing institutions as well as changing attitudes. Hence, the social elevation of *vassus* and *thegn*, the increasing provision of pastoral care within the *parochia*, are implicit in the changing use of these terms. This paper is about words and about the implications of the use of certain words in sixth-, seventh- and early eighth-century Ireland: particularly, words used by Latin writers when referring to the powers of clerics.[1] Though some of these points have been made before, they raise questions of the relationship between ecclesiastical and secular power which will bear more investigation, and they relate the Irish experience to a characteristic problem of many areas of Europe in the Middle Ages: how separate were the spheres of spiritual and temporal government?

Our understanding of the nature and development of the early Irish church as such has been considerably deepened in the past two decades. We know that conversion appears to have taken most of the fifth and sixth centuries and that the early church was diocesan, organized like the continental church, drawing many of its rulings from continental canonical collections, emphasizing the power and role of bishops. In the course of the sixth and seventh centuries many monastic foundations were made and, ultimately, the emergence of powerful monastic federations, a development noticeable in some areas in the seventh century but far from usual before the eighth century, assisted the transfer of fiscal and jurisdictional powers from many bishops to the major abbots. Although it is possible to overemphasize the distinctiveness of the Irish church, it is nevertheless reasonable to note that it subsequently became characterized by an unusual administrative structure, in which dioceses were often insignificant or non-existent, real powers of direction and control lay in the hands of abbots, and many bishops performed no more than sacred ritual functions. It was also characterized by the unusually close relationship between royal kindreds and ecclesiastical foundations. Again, the phenomenon is not peculiar to Ireland but the interrelationship was a tightly woven one, in which the succession to ecclesiastical office was often confined to branches of powerful lay families (whether or not the clergy was celibate), to the extent that in the late eighth, ninth and tenth centuries secular and ecclesiastical political interests were often identical. Abbots might fight with each other, often over jurisdiction, or join in secular battles, and kings became abbots, vice-abbots and bishops. Hence, Cathal, who died in 819, king of the Uí Cheinselaig, was also vice-abbot of Ferns; Ólchobar, abbot of Emly, became king of Cashel in 848; Muiredach, king of Airthir, who died in 863, was vice-abbot of Armagh; Bishop Cormac took the kingship of Cashel in 908; and so on.[2] Such is the long-term development which provides the context for the ideas which are the subject of this paper.

The words which express the ideas are those used in the early Saints' Lives, especially the 'Life of Patrick' by Muirchú, of the late seventh century;[3] in the *Book of Armagh*, material of seventh- and eighth-century date in a manuscript of 807, especially the so-called 'Life of Patrick' by Tírechán,[4] the additions to that Life – commonly known as the Additamenta,[5] and the passage known as the 'Liber Angeli';[6] in ecclesiastical canons, especially from two Irish synods of the sixth century – collections known as *Pa.I* and *Pa.II* respectively[7] – and the large collection of continental and Irish material of several centuries in the early eighth-century 'Collectio Canonum Hibernensis';[8] and in the penitentials, especially those of Vinnian and Columbanus in the sixth century.[9] Also relevant are the principal collections of Irish annals, of which a high proportion of early entries appear to be based on an Iona record, kept through much of the seventh century until c. 740;[10] while the corpus of glosses in Old Irish, particularly those of the Würzburg glossator on the epistles of St Paul, from the mid-eighth century, provides some insight into the perception of Irish speakers – in this case continental Irishmen – of the meaning of Latin texts.[11] These were all, presumably, ecclesiastical writers and in so far as their approach is consistent it may be presumed to reflect the views of a significant proportion of the founders and formers of the early Irish church.

It is natural to begin with *princeps*. It literally means 'first, chief' and is a word of very wide use: it applied not only to the emperor in classical Rome but to all sorts of ruler in early medieval contexts – kings, dukes, counts, heads of households, and so on.[12] In Ireland, as has frequently been noted, *princeps* was used of heads of monastic houses – abbots – and, despite the word's widespread occurrence in the sense 'principal' in early medieval Europe, this constitutes a particularization which is exceptional.[13] It occurs with this meaning in some early Eastern monastic material – possibly the source of the practice – and occasionally in Welsh contexts;[14] it is not normally to be found with this sense in other areas of Europe. Correspondingly, the *principatus*, 'principate', of the monastic house of Iona is frequently mentioned in eighth- and ninth-century entries of the *Annals of Ulster*: 'Dunchad principatum Iae tenuit' (s.a.706); 'Cillenius longus ei in principatum Iae successit' (s.a.723); 'Bresal . . . abbas Iae, anno principatus sui xxxi dormiuit' (s.a.800).[15] 'Principate' refers to the office and authority of abbot. Earlier, in the sixth century, it was a bishop whose sphere of authority might be referred to as *principatus*:

> Aepiscopus quislibet qui de sua in alteram progreditur parruchiam nec ordinare praesumat nisi permissionem acciperit ab eo qui in suo principatu est [Any bishop who goes from his own to another's *parruchia* should not presume to ordain unless he has received permission from him who is in his own principate].[16]

A comparable usage is to be found in the Armagh Additamenta in the story of Foirtchern's refusal to accept the *principatus* of the church at Trim: his father Fedelmid had been converted and had given land and goods to Patrick and his companion Lommán; Lommán and Foirtchern built a church on the land at Trim, but the latter refused to accept responsibility for the church, since it had been his father's inheritance which had been given to God and Patrick; Lommán thereupon refused to give Foirtchern his blessing 'nissi acciperis principatum aeclessiae meae'; Foirtchern subsequently held the *principatus* for three days before handing the church over to the *peregrinus* Cathlaid.[17] Ecclesiastical authority, which in this case was the successor to secular power over property, is again conceptualized as *principatus*, a 'principate'.

The characterization of the cleric as 'head, chief' and hence 'ruler', and of his authority as a 'principate', is reflected in other comparable usages. Both Muirchú and Tírechán wrote of Patrick's kingdom, *regnum*, which would overcome all others and to which Benignus, his successor, was heir: 'heres regni mei est'.[18] Likewise, the Additamenta record that Coirpre offered and gave to Patrick not merely lands and control over them but his kingdom itself: 'et regnum offerebat cum eis Coirpre Patricio'.[19] The 'Liber Angeli', accordingly, claimed that Patrick had been given the *gentes*, 'peoples', of Ireland and referred to its supposed division of supreme ecclesiastical authority in Ireland between Patrick and Brigit in terms of rule – *monarchia*.[20] Even Bede, when writing of Irish Iona, chose terms appropriate to secular political authority: Iona 'omnium Pictorum monasteriis . . . arcem tenebat'; 'regendisque eorum populis praeerat'; and the island had an abbot priest as *rector*.[21] These are stronger terms than those he normally employed when referring to the authority of bishops and abbots and the recent suggestion that he was using Irish sources for his discussion of Iona implies that his work here reflects Irish attitudes.[22] The glossators were often explicit in their associations: when the Würzburg glossator of I Timothy 3 expanded upon the qualities expected of bishops he added a note to verse five, to the effect that a bishop should keep his house in order since he must ultimately have the leadership (*toisigecht*) of a multitude; this is a term that the Milan glossator used of the function of kings.[23] Of course, government is a function not uncommonly associated with clerics in medieval Europe, but the Würzburg glossator of Corinthians carried this to extremes by glossing *gubernationes*, as it occurred in a list of the gifts of God, with the words *principes uel secndapid*, in other words 'abbots or their deputies'.[24] The notion of governors seems to have suggested monastic officials in the first instance, not merely as an analogy.

In these passages, then, it is the ruling and governing capacities of clerics that are emphasized by the choice of words. The terminology of rule in secular kingdoms has been used to describe the functions of clerics, and apparently employed as a matter of course. Hence, when the glossator read about governors his first thought was of abbots. Indeed, the use of *princeps* for 'abbot' could hardly have become so common without the analogy of the secular ruler in mind, and a clear awareness of this analogy was demonstrated when the attributes of kings were attached to abbots. This occurs most notably in sections of the 'Collectio Canonum Hibernensis' which deal with the powers of abbots. Quoting an Irish synod, and headed 'De Principatu', book 37 of the 'Collectio' describes the qualities of an abbot in phrases similar to those identifying the qualities of kings in the seventh-century tract called 'De Duodecim Abusivis' and related works. These passages of the 'Collectio' refer to the abbot as *princeps*, and the context makes it quite clear that *princeps* does indeed mean abbot and not secular prince; hence, we find *principatu ecclesiae*, prescriptions that *principes* should care for their churches, and the opposition of *princeps* and laity. The canons ordain that the abbot should be sustenance, governor, anchor, righteous persecutor, sun and water to the flock:

> Oportet omnem principem, ut terra sit ad sustinendum, gubernator sit ad corrigendum, anchora sit ad sustentandum, malleus sit ad percutiendum . . . sol sit ad illuminandum, ros sit ad madefaciendum.[25]

'De Duodecim Abusivis' instructs the king, *rex*, to defend widows and not oppress the poor, to defend the country against adversaries, and prescribes that his justice be bulwark, peace, calm weather, fertility:

> Justitia regis . . . Pax populorum est, tutamen patriae, munitas plebis . . . cura languorum, gaudium hominum, temperies aeris, serenitas maris, terra fecunditas.[26]

Vernacular tracts like *Audacht Morainn*, produced round about the year 700, reiterate the theme and the attitude. It is the virtue of the ruler (*flaithem*) that will banish plagues and lightning, secure peace, ensure ample supplies of fruit, milk, corn and fish.[27] The attributes of the *princeps* in the 'Collectio' are the distinctive qualities of kings and rulers in contemporary Irish tracts, a range of ideas subsequently developed in continental Europe in the context of political theorizing about the role of kings.[28] What is distinctive about the genre – known, appropriately enough, as the *Specula Principum*, *Fürstenspiegeln* – is the image of the ruler not merely as defender and protector of the people, but as guarantor of the good behaviour of the elements and of the fertility of the land. In the 'Collectio', the distinctive expectations of the secular ruler are applied to the ecclesiastical ruler too: he must be sun and water as well as defender and support.

The terms used in referring to the powers of clerics therefore suggest that the writers regarded them as they regarded secular rulers and saw their powers in much the same light as secular powers. The association of ideas was explicitly indicated when kingly qualities were expected of abbots. In many ways this is scarcely surprising, for the Old Testament provided models of the priest king and the analogy between temporal and spiritual powers had already been suggested by the Gospels: Christ may not have been 'king of the Jews', but his Father had a kingdom; the kingdom of heaven awaited the poor in spirit and was like a grain of mustard seed which grew to become a great tree; the kingdom of God was the end to be sought, even above the requirements of day-to-day living. 'But seek ye first the kingdom of God, and his righteousness'.[29] The Bible presented the ultimate Christian experience in terms of membership of a kingdom, and other writers duly took up the message. For Augustine, Christ was king of the city of God.[30] For Benedict, his monks were heirs of the kingdom of heaven.[31] For Bede in England, the most devout of converts became 'citizens of the heavenly kingdom'.[32] For Wulfstan, much later, discussion of earthly kingship naturally followed from that of heavenly.[33] A comparable contrast between the earthly and heavenly kingdoms is suggested by the Prologue to the Irish *Martyrology of Oengus*: the kings and kingdoms of the earth are as nothing to that of heaven.[34] Indeed, for the Irish glossators of the Bible Christ was *tuissech* (leader) and God was *airchinnech* (chief) and the kingdom of God was his *flathemnacht* (area of rule).[35] The Bible's analogy was clearly understood and absorbed by Irish clerics.

Does the language used of clerics in early Christian Ireland therefore indicate any more than an acceptance of the Gospel message, an appreciation of the analogy already suggested? There are some indications that the Irish attitude was more than an acknowledgment of this. The Prologue to the *Martyrology of Oengus* notes how the kingdoms dependent on Tara, Rathcróghan, Aillenn, Emain Macha have fallen while the monasteries of Armagh, Clonmacnois, Kildare, Glendalough and Ferns have thrived. Moreover, the very high status of clerics in early Irish society has often been noted: priests had a status equivalent to kings and a bishop status equivalent to that of an overking, in the seventh/early eighth-century *Uraicecht Becc*. A bishop was entitled to the same size of retinue as a king in *Críth Gablach*, the early eighth-century tract which also states explicitly that a bishop has a higher dignity than a king.[36]

Besides these well-known examples, the early claims of clerics include claims of unusual political powers. It was claimed in the 'Liber Angeli', for example, that the 'free' churches and provinces of Ireland owed a special tax, *census*, to Patrick, i.e. Armagh, since *ius* had been decreed to the ruler of Armagh.[37] With *ius* came fiscal powers, possibly an alternative expression of the range of associations expressed in the more common *lex* or *cáin* of Patrick and others – a term meaning both 'ordinance' and 'tribute'. (The use of the single term for both implies that the ordinance-making power had some fiscal import. Indeed, the very phenomenon of the *cána*, promulgated so often in the eighth century, bears witness to the fiscal and legislative powers of major abbots, and to the special protection of the great churches – though it should not be forgotten that they were often promulgated together with kings.[38]) Whatever the reality of the powers of seventh- and eighth-century Armagh, the formulation of the claim of *ius* and *census* in the 'Liber Angeli' is a political formulation: Armagh has rights which can provide a fiscal benefit, which can supply more than do the usual proprietary powers.[39] By virtue of a supreme *ecclesiastical* authority Armagh expected more than the render from its own lands; ecclesiastical authority – in this case supra-authority, quasi-metropolitan – should bring powers greater than those of the ordinary landlord. Correspondingly, therefore, the canonist of the 'Collectio' assumed that Irish monks owed tax, *census*, to their abbot if they did not owe it to a king.[40] King and abbot are alternatives: *census* goes to the king *or* to the abbot. The attitude of the canonist is understandable, given the quotations from Ambrose and Augustine in the collection on the necessary immunity of churches from taxation.[41] If churches were not themselves taxable, it was a relatively small step to suppose that they had taxing powers. Irish canonists, more extremely than those of other parts of Europe, may have read the fathers as advocating not merely the immunity of churches but as endowing churches with fiscal rights.

A further political claim is evidenced by the same sources, as also by the canons from the first synod attributed to Patrick (*Pa.I*) and early penitentials. *Pa.I* pronounced that there should be penalties for Christians who took offenders to court rather than church:

> Christianus cui dereliquerit aliquis et prouocat eum in iudicium et non in ecclesiam ut ibi examinetur causa, qui sic fecerit alienus sit.[42]

In the still young Christian community of the sixth century, the leaders attempted to insist that Christians should resolve their disputes by clerical decision rather than by recourse to normal secular procedures, or risk rejection by the community; in other words, the leaders attempted to establish a monopoly of jurisdiction in civil cases. The 'Penitential of Vinnian' argued further that a layman guilty of bloodshed should not only do penance for 40 days but should give *pecunia* to the man he had struck, according as a priest (*sacerdos*) or judge decided.[43] It envisaged the possibility, therefore, that secular compensation might be determined by clerics rather than secular judges. The compiler of the

'Collectio' duly argued that theft in church should be left to the judgment of a priest (*sacerdos*) and that clerics should not appear in secular courts without the permission of their bishops, and quoted Rufinus at length on the need for clerical immunity from secular courts.[44] Always more extreme, the 'Liber Angeli' claimed jurisdiction for the bishop of Armagh not merely in cases of harm to the community of Armagh but also in difficult cases which the judges of Ireland could not resolve:

> ad libertatem examinis eiusdem airddmachae praesulis recte iudicantis perveniet caussa totius negotionis caeteris aliorum iudicibus praetermissis . . . quaecumque causa ualde difficilis exorta fuerit atque ignota cunctis scotorum gentium iudicibus ad cathedram archiepiscopi hibernensium, id est patricii, atque huius antestitis examinationem recte refferenda.[45]

These varying claims comprise, therefore, an early attempt to separate the Christian community from secular jurisdiction or at the least to place the powers of the priest on a level with those of secular judges; the reservation of certain classes of offence for ecclesiastical judges; and an attempt to create an appellate jurisdiction of near-papal dimensions, as is explicitly acknowledged. These are rights of jurisdiction far in excess of those of the normal landed proprietor, with his powers of restraint over dependents, on a scale which might well have been suggested by fourth-century continental precedents.[46] If admitted, they would have endowed clerics with exceptional powers, which would have seemed a real intrusion in the juridical framework, a major disturbance to the customary and proper distribution of functions. The corollary of this lies in the attempts of the earliest ecclesiastical legislators to attack the values of secular society: an insistence not merely on monogamy but on continence, and on monogamy even in the case of barrenness and separation; injunctions to free slaves; all were severe attacks, designed to create an alternative society.[47]

The same sources claimed power over persons for abbots and bishops. The second synod attributed to Patrick (*Pa.II*) had the monk *sub potestate* his bishop or abbot.[48] In the Irish material of the 'Collectio' an abbot was *dominus* in relation to a monk, who had no liberty except through permission of the abbot: like the slave or foreigner, he could not make bequests nor act as *fideiussor*,[49] while the secular law tracts prescribed that the abbot might veto contracts made by his *manaig* (monastic clients and monks).[50] There are echoes here of Roman *potestas patris*, the notion that no-one with a male ascendant alive (through the agnatic line) could perform valid legal acts in respect of property, a notion which meant in effect that many free adults had no separate private legal status. Of course, limitations on monastic freedom are to be found in many European contexts: the Benedictine Rule exhorts its monks to live by the commands of someone else rather than by their own wills, for the abbot had undertaken the government of their souls.[51] Gratian cited sixth-century canons to the effect that no monk should undertake business transactions, except for the purposes of the monastery, at the abbot's command.[52] The terms used of the relationship between abbot and monk in these cases, however, are not so extreme as those of the Irish canons; and in so far as terms and practices *do* echo those of Roman law then they share the peculiarity of that law. Such powers over persons were unusual, and recognized as such by Roman lawyers and later commentators alike.[53]

In the Roman case the private legal status of a person *in potestate* did not theoretically affect his political status: he could become a consul; and it might be argued that in Ireland power over persons has no political implication. Parts of Muirchú's 'Life of Patrick', however, indicate that he associated power over persons with political submission. Muirchú translated his theme of submission into a narrative, attributing coercive powers to Patrick, adapting and amplifying Patrick's *Confessio* to make the point. According to Muirchú, Patrick's former owner, the pagan Miliucc, burnt himself and all his substance rather than submit to Patrick, for he was afraid that his former slave would force him to a practice that he did not want; and he did not wish to become a subject of this former slave. The tale assumes that belief in Christianity implied submission to its officers: if Miliucc believed, then he must become Patrick's subject; roles would be reversed. The former slave would become master; the master would lose his power: 'ne servo subiectus fieret et ille sibi dominaret'. Later, Muirchú took up the same theme: the Paschal fire lit by Patrick was itself the generator of Christianity and compelled people to submit; Patrick and his kingdom would overcome all; they would seduce the men of Láegaire's kingdom, replace all other kingdoms and reign for ever. Here again Christian kingdom and (pagan) secular kingdom appear as alternatives. Here the submission implied in power over persons has been translated into political dominance. The political power of clerics is acknowledged by clothing them with coercive power.[54] Hence, Láegaire's queen says the king will come and bow the knee before Patrick as an act of acknowledgment, and of submission.[55]

The choice of words, therefore, appears to be significant; it represents a view of the proper role of the cleric. Both words and early claims suggest that some people saw the cleric as ruler in some more than spiritual sense, with the powers and obligations of kings, with powers of taxation and of superior jurisdiction.[56] Of course, if we are to believe the prescriptions of the law tracts, the powers and obligations of kings were very limited anyway. They appeared to have some rudimentary fiscal right;[57] they sometimes acted as judges, though there was a respected and powerful class of professional judges; they called assemblies, represented the *tuath* in its external relations, led the host; they were empowered to bind the *tuath* by special ordinances – i.e. to enforce law – in times of crisis after military defeat or famine; as overkings they might bind their subject kings; they might enforce religious law.[58] But they represented only one of several sections in the *tuath* which had political authority: a noble, like a king, was also a *flaithem*; both had *flaith* (authority) and both had duties of protection and restraint.[59] By definition the king had the greatest political authority – 'why is a king so called? because he extends over his people with coercive power'[60] – but it was not confined to him. Hence, the writer of *Audacht Morainn* used *flaithem* rather than *rí* when classifying qualities of kings.[61] Hence, the glossators characteristically used *flaithem* not *rí* for *rex*, and *flaith* or *flaithemnacht* for *regnum*: the type of authority kings held, even if greater than that of others, was the same as others' and was distinguished from the position of king. Bishops and abbots, therefore, were seen to possess *flaith* too, like nobles and kings, but in some respects their political authority was seen as greater even than that of kings. Correspondingly, therefore, in some contexts there is implied the alienation of political rights from kings to abbots or bishops. The monk was *sub censu* abbot *or* king; released from the fiscal demands of the king he was open to the fiscal demands of the abbot. The land of one grant recorded in the Additamenta was literally liberated from the royal power: 'obtulerunt . . . quintam partem Caichain deo et Patricio et liberavit rex deo et Patricio'.[62] This is more than the standard formula of English and European charters – *libera ab omni regali servitio/tributo/vectigali* etc.; it implies an act of liberation; the king released land and people from his own power and permitted them to be incorporated in that of someone else.[63] Thus, freed from royal power, the *paruchia Patricii* itself became a *regnum*. Hence, Patrick's future kingdom, symbolized by the lighting of the Paschal fire, would seduce the men of other kingdoms. Hence the glossator of Romans 13, on subjection to power, added to the content of his text. The text argued that all power came from God; resistance brought punishment; secular rulers were the agents of God and executors of his wrath; it was therefore the duty of the good Christian to pay tribute and to fear them if he did evil. The glossator reiterated most of this, but added that Paul clearly did not consider 'bad power' as power, and that service was only proper to those who did good.[64] Resistance to secular rulers was undoubtedly envisaged by some Irish clerics. Similarly, the gloss on Romans 1:8 implies that believers were immune from the powers of secular political agents (*ardlathi* 'chief rulers').[65] The practical implications of resistance may have been to join the alternative, Christian society – the kingdom of God on earth.

It appears then that some Irish clerics took the biblical notion of the kingdom of Heaven literally, more literally than most, and supposed that entry into Christian society in *life*, even as a layman, meant entry into the kingdom already; the establishment of Christian communities may have implied in some literal sense the acquisition of kingly rights and powers for their leaders. This is not so difficult to comprehend. The Christian faith offered a key to well-being, one of the prime functions of kings if we are to believe the import of the vernacular tracts:[66]

> Tell him, it is through the justice of the ruler that plagues and great lightnings are kept from the people.
>
> It is through the justice of the ruler that he secures peace, tranquillity, joy, ease, and comfort . . .
>
> It is through the justice of the ruler that abundances of great tree-fruit of the great wood are tasted.[67]

Moreover, in as much as the so-called sacred functions (law-making, divination, poetry and so on) were shared in Ireland between kings and druid, faithe and filid (and later lawyers – brithemain – too), the Christian clergy had a claim upon more than kingly powers. They had powers of law-making, divination and sacrifice.[68] A king was only one of a number of judges and only gradually acquired the power to make law as well as hear its declaration.[69] Abbots and bishops had both legislating power, in synod (even if they viewed themselves as the mouthpiece, merely, of the old law) and powers of judgment. They obviously performed religious offices. Potentially they were more powerful than kings; in so far as they exercised powers of jurisdiction in accordance with the prescriptions of the canons they achieved that position. Moreover, in so far as the distinctively kingly aspect of political authority may be defined as the capacity of kings for law enforcement, by the eighth century abbots shared that too: they joined with kings in enforcing the *cána*. There is, therefore, as one might expect, evidence of opposition to the Christian mission – not merely the deafness of the pagans who would not hear but active opposition. Patrick himself recorded that even though he had given presents to kings they had seized him and his belongings and kept him in irons for 14 days; his converts had had to endure persecution and the reproaches of their parents.[70] Two centuries later, Muirchú could still present conversion as a matter for conflict: Láegaire sent his followers to capture Patrick; when Patrick had won the formal contest which ensued, Láegaire still rushed at him in the hope of removing him. Miliucc, *rex*, not only burned himself rather than submit, but by his action brought a curse on his descendants, such that they should not in future possess the kingdom.[71] If Christianity were itself a threat, opposition is understandable, as is the long period which it took to convert Ireland.

Such attitudes clearly did not continue long. If early abbots and bishops claimed such powers, and even began to exercise them, it can only have been a short time before kings began to appropriate clerical powers. The ultimate accommodation of secular principles in ecclesiastical law has been well noted.[72] The increasingly close relationships between kingly families and principal ecclesiastical foundations, the emergence of bishop kings and abbot kings, must have been partly the result of early clerical attitudes. Royal families not only struggled to maintain an interest in their properties; they struggled to maintain an interest in their royal powers.

The choice of words which emphasized the role of cleric as ruler in sixth-, seventh- and eighth-century Irish Latin sources does not seem to have been accidental. It expressed an early view of the cleric in his proper role of governor: clerics were a type of *flaithem*, as kings and nobles were, and in some respects were a superior type. The conversion period must therefore have seen kings and clerics as rivals. In the period of the early established church Christian kings and clerics may well have adopted an attitude of coexistence: the phenomenon of multiple kingships and the accepted institution of overkingship meant that kings *could* have superiors. In the long term, however, ecclesiastical and secular were increasingly accommodated and the view of clerics as governors may well have been instrumental in determining the long-term attitude of kingly families to ecclesiastical foundations, and thereby in conditioning the acquisition of superior powers by abbots.[73] More than this, the phenomenon raises interesting questions. How far was this Irish attitude really in contrast with clerical attitudes in the rest of Europe? After all, many of the claims owe their formulation to continental precedent, often explicitly acknowledged in the canonical collections; attitudes to jurisdiction and to the *census* are notable in this respect. And, we have only to look at the papal state to remember that comparable developments are not completely lacking on the continent. It still remains to describe precisely an Irish abbot's powers over his monks, and especially over the lay flock, and to probe the question of immunities, if the comparison is to be made more precisely. The rights and powers of Irish kings need specification not just from the prescriptions of the law tracts but in greater practical detail. The relationship between the early Irish conceptualization of political power and our own conceptualization of it remains a fundamental problem, as does the determination of the distribution of real political power. We may certainly look forward to the resolution of such problems in the work of the current generation of Irish historians.

NOTES

1. Early versions of this paper have been read to students in Cambridge and in University College Cork and I am most grateful to them for their comments in the discussions which ensued, as well of course as to those who attended the St Andrews Symposium. I am also indebted to my friends Fergus Kelly, Jinty Nelson, Chris Wickham, Richard Sharpe and Tom Davis for their comments on written drafts of this paper.
2. See K. Hughes, *The Church in Early Irish Society* (1966) for full discussion of this development; and D. A. Binchy, 'Patrick and his biographers', *Studia Hibernica*, II (1962), 63f., for some valuable comment on wars between abbots. Fergus Kelly points out, with reference to the slow conversion of Ireland, that druids were still active as late as the eighth century; see *Bretha Crólige*, ed. D. A. Binchy, *Ériu*, XXII (1971), 41, §51.
3. *Liber Ardmachanus. The Book of Armagh*, ed. J. Gwynn (Dublin and London, 1913), fos. 2 8v, 20; also *St Patrick, His Writings and Muirchu's Life*, ed. and trans. A. B. E. Hood (1978). The Life was written for Bishop Aed of Sletty, who died in 700 and who was associated with Armagh some time between 663 and 688. See K. Hughes, *Early Christian Ireland: Introduction to the Sources* (1972), 229–32. See also *The Patrician Texts in the Book of Armagh* (ed. L. Bieler, Scriptores Latini Hiberniae, 10: Dublin, 1979), 60–122, which appeared after this paper was prepared for press.
4. *Patrician Texts*, ed. Bieler, 122–62. The work was written after 664/8, drawing upon the writings of Ultan, who died in 657. See J. Kenney, *Sources for the Early History of Ireland* (Columbia, 1929), 329–31.
5. *Patrician Texts*, ed. Bieler, 166–78. See Kenney, *op. cit.*, 334f.
6. *Patrician Texts*, ed. Bieler, 184–90. See Hughes, *Church in Early Irish Society*, 275–81.
7. *The Irish Penitentials*, ed. L. Bieler (Dublin, 1963), 54–8, 184–96. See Hughes, *Church in Early Irish Society*, 44–50, for discussion of the date of the first synod,

and *idem*, 'Synodus II S. Patricii', in *Latin Script and Letters A.D. 400–900*, ed. J. J. O'Meara and B. Naumann (Leiden, 1976), 141–7.

8. *Die Irische Kanonensammlung*, ed. F. W. H. Wasserschleben (Leipzig, 1885). See Hughes, *Early Christian Ireland*, 67f.
9. *Irish Penitentials*, ed. Bieler, 74–106.
10. *Annals of Ulster*, ed. W. Hennessy (Rolls Series, 1887). See Hughes, *Early Christian Ireland*, 99–128 and 142–8, and A. P. Smyth, 'The earliest Irish annals', *Procs. Royal Irish Acad.*, LXXII C (1972), 1–48, for discussion of date and provenance.
11. *Thesaurus Palaeohibernicus*, ed. W. Stokes and J. Strachan (2 vols., 1901–3), esp. I, 499–712.
12. Du Cange, *Glossarium mediae et infimae Latinitatis*, ed. G. Henschel, V (Paris, 1845), and J. F. Niermeyer, *Mediae Latinitatis lexicon minus* (Leiden, 1976), both s.v. *princeps*.
13. See Hughes, *Church in Early Irish Society*, 126, 158.
14. See J. F. Niermeyer, *Mediae Latinitatis lexicon*, s.v. *princeps* (9). For Wales in the seventh century and for the tenth-century Welsh or Cornish Colloquy, see Wendy Davies, *An Early Welsh Microcosm* (1978), 125; the term also occurs in eleventh-century Welsh Saints' Lives: *Vitae Sanctorum Britanniae et Genealogiae*, ed. A. W. Wade-Evans (1944), 124, 134, 166.
15. *Annals of Ulster*, ed. Hennessy, I, 156, 174, 284. The usage does not occur in the seventh century.
16. *Pa.I.*30, *Irish Penitentials*, ed. Bieler, 58.
17. *Patrician Texts*, ed. Bieler, 168.
18. *Patrick, Writings and Muirchu's Life*, ed. Hood, 68: 'et ille qui incendit et regnum superveniens a quo incensus est in hac nocte superabit nos omnes et te'; *Patrician Texts*, ed. Bieler, 86, 126.
19. *Ibid.*, 174.
20. *Ibid.*, 184, 190; 'O mea Brigita paruchia tua in prouincia tua apud reputabitur monarchiam tuam in parte autem orientali et occidentali dominatu in mea erit'.
21. *Venerabilis Baedae Historia Ecclesiastica Gentis Anglorum*, ed. C. Plummer (1896), 132, 134.
22. A. A. M. Duncan, 'Bede, Iona and the Picts', in *The Writing of History in the Middle Ages*, ed. R. H. C. Davis and J. M. Wallace-Hadrill (1981), 1–42.
23. *Thesaurus Palaeohibernicus*, ed. Stokes and Strachan, I, 682; cf. the Milan glossator of Psalm 67, *ibid.*, 287, line 27.
24. I Cor. 12:28; *Thesaurus Palaeohibernicus*, ed. Stokes and Strachan, I, 574, line 24.
25. *Die Irische Kanonensammlung*, ed. Wasserschleben, 132.
26. *Pseudo-Cyprianus de xii abusivis saeculi*, ed. S. Hellmann (Texte und Untersuchungen zur Geschichte der Altchristlichen Literatur, XXXIV, Leipzig, 1909), 51–3.
27. *Audacht Morainn*, ed. Fergus Kelly (Dublin, 1976), 6. The tract uses *flaithem* (ruler) rather than *rí* (king) in the passages that classify qualities (see below, pp. 90–1). See also F. J. Byrne, *Irish Kings and High-Kings* (1973), 7–27.
28. See H. H. Anton, *Fürstenspiegel und Herrscherethos in der Karolingerzeit* (*Bonner Historische Forschungen*, XXXII, Bonn, 1968), and the discussion of J. M. Wallace-Hadrill, 'The *Via Regia* of the Carolingian age', in *Trends in Medieval Political Thought*, ed. B. Smalley (1965), 22–41.
29. Matt. 5:3; 13:31–2; 6:33.

30. Augustine, *De Civitate Dei*, xvii. 4.
31. *La Règle de Saint Benoît*, ed. A. de Vogüé and J. Neufville, I (Paris, 1972), 424 (Prologue).
32. Bede, *Historia Ecclesiastica*, iii.22 (ed. Plummer, 172).
33. *Die 'Institutes of Polity, Civil and Ecclesiastical'*, ed. K. Jost (*Schweizer Anglistiche Arbeiten*, XLVII, Bern, 1959), 39–51.
34. *The Martyrology of Oengus*, ed. Whitley Stokes (Henry Bradshaw Society, XXIX, 1905), 17–31.
35. *Thesaurus Palaeohibernicus*, ed. Stokes and Strachan, I, 669, line 22; 683, line 25; 710, line 28; 520, line 21, for example.
36. *The Martyrology of Oengus*, ed. Whitley Stokes, 24f.; *Críth Gablach*, ed. D. A. Binchy (Dublin, 1941), 23f.; see also Hughes, *Church in Early Irish Society*, 80, 134.
37. *Patrician Texts*, ed. Bieler, 186; see Hughes, *Church in Early Irish Society*, 111–14.
38. *Ibid.*, 149–53, 168.
39. It will, of course, be noted that Armagh is a particular case. By the late seventh century the church of Armagh was claiming wide control over existing ecclesiastical institutions, and, as in its relationship with Kildare, attempting to define the extent of its control as against that of other major churches. It was therefore seeking to establish a pre-eminent position within the ecclesiastical world, and many of Armagh's claims might be seen as an aspect of purely ecclesiastical politics. However, it is by virtue of supreme *ecclesiastical* authority, not other, that Armagh claimed to expect more; further, it is commonly argued that Armagh behaved as an *over*king (*ruiri*) in this respect, and indeed Dr Binchy explicitly distinguished between the overkingly powers claimed over the *paruchia* (wide area) and kingly powers (as of the *rí tuaithe*) claimed over the *termonn* (immediate area); and further, of course, the examples are not confined to Armagh material. See Hughes, *Church in Early Irish Society*, 87f., 113f., 130; Binchy, *op. cit.* in n. 2, 60f.
40. *Die Irische Kanonensammlung*, ed. Wasserschleben, 160. I am assuming that the requirement of at least one secular law-tract that the *tuath* support the king and retinue when on public business is in effect a statement of fiscal rights; *Críth Gablach*, ed. Binchy, 23f.
41. *Die Irische Kanonensammlung*, ed. Wasserschleben, 79; 'Ambrosius: Ecclesia catholica libera est ab omni censu; si autem gravetur causa mali principis, debet revertere ad priorem libertatem'.
42. *Pa.I.*21, *Irish Penitentials*, ed. Bieler, 56.
43. Pen. Vinn. 9, *ibid.*, 76. Cf. *iudice sacerdote* etc. in the 'Penitential of Cummean', *ibid.*, 116, 118, 122.
44. *Die Irische Kanonensammlung*, ed. Wasserschleben, 72f., 101.
45. *Patrician Texts*, ed. Bieler, 188.
46. There are quotations from fourth-century synods in the 'Collectio'; see A. H. M. Jones, *The Later Roman Empire, 284–602*, I (1964), 480f., for discussion of the judicial powers of bishops acquired and exercised in the fourth century. For landed proprietors, see *Críth Gablach*, ed. Binchy, 13.
47. Pen. Vinn., 35, 36, 41, 40, 43, 44, 22, and Pen.Columb., B20, *Irish Penitentials*, ed. Bieler, 80, 86–90, 104.
48. *Pa.II.*17, *ibid.*, 190.
49. *Die Irische Kanonensammlung*, ed. Wasserschleben, 160, 57, 122. Richard Sharpe

points out to me the use of *dominatrix* for 'abbess' in eighth-century annals; *Annals of Ulster*, ed. Hennessy, 186, 238.

50. See Hughes, *Church in Early Irish Society*, 137.
51. *La Règle de S. Benoît*, ed. de Vogüé and Neufville, I, 440–2, 450, 466 (cc. 2, 5).
52. *Corpus Iuris Canonici*, ed. E. Friedberg, I (repr. Graz, 1955), 770.
53. I am indebted to my colleague Andrew Lewis for a very helpful discussion on Roman law.
54. *Patrician Texts*, ed. Bieler, 78–80, 84–8.
55. *Ibid.*, 90. Cf. *Críth Gablach*, ed. Binchy, 24. Power over persons would be regarded as a private matter in most European societies until a very modern period – hence glosses express the power of king over queen, master over servant, God over man, by using *coimdiu* ('lord') and not *flaithem* ('ruler', of political authority) – but this does not stop the powers being political: *Thesaurus Palaeohibernicus*, ed. Stokes and Strachan, I, 222, 675ff. Hence in 'De xii Abusivis' the 'dominus sine virtute' is a separate category. There is some comparable material about Scotland in the 'Life of Kentigern'; King Rhydderch is said to have done homage to the saint, given up dominion over his whole kingdom ('eique dominium et principatum super universum regnum suum tradidit'), and wished the saint to be called king; henceforth, the 'prince' of the Cumbrian kingdom was always subject to the bishop. This is clearly influenced by the story of Constantine and Sylvester, and includes reference to such relatively late institutions as homage, but it may nevertheless reflect something of an earlier attitude. See A. O. Anderson, *Early Sources of Scottish History, AD 500 to 1286*, I (1922), 134.
56. I am not trying to suggest that powers of taxation and jurisdiction did not become private property in Europe in the early medieval period, but this does not stop them being essentially political powers, and the concurrence in Ireland is extremely early.
57. See above, n. 40, and D. A. Binchy, *Celtic and Anglo-Saxon Kingship* (1970), 18, 20.
58. *Críth Gablach*, ed. Binchy, 20f.; see Byrne, *op. cit.* in n. 27, 30–4, 41–5; Binchy, *Celtic and Anglo-Saxon Kingship*, 16–21. But see also D. Ó'Corráin, 'Nationality and kingship in pre-Norman Ireland', in *Nationality and the Pursuit of National Independence*, ed. T. Moody (*Historical Studies*, XI, 1978), 1–35, for some evidence of practical behaviour.
59. *Críth Gablach*, ed. Binchy, 13.
60. *Ibid.*, 18.
61. See above, n. 27.
62. *Patrician Texts*, ed. Bieler, 172. Dr Binchy, it may be noted, went as far as to say that the abbot of Armagh acted as *rí tuaithe* in the *termonn* of Armagh, though he did not discuss his statement; see above, n. 39.
63. This seems to imply the alientation of *all* royal rights, and in effect claims an immunity on a vast scale. How far this represents a difference from English and continental practice depends on one's view of the totality and political import of continental immunities; there was, of course, much variation; see F. L. Ganshof, *Frankish Institutions under Charlemagne* (New York, 1970), 45–50, for a brief summary. For England, the controversial but stimulating work of Eric John focuses the problem, *Land Tenure in Early England* (1960); see also the comments of and references cited by N. Brooks, 'The development of military obligations in eighth- and ninth-century England', in *England before the Conquest*, ed. P. Clemoes and K. Hughes (1971), 69–84, esp. 73, n.2.

64. *Thesaurus Palaeohibernicus*, ed. Stokes and Strachan, I, 533f.
65. *Ibid.*, I, 499, lines 14–17.
66. See the comments of Fergus Kelly, *Audacht Morainn*, xviif., and Binchy, *Celtic and Anglo-Saxon Kingship*, 9–11.
67. *Audacht Morainn*, ed. Kelly, 7.
68. See Binchy, *Celtic and Anglo-Saxon Kingship*, 15f., and Clare Stancliffe, 'Kings and conversion: some comparisons between the Roman mission to England and Patrick's to Ireland', *Frühmittelalterliche Studien*, XIV (1980), 59–94. I am indebted to the author of the latter for letting me see her paper in advance of publication. Donnchadh Ó'Corráin's very reasonable arguments that the Church was *not* the political rival of kings would seem to me to be germane to the established Church rather than the early Church (*art. cit.* in n. 58, 16f.). However, I agree that the 'Collectio' advocates that Christian kings should have judicial powers, though I do not think that this affects my argument. I would suggest that the clergy were not trying to replace *all* kings, but saw themselves, in the multiplicity of kingdoms, initially as alternatives to pagan kings and subsequently either as superior to (but not replacing) Christian kings or as kings side by side with them, with different territorial responsibility. Such an attitude was quite possible given the dual phenomenon of the large number of kingdoms in early Ireland and the notion and practice of overkingship. (See further above, p. 92.)
69. See Binchy, *Celtic and Anglo-Saxon Kingship*, 15–19.
70. *Patrick, Writings and Muirchu's Life*, ed. Hood, 31, 33 (cc. 42, 52). Clare Stancliffe, *op. cit.* in n. 68, commenting on hostility to the missions, points out that kings had only limited powers over the law, and could not therefore, even if they wished to, protect the church as did the Anglo-Saxon kings.
71. *Patrician Texts*, ed. Bieler, 84–98, 80. Cf. the comments of Richard Sharpe on the borrowing of *laicus* into Old Irish in this period, on its changing meaning and on the increasing association of paganism with brigandage in the seventh and eighth centuries. *Ériu*, XXX (1979), 75–92.
72. See Hughes, *Church in Early Irish Society*, 129.
73. *Ibid.*, 79–90 and 157–72 for discussion of developments, and also Hughes, *Early Christian Ireland*, 72–5.

The Study of Latin Texts in late Anglo-Saxon England

[1]

The Evidence of Latin Glosses

MICHAEL LAPIDGE

It has become conventional of late to describe Latin manuscripts of the Anglo-Saxon period, which contain poetic texts known otherwise to have been read at that time, as 'classbooks'. Thus Oxford, Bodleian Library, MS Auct.F.4.32 was described by its editor as 'St Dunstan's classbook'.[1] Another well-known manuscript, Cambridge, University Library, MS Gg.5.35, a huge compendium of Christian–Latin and early medieval Latin poetry, has recently been catalogued in detail and characterized by its cataloguers as a 'Canterbury classbook'.[2] Clearly the word 'classbook' carries with it the implication that the book in question saw service in an Anglo-Saxon classroom – either as the master's copy, from which the lesson was expounded, or as the student's copy, by which the 'set-texts' were studied. And this assumption has the consequent implication that glosses found in such 'classbooks' preserve some record of how the texts were taught and studied; in other words, there is the implicit assumption that by studying these glosses one may be able to glimpse something of the procedure of an Anglo-Saxon classroom, and to learn how the Latin poets were studied by the Anglo-Saxons. It is this last implication which I wish to investigate here: to ask what the glosses in so-called 'classbooks' have to tell us about the manner in which Latin was studied in Anglo-Saxon England. I shall confine my attention to Latin glosses;[3] for practical reasons, I shall be dealing only with glossed manuscripts of the later Anglo-Saxon period (tenth and eleventh centuries).

Given the extreme poverty of our knowledge concerning procedure in the Anglo-Saxon classroom, the evidence of Latin glosses assumes the greater importance. It is well to recall the words of Pierre Riché, as he set out to describe 'techniques scolaires' in early medieval education: 'Disons tout de suite', he writes in his comprehensive *Éducation et culture dans l'Occident barbare*, 'que nous ne possédons aucun traité théorique, aucun manuel scolaire, aucun cahier d'écolier, aucune représentation iconographique de l'école'.[4] One is therefore obliged to ask: how were the classbooks used? Did the master read from one book, and students follow his lesson in books of their own? No surviving text can answer these questions satisfactorily, let alone definitively; but there is one text from late Anglo-Saxon England which can, perhaps, throw some light on these obscurities: I speak of the *Colloquia* of Ælfric Bata,[5] a student of the more famous Ælfric of Cerne and Eynsham, who taught in a monastic school (quite where is unknown) during the first part of the eleventh century. Bata's *Colloquia* are fictional dialogues purportedly spoken by young students to enable them to learn vocabulary; to enliven this dull scholastic exercise, Bata gives the students in his colloquies some vivid characterization. His students appear as an extremely lively group who revile each other at great length in highly abusive language,[6] misbehave in numerous ways, and are duly punished by whippings (frequently described in minute detail[7]) for their boisterous behaviour. One episode early in the colloquy has to do with books and 'set-texts':

> You there, brother! – hand me my book, and sit beside me on this bench and read out your set-piece [or 'assignment': *tuum acceptum*[8]], so that you'll be able to regurgitate it quickly.
>
> I'm coming; I'll do as you say.
>
> Be a good lad: hand me your book, so that I can read in it the passage I learned yesterday, since I couldn't find my book anywhere, nor do I dare go look for it because of our master, since he's very severe with us.[9]

To this the first student – who appears to be the classroom swot – replies indignantly as follows:

> Why ask me? Certainly I have no wish to pass you my book, nor do I care whether you have yours or not. Why did you want to lose yours? All day long you've been wandering here and there, up to no good, nor do you wish to read with us of your own accord, nor chant willingly, nor write on a wooden tablet (*tabula*) nor on a sheet of papyrus (*scedula*) nor on any parchment-scrap (*pergamenum*) nor

> in a quire (*quaternio*) . . . Believe me [says the swot in conclusion] I'm going to rat on you (*accusare*) to the master.[10]

In spite of its high spirits, this passage has some puzzling implications. It seems to state that each student is reponsible for memorizing a set passage each day, and that he learns this passage from a book (*liber*, so it would seem, refers unequivocally to a 'book') in his own possession. Yet I suspect that few scholars today would be prepared to believe that each student possessed his own manuscript containing the set-texts: one obstacle is that, out of the thousands upon thousands of early medieval manuscripts that have been preserved, only one or two have been conjecturally described as 'student copies'.[11] Yet we could well expect that hundreds (if not thousands) of identifiable student copies would survive, if indeed each student had had his own personal copy of whatever text was being read in the monastic school.

The more usual theory is that each medieval student copied the set-text (as it was being dictated by a master)[12] on to wax (or wooden) tablets – the *tabula* in Bata's *Colloquia* quoted above. Archaeological evidence supports this theory to some degree: tablets have been found in a good state of preservation in Ireland,[13] and styluses have been found through excavation at Whitby.[14] Yet here too there are problems. We can be fairly certain that Vergil's *Aeneid* was studied in monastic schools throughout the Anglo-Saxon period. Aldhelm, Bede,[15] Alcuin, Frithegod and Wulfstan of Winchester all apparently knew the poem by heart. Now Vergil's *Aeneid* is nearly 10,000 lines long. How many wax tablets would be needed to record a complete transcription? Or how long would it take to memorize the *Aeneid* piece-meal in assignments (*accepta*) of, say, 20–40 lines per day – the approximate number which could be copied on to a double tablet? I see no way of answering these questions. And the problem is compounded by manuscript evidence. So far only one complete manuscript[16] and a number of tiny fragments[17] of Vergil have been identified as having been written or available in Anglo-Saxon England. This number is astonishingly small for an author who was unquestionably read intensively throughout the period. The complete manuscript in question, Rome, Biblioteca Apostolica Vaticana, MS Reginensis lat. 1671,[18] shows little sign of intensive use: its parchment is crisp and clean, and it contains few glosses. Manuscript evidence, then, gives no clue as to how the great Anglo-Saxon masters acquired their knowledge of Vergil, nor does it allow any glimpse of how Vergil was studied in Anglo-Saxon schools.

Faced with this embarrassing poverty of information about the workings of Anglo-Saxon schools, it has seemed potentially more productive to turn from Vergil to authors whom we know were studied in Anglo-Saxon schools but who are also well represented by surviving Anglo-Saxon manuscripts. I propose to examine the Anglo-Saxon manuscripts of five works which formed part of what may be called the Anglo-Saxon curriculum:[19] the anonymous Late Latin *Disticha Catonis*, Prosper of Aquitaine's *Epigrammata*, Juvencus's *Libri Evangeliorum Quattuor*, Caelius Sedulius's *Carmen Paschale*, and Arator's *De Actibus Apostolorum*. We know that each of these works was studied in Anglo-Saxon times, since each is cited or paraphrased by various Anglo-Saxon authors.[20] We may hope to gain some knowledge of how these authors were interpreted and studied by Anglo-Saxons by examining the Latin glosses which accompany their work in manuscripts of English origin or provenance. My method has been to compare the glossing of certain limited passages (usually not more than ten lines) of these authors in all surviving Anglo-Saxon manuscripts; in certain cases, as a sort of external control, I have also compared the glossing in manuscripts of continental origin and provenance. I should state at once that my results can only be considered tentative in the extreme, given the partial and restricted nature of my scope. More than 100 manuscripts of Arator survive, many of them glossed; I have collated fewer than ten, and for these ten, only a fraction of the poem's total length. Whether anyone will ever wish to undertake a full collation of the glossing in all surviving manuscripts even of the authors I have named (there are many more authors worthy of such study), I doubt. Nevertheless, I hope that my very tentative results may suggest that such collation would shed a good deal of light on how school-texts were studied and transmitted in the early Middle Ages.[21]

I begin with the *Disticha Catonis*.[22] These are a four-book collection of moral maxims, each consisting in two hexameters, which was probably composed in the third or fourth century A.D. Though their moral tone is serious, their author was clearly not Christian. They were intended for a young audience from the outset, but, because they were not specifically Christian in inspiration, they were not used for elementary instruction in the early Middle Ages (they are unknown to Aldhelm and Bede, for example). However, in Carolingian times it was realized that the *Disticha Catonis* could properly be used for elementary instruction,[23] and from that period onwards they formed an essential part of the school curriculum, a position they maintained until the late Middle Ages[24] (there are numerous fourteenth-century manuscripts, and it will be recalled that the carpenter in Chaucer's *Miller's Tale* 'knew nat Catoun, for his wit was rude'[25]). They were certainly read by the young in late Anglo-Saxon schools. In the above-mentioned *Colloquia* of Ælfric Bata, for example, the master's first appearance on the scene is accompanied by the admonition to learn the set-pieces well so that the students may ultimately be able to teach others, since 'to read books [*legere*] and not to comprehend them, is to neglect [*neglegere*] them' – *secundum Catonis sententiam.*[26] Similarly, Byrhtferth states explicitly in his *Enchiridion* that he 'will now direct his words to the young monks, who have occupied their childhood with scientific books. To touch on a few out of many – they have analysed Sergius and Priscian, and gone carefully through the *Disticha* of Cato, the bald man . . .'[27] Further evidence of the study of this text is the fact that a partial Old English translation of the *Disticha Catonis* was made late in the Anglo-Saxon period and survives in three manuscripts.[28] There are several surviving manuscripts of the Latin text of the *Disticha Catonis* from Anglo-Saxon England (though not perhaps as many as one would expect): two from St Augustine's, Canterbury (London, British Library, MS Cotton Vespasian D.vi (s.x^{med})[29] and Cambridge, University Library, MS Gg.5.35 (s.xi^{med})[30]); one from Christ Church, Canterbury (Cambridge, Trinity College O.2.31 (1135) (s x/xi)[31]); and one of unknown origin and provenance (Oxford, Bodleian Library, MS Rawlinson G.57 (SC 14788) (s. xi^{2})[32]). Of these, Vespasian D.vi contains no glosses at all, and Rawlinson G.57's text of the *Disticha Catonis* is acephalous. The remaining two Canterbury manuscripts – one from St Augustine's, one from Christ Church – are rather lightly glossed, and the glossing is of an elementary sort, as can be seen from two brief extracts from Book I:

Cambridge, Trinity College O.2.31 (1135), f.35r

mens
I.1 Si deus est animus nobis ut carmina dicunt
s. deus s. ante omnia
Hic tibi precipue sit pura mente colendus.

quam dormias
I.2 Plus uigila semper nec somno deditus esto
nutrit.fouet
Nam diuturna quies uitiis alimenta ministrat.

opprimere.refrenare.sedare
I.3 Virtutem primam esse puto compescere linguam
per rationem
Proximus ille deo est qui scit ratione tacere.

Cambridge, University Library Gg.5.35, f.407v.

sapientia s.gentilium
I.1 Si deus est animus nobis ut carmina dicunt
s.deus sincera
Hic tibi precipue sit pura mente colendus.

I.2 Plus uigila semper nec somno deditus esto
confert
Nam diuturna quies uitiis alimenta ministrat.

.i.scio
I.3 Virtutem primam esse puto compescere linguam
Proximus ille deo est qui scit ratione tacere.

Several points should be borne in mind. First, in each case, the glosses have been copied by the scribe who was copying the text; this implies that the glosses were found already in the exemplar(s).[33] Second, although Christ Church and St Augustine's were near to each other and were in close intellectual contact in the tenth and eleventh centuries, the interlinear glosses in their copies of the *Disticha Catonis* are apparently independent: there is only one shared gloss (*hic*: *scilicet deus* in I.1) and a number of discrepant interpretations (e.g. *animus* glossed variously as *mens* or *sapientia* in I.1, or *ministrat* glossed either as *nutrit.fouet* or as *confert* in I.2). Third, the glosses in these two manuscripts (at least for the first few distichs of Book I) do not betray the influence of the *Expositio super Catonem* of Remigius of Auxerre, the great Paris master who died in 908.[34] Remigius's commentary on the *Disticha Catonis* was certainly known at Canterbury before 1066, since it is found in a book-list which was copied into a manuscript at St Augustine's c. 1000,[35] and is preserved (partially) in a manuscript of uncertain origin which was at St Augustine's by the late Anglo-Saxon period, now Cambridge, Gonville and Caius College, MS 144/194.[36] It is probable that the entry in the book-list refers to this very manuscript. In any case, the authors of the interlinear glosses in the two manuscripts quoted above do not appear to have had recourse to Remigius's commentary. One might suspect, therefore, that the glosses preserve some record of a classroom exposition of the *Disticha Catonis*. Glossed manuscripts of other school-texts cast doubt on suspicions of this sort.

Another text which was similarly used for elementary and moral instruction in Anglo-Saxon schools – indeed it is found adjacent to the *Disticha Catonis* in the Christ Church manuscript just mentioned – is the *Epigrammata* of Prosper of Aquitaine,[37] the close adherent of St Augustine's doctrine who flourished in the first half of the fifth century. His epigrams are concise, elegiac renderings of selected *sententiae* of St Augustine. Because of their simple language and pious sentiments, they were quickly adopted for classroom use, and appear to have been studied throughout the Anglo-Saxon period. They are cited at length by Aldhelm in the prose *De Virginitate*[38] and by Bede in the *De Arte Metrica*;[39] Prosper is mentioned by Alcuin among the Christian-Latin poets who were represented in the library at York,[40] and Byrhtferth quoted one of Prosper's epigrams near the end of the Anglo-Saxon period.[41] In fact every literate Anglo-Saxon appears to have studied Prosper's epigrams, and it is surprising that a text so widely known in the Middle Ages has received so little scholarly attention: the only edition of this important medieval school-text was published by the Benedictines LeBrun and Mangeaut as long ago as 1711.[42] The *Epigrammata* are preserved in several pre-Conquest English manuscripts:[43] two written at Christ Church (Cambridge, Trinity College, MS O.2.31 (1135) (s.x/xi)[44] and London, British Library, MS Harley 110 (s.x^{ex})[45]), one written at St Augustine's (Cambridge, University Library, MS Gg.5.35 (s.xi^{med})[46]), and one written in Anglo-Saxon square minuscule of mid-tenth-century date and Winchester provenance, but unknown origin (Cambridge, Corpus Christi College, MS 448[47]). Finally, two leaves of another English manuscript survive in London, British Library, MS Cotton Tiberius A.vii (s.xi^{1});[48] these leaves are heavily glossed in Old English, but their origin and provenance are unknown.

That Prosper's *Epigrammata* were used for elementary grammatical instruction is revealed by the nature of the glossing which accompanies the prefatory epigram[49] to the collection in one of the Christ Church manuscripts:

Cambridge, Trinity College O.2.31 (1135), f.1r

quam rem cuius rei unde
Haec Agustini ex sacris epigrammata dictis
quo modo que res
Dulcisono hrethor componens carmine Prosper
hoc est tamquam que res
Floribus ex uariis ceu fulget nexa corona
hoc est propter quam rem s.o s.epigrammata
Unde ego te lector relegis quo haec sedulus oro
s. quid oro
Intentas adhibere sonis celestibus aures.

The glossing here might be described as 'grammatical' or 'morphological': *quam rem* in the first line indicates that *haec* is accusative, *cuius rei* that *Agustini* is genitive, *que res* that *hrethor* in line 2 is nominative, *quo modo* that *dulcisono . . . carmine* is ablative, and so on. Here, one might think, the Anglo-Saxon classroom of a thousand years ago comes alive: we seem to hear the master questioning the students on the various cases of the noun. But the master's lesson – if such it was – was a very short one indeed, for here, as in so many glossed pre-Conquest manuscripts, the detailed morphological glossing terminates abruptly at the end of the prefatory epigram. Thereafter, Latin glossing in this Christ Church manuscript (as in some other pre-Conquest manuscripts of Prosper) is sporadic and unsystematic, apparently quite random. It cannot be entirely random, however, as may be seen by comparing the glosses in the four[50] pre-Conquest manuscripts to one (randomly selected) epigram: no.II, *De Hominibus Diligendis*.

Cambridge, Corpus Christi College 448, f.2r

s. o tu homo
Nature quisquis proprie non spernis honorem
s. ea
In quocumque hominum que tua noscis ama
s. ama s. sua
Sic tamen ut prauos uitet concordia mores
.i.non
Nulla que sint pacis federa cum uitiis.

Cambridge, Trinity College O.2.31 (1135), f.1v

s. o tu
Nature quisquis proprie non spernis honorem
in quocumque hominum que tua noscis ama
s. ama
Sic tamen ut prauos uitet concordia mores
Nulla que sint pacis federa cum uitiis.

London, British Library, Harley 110, f.3v

s. o tu
Naturae quisquis propriae non spernis honorem
s. ea
In quocumque hominum quae tua noscis ama
s. ama
Sic tamen ut prauos uitet concordia mores
Nulla que sint pacis federa cum uitiis.

Cambridge, University Library, Gg.5.35, f.127r

s. o tu
Natura quisquis propriae non spernis honorem
In quocumque hominum quae tua noscis ama
Sic tamen ut prauos uitet concordia mores
Nulla que sint pacis federa cum uitiis.

It would seem an extraordinary coincidence that here, some way into the collection, among pages of scantily glossed epigrams, all manuscripts should display the gloss *scilicet. o tu* (*homo*) over *quisquis* in the first line, or *scilicet. ama* in the third line. These glosses are not the random annotations of various Anglo-Saxon masters. The coincidence can only be explained by assuming that these glosses to Prosper's *Epigrammata* all derive from a common source – say, a set of interlinear glosses accompanying a text of Prosper which may have been the ancestor of all four English manuscripts.[51] This suggestion has some confirmation in the fact that in three of the manuscripts the glosses have been entered by the main scribe who copied the text.[52] Unfortunately, until the text *and glosses* of Prosper's *Epigrammata* have been fully collated, it is not possible to comment on the manuscript affiliations, nor even to ascertain whether the two Christ Church manuscripts are related to each other. For the time being, the fact that the Latin glosses appear to derive from a common source and apparently travelled with the text, should make us wary of assuming that they reflect the classroom procedure of an Anglo-Saxon master.

The situation becomes somewhat clearer with respect to manuscripts of Juvencus's *Libri Evangeliorum Quattuor*.[53] Juvencus was a Spanish priest, whose hexametrical version of the gospel account of the life of Christ was dedicated to the emperor Constantine c. 330 and became one of the most widely read texts of the early middle ages. In Anglo-Saxon England, Juvencus was quoted by Aldhelm and Bede,[54] was listed by Alcuin among the Christian-Latin poets in the York library,[55] and appears to have been studied by tenth-century Anglo-Latin poets as well.[56] A number of manuscripts of Juvencus from the pre-Conquest period has survived, even though few of these were written in England. Some fragments of one very early manuscript, perhaps written in England in the late seventh century, are preserved in Cues, Hospital-bibliothek, MS 171.[57] Another very early manuscript, now Cambridge, Corpus Christi College, MS 304, written in uncial probably in Italy in the early eighth century,[58] was in England at least by the late tenth century, when a number of glosses was added to the first few folios; it has been thought identical to the 'Iuuencus in Romana scriptura' listed in the twelfth-century catalogue of books from Christ Church, Canterbury.[59] Another manuscript now preserved in Cambridge, University Library, MS Ff.4.42, was written at an unidentified centre in Wales in the ninth century[60] and was subsequently glossed by a wild profusion of Insular scribes writing in Old Welsh, Old Irish and Latin; at some point before c. 1000 the manuscript had migrated to England (to which monastic library is unknown) where some further glosses were added in an Anglo-Caroline hand.[61] London, British Library, MS Royal 15.A.XVI, was also written in the late ninth century, possibly in northern France, but was at St Augustine's, Canterbury, by the late tenth century, when English scribes added some replacement leaves.[62] From the late Anglo-Saxon period there is a copy of Juvencus in the aforementioned manuscript from St Augustine's, Canterbury, now Cambridge, University Library, MS Gg.5.35 (s.xi^{med}).[63] In assessing the dissemination of the texts of Juvencus in late Anglo-Saxon England, one should consider two further manuscripts, both probably of English origin: Oxford, Bodleian Library, MS Barlow 25 (SC 6493) (s.x),[64] and Paris, Bibliothèque Sainte-Geneviève, MS 2410 (s.x/xi);[65] however, because neither of these texts of

Juvencus contains glosses, I shall have no further occasion to discuss them here. I might also mention two other manuscripts of Juvencus in British libraries which I have consulted for purposes of comparison but which give no indication of having arrived in England before the Conquest:[66] London, British Library, MS Harley 3093 (France (?), s.xi)[67] and Add. 19723 (Germany, s.x.).[68]

How are the glosses in these various manuscripts of Juvencus related? First, those in several of the continental manuscripts as well as in Royal 15.A.XVI appear to bear no relationship to each other or to manuscripts which were certainly in England in the late Anglo-Saxon period. Between two of those which certainly were in England at that time there is an undoubted relationship. I quote the first 12 lines of Book I of the *Libri Evangeliorum Quattuor* with the accompanying glosses in these two manuscripts:

Cambridge, Corpus Christi College 304, fos. 5v–6r

.i.ferus
Rex fuit herodes iudaea in gente cruentus

s. fuit .i. custos
Sub quo seruator iusti templique sacerdos

ordine solicitudo custodiri
Zacharias uicibus cui templum curat ueri

electorum sacerdotum
Digesto instabat lectorum ex ordine uatum

.i.elizabet
Huius inherebat thalamis dignissima coniux

s.erat .i. iusti
Cura his ambobus parilis moderaminis aequi

.i.nominatiuus casus
Ambos adnexos legis precepta tenebant

.i. labentibus
Nec fuit his soboles iam tum uergentibus annis

acceptus
ideo .i.non fuit Cratius ut donum iam desperantibus esset

.i.euntu templi secretis
Sed cum forte adytis arisque inferret odores

uel -e s.est s.-sus
Zaccharias uidit caelo discendere aperto
s.uisus est
Nuntius et soli iussas perferre loquellas.

Cambridge, University Library, Gg.5.35, f.1v

Rex fuit herodes iudea in gente cruentus
s.fuit custos .i.iustitie
Sub quo seruator iusti templique sacerdos
ordine sollicitudo custodire
Zacharias uicibus cui templum cura tueri
electorum sacerdotum
Digesto instabat lectorum ex ordine uatum
se
Huius inherebat thalamis dignissima coniunx
s.erat .i.equa .i.iusti
Cura his ambobus parilis moderaminis aequi
nominis casus
Ambos annexos legis precepta tenebant
labentibus uel uertentibus
Nec fuit his soboles iam tunc uergentibus annis
acceptius
.i. ideo non fuit Gratius ut donum iam disperantibus esset
.i.euentu templi secretis .i.censum
Sed cum forte aditis arisque inferret odores
s.est
Zacharias uisus celo descendere aperto
nuntiare
Nuntius et soli iussas perferre loquelas.

The glosses in CCCC 304 were added in England in the late Anglo-Saxon period; those in Gg.5.35 were copied by the main scribe. Now it is clear that the text of Gg.5.35 cannot derive from the earlier manuscript (note the significant textual variant *uisus/uidit* in line 11), and I doubt whether the glosses in either manuscript can have been copied from the other (note *custodire/custodiri* in line 3, *nominis casus/nominatiuus casus* in line 7, *acceptius/acceptus* in line 9 and *euntu/euentu* in line 10).[69] Nevertheless, there are so many striking agreements – such as the glosses *seruator*: *custos*, *uicibus*: *ordine*, *cura*: *sollicitudo*, *tueri*: *custodire*, *lectorum*: *electorum*, *uergentibus*: *labentibus*, the marginal note *.i. ideo non fuit*, *adytis*: *templi secretis*, and so on – that we are obliged to conclude that the glosses in these two manuscripts derive independently from a common source. Given the Canterbury provenance of both manuscripts, one might suspect *a priori* that these glosses originated at tenth-century Canterbury and were the work of a Canterbury master; but the evidence of Cambridge, University Library Ff.4.42, a manuscript of undoubted Welsh origin, rules out such a suspicion. Here is the same passage from Ff.4.42 with its plethora of glosses:[70]

Cambridge, University Library, Ff.4.42, f.2v (see plate I)

eƀ pelicius interpretata spdistinis
Rex fuit erodes Iudea in gente cruentus

s.fuit custos .i.iustitie ł iuris .i.salamonis
sub quo seruator iusti templique sacerdos

ł.memor Domini *ł.sortibus*
eƀ benedictus annis successionibus s.solicitudo .i.defendere
Zacharias uicibus cui templum cura tueri *custo-dire*

.i.deposito .i.electorum .i.sacerdotum
preclaro ł composito degesto instabat lectorum ordine uatum

s. Zacharie
huius inhaerebat thalamis dignissima coniux

s.fuit .i.simils .i.equitatis.*iusti*
cura his ambobus parilis moderaminis aequi

ambos annexos legis precepta tenebant

.i. filius
nec fuit his soboles iam tunc uergentibus annis

s. quia in iuuentute ł creationis .i.zacharias et elisabet
gratius ut donum iam desperantibus esset

.i.templis ara pro offerret .i.oblationes
sed cum forte aditis arisque inferret odores

.i. est
Zacharias uisus caelo descendere aperto

.i.angelus .i.Zacharia *s.a Deo* narrare
nuntius et soli iusus perferre loquelas.

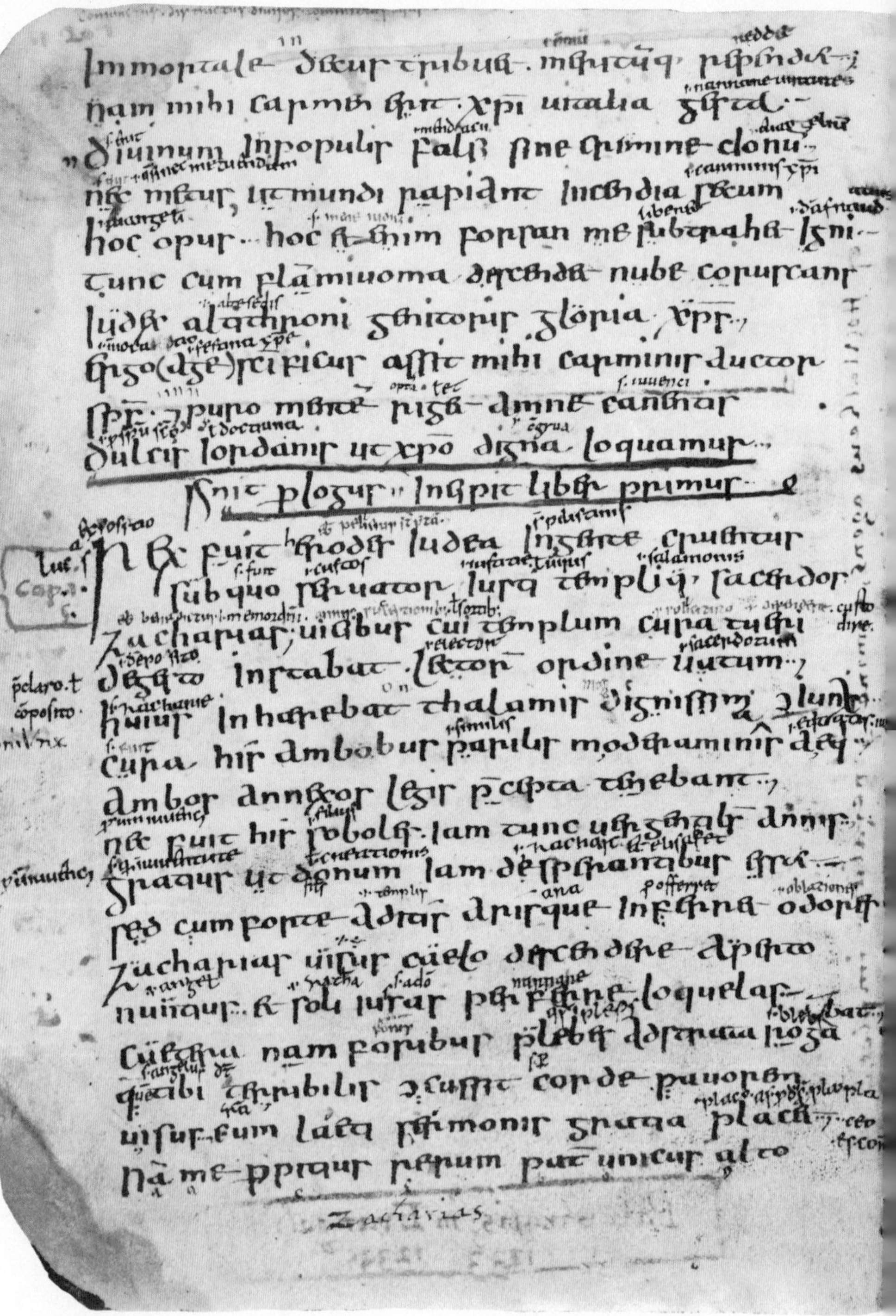

I. Cambridge, University Library, Ff.4.42, f.2v: Juvencus, *Libri Evangeliorum Quattuor*, beginning of Book I.

At least three (and probably more) glossators have been at work on this passage,[71] and I have attempted to distinguish their contributions as follows: the first, no underlining; the second, underlined once; the third in italics. The first of the glossators approached the text in a scholarly manner, and attempted among other things to supply meanings for the Hebrew names which he found there; thus, for example, he glosses the name *Herodes* as *(H)eb(raice) pelicius*.[72] The second glossator (who was working at the text before it left Wales) is more interesting for our purposes, for a number of the glosses he added agree exactly with those found in the above-mentioned Juvencus manuscripts from Canterbury: *scilicet fuit* on *quo*, *custos* on *seruator*, *iustitie* on *iusti*, all in line 2; *solicitudo* on *cura* in line 3, *electorum* on *lectorum* and *sacerdotum* on *uatum* in line 4. Apparently this Welsh glossator had access to the same core of Juvencus glosses that was later copied into manuscripts at Canterbury. This would imply in turn that the glosses were in existence no later than the beginning of the tenth century. It is perhaps worth noting as well that, when the manuscript came to England, the third glossator (writing a fine and distinct Anglo-Caroline script) added two further glosses which appear to derive from the same common core: *custodire* on *tueri* in line 3, and *iusti* on *aequi* in line 6. Clearly these Juvencus glosses enjoyed a wide circulation in the British Isles, and equally clearly, one must look back to some time before the tenth century to discover their origin.

A similar situation is encountered with respect to glossed manuscripts of Caelius Sedulius's *Carmen Paschale*,[73] one of the most widely read school-books in Anglo-Saxon times. Sedulius was one of Aldhelm's favourite authors: he quoted him frequently, and modelled his *opus geminatum* on virginity on Sedulius's similarly-structured work.[74] Bede knew and quoted Sedulius,[75] and Sedulius figures among the Christian-Latin poets listed by Alcuin in the York library.[76] In the tenth century, Wulfstan of Winchester plagiarized many lines directly from Sedulius.[77] Not surprisingly, a number of manuscripts of the *Carmen Paschale* survive which can be attributed to Anglo-Saxon England. The earliest, Cambridge, Corpus Christi College, MS 173, was written in an unknown centre sometime during the eighth century, but was in the possession of Frithestan of Winchester by the early tenth century;[78] it is densely glossed in both Latin and Old English.[79] London, British Library, MS Royal 15.B.XIX, part 1, was written at Christ Church, Canterbury, in the late tenth century by the same scribe as wrote the Harley manuscript of Prosper mentioned earlier.[80] The compendium of school-texts from St Augustine's, Canterbury, now Cambridge, University Library, MS

Gg.5.35, contains (as one would expect) a text of the *Carmen Paschale*.[81] A fragmentary manuscript of Sedulius, perhaps written at Worcester in the late tenth century and now preserved in Oxford, Bodleian Library, MS Lat. theol. c.4 (SC 1926*),[82] contains both marginal and interlinear glosses. There are also three manuscripts of Sedulius which were certainly written in late Anglo-Saxon England, but whose place of origin cannot be specified: Edinburgh, National Library, MS Advoc. 18.7.7 (s.x/xi),[83] Paris, Bibliothèque Nationale, MS lat. 8092 (s.xi^{1}),[84] and Paris, Bibliothèque Sainte-Geneviève, MS 2410 (s.x^{2}).[85]

Another index to the way Sedulius's *Carmen Paschale* was studied in late Anglo-Saxon England is provided by surviving manuscripts of the extensive commentary on this poem by Remigius of Auxerre.[86] Two such manuscripts of the commentary are in question: Cambridge, Gonville and Caius College 144/194, a tenth-century manuscript mentioned previously as containing a fragment of Remigius's commentary on the *Disticha Catonis*, which is of unknown origin but certainly was at St Augustine's by the eleventh century;[87] and Salisbury, Cathedral Library, MS 134, written in Anglo-Caroline script (though the scriptorium which produced it is unknown) and datable to c. 1000;[88] in this manuscript Remigius's commentary is described as *Commentum Remegii super Sedulium* (f.1r). In a Worcester book-list of the late eleventh century is found the entry *Commentum Remigii super Sedulium*;[89] it is possible (judging from the title of the work in the manuscript) that the Salisbury Cathedral manuscript is identical with the entry in the Worcester book-list. In any case there is sound evidence for believing that Remigius's commentary on the *Carmen Paschale* was known in late Anglo-Saxon England. With this in mind, we can turn to the interlinear and marginal glosses in the Anglo-Saxon manuscripts of Sedulius.

The text of Sedulius's *Carmen Paschale* in Cambridge, University Library Gg.5.35, is provided with abundant interlinear glosses. On close inspection, it becomes apparent that these glosses have been copied directly from Remigius's *Commentum super Sedulium*, as may be seen by comparing the glosses to the first five lines of Book I with Remigius's commentary as it is preserved in Salisbury Cathedral 134 and Cambridge, Gonville and Caius College 144/194.

Cambridge, University Library, Gg.5.35, f.53v

mendacia
Cum sua gentiles studeant figmenta poetae
grandiloquis carminibus ornare uigili
Grandisonis pompare modis tragicoque boatu
Ridiculo ucgctc seu qualibet arte canendi
nec loquendarum uitia
Seua nefandarum renouent contagia rerum
recordationes consuetudine
Et scelerum monimenta canant rituque magistro.

Salisbury Cathedral 134, f.6r; Gonville and Caius College 144/194, f.9r

Cum sua gentiles: gentiles dicuntur qui ita permanent ut nati sunt.
figmenta: .i.mendacia et suas compostiones.
grandisonis: .i.grandiloquis carminibus. Tres sunt caracteres – humilis, mediocris, grandiloquus – quos Virgilius tangit.
pompare: .i.ornare.
tragico: .i.uili. Tragos enim hyrcus, hinc etiam tragemata grece, .i.uilia munuscula. Colobida ebreice, bellaria latine.
ridiculo: .i.ioco.
Gete: persona comica est apud Terentium. Missi (*leg.* Mysi) sunt populi ioculatores, lusibus nimiis studentes.
nefandarum: .i.nec loquendarum.
contagia: .i.uitia, scelera. Contagium est morbus porcinus dictus, quod unius contactu in plures diffundatur. Idem est et porrigo a porrigendo, eo quod ab imo in alios porrigat.
monumenta: .i.recordationes. Monumenta dicitur memoria, eo quod moneat mentem.
ritu: .i.consuetudine magistrali.

The St Augustine's scribes responsible for this part of Gg.5.35[90] seem to have been copying their text of Sedulius from one manuscript and their interlinear glosses from another – a procedure which might account for the numerous errors of transcription in their work.[91] If this hypothesis is correct – and one cannot rule out the possibility that the scribes' exemplar of the *Carmen Paschale* already contained interlinear glosses derived from Remigius's commentary – then it is an open possibility that their exemplar of Remigius was in fact Gonville and Caius 144/194, a manuscript which was at St Augustine's by the time CUL Gg.5.35 was written there (c. 1050). A similar procedure appears to have been followed by the scribe of the fragmentary manuscript of Sedulius, Oxford, Bodleian Library, Lat. theol.c.4. As Bishop has demonstrated,[92] the marginal and interlinear glosses in this manuscript derive directly from Remigius's commentary. Now Lat. theol.c.4 was possibly written at Worcester in the late tenth century, and it will be recalled that Salisbury Cathedral 134 (s.x/xi) is possibly identical with the *commentum Remegii super Sedulium* in a late eleventh-century Worcester book-list; it may have been there earlier. Here, too, it is possible that the scribe of Lat. theol.c.4 copied the glosses to the *Carmen Paschale* directly from Salisbury Cathedral 134 (or its immediate archetype). Latin glosses in other pre-Conquest manuscripts of Sedulius do not reveal such direct debts to the commentary of Remigius,[93] though it is possible that when his commentary has been published and its transmission more fully understood, greater indebtedness will be apparent. For the time being, there is evidence to show that the *Carmen Paschale* was studied in late Anglo-Saxon England by means of Remigius's commentary. In the case of Sedulius manuscripts, therefore, the Latin glosses are not the *ad hoc* reactions of Anglo-Saxon readers to the poem, nor the lecture notes of Anglo-Saxon masters: they are the residue of a commentary composed in Francia over a century earlier.

I come finally to the last author under discussion whose works were studied in Anglo-Saxon schools and are preserved in glossed English manuscripts: Arator, whose *De Actibus Apostolorum*,[94] dedicated to Pope Vigilius in 544, became at once a classic of Christian-Latin poetry. Aldhelm had studied Arator;[95] Bede quoted Arator in his *De Arte Metrica* and based his *Expositio* on the Acts of the Apostles very largely on Arator's *De Actibus Apostolorum*;[96] Alcuin listed Arator among the Christian-Latin poets in the York library,[97] and in the early eleventh century Byrhtferth of Ramsey quoted his verse.[98] One might, therefore, expect to find a large number of Anglo-Saxon manuscripts of Arator. But although some dozen of the 100 or so surviving manuscripts of Arator[99] are preserved in British libraries, few of them appear either to have originated or to have arrived in the British Isles before 1066.[100] Those which are certainly of pre-Conquest English origin are as follows: Cambridge, Trinity College, MS B.14.3 (289) of the late tenth century (s.x^{ex}) from Christ Church, Canterbury;[101] Oxford, Bodleian Library, MS Rawlinson C.570 (SC 12415) (s.x/xi)[102] and Cambridge, University Library, MS Gg.5.35 (s.xi^{med}),[103] both from St Augustine's, Canterbury; and Paris, Bibliothèque Nationale, MS lat. 8092 (s.xi^{1}), from an unidentified centre.[104] To these one may perhaps add London, British Library, MS Add. 11034 (probably s.x), of possible English origin.[105] I shall also include London, British Library, MS Royal 15.A.V (s.xi^{ex}) in my discussion because, although the manuscript was manifestly written after the Norman Conquest in the late eleventh century, it was, from the evidence of its script, written in England by an English scribe.[106] Some of these English manuscripts contain virtually no glossing (Rawlinson C.570 and part II of Royal 15.A.V), but others are glossed sufficiently to enable a collation to be made; for purposes of comparison I have also collated the various continental manuscripts of Arator now in British libraries.

Even a cursory collation will indicate that there were various sets of Arator glosses which travelled with the text.[107] I shall consider only one such set which appears to be most fully attested in the marginal and interlinear glossing found in Cambridge, Trinity College, MS B.14.3 (289). To facilitate discussion I present here a schematic and somewhat abbreviated version of the glosses which accompany the first 12 lines of the prefatory *Epistola ad Florianum* in this manuscript; a facsimile of the folio in question is given in Plate II (p. 119).

Cambridge, Trinity College, B.14.3 (289), f.5r

.i.perfectis florem dico .i.natum
Qui meriti florem maturis sensibus ortum

.i. in superficie tui nominis s. o s.ut a flore
Nominis ore tui iam floriane tenes

florianus dicaris quia florianus es tu et nomine et merito. Deinde per parenthesim interpositam dictionem exponit quomodo est ille florianus actu

.i. iuuenis .i.primeuo euo positus
Nam primeuus adhuc senibus documenta dedistis

Primeuos dicimus homines ex primo et euo sicut equeuos equales etate

s. documentis .i.profectus illorum bonus
E quibus in caelum uita pararet iter

.i.intende meum opus s.metri .i.uacillanti
Ad carmen concurre meum pedibusque labanti*

Distat inter occurro aliquem .i. obuio et concurro .i.prebeo auxilium .i.constructione et sermone

.i. de larga pietate .i.miti sensu
Porrige de placido sepe fauore manum

*labanti .i. titubanti labo breuem habet la. labor longam

.i.uili ingenio .i.profunda
Ieiuno sermone quidem sed pinguia* gesta

*pinguia .i. plena misteriis apostolorum

.i. ueluti .i.magnitudine
Scripsimus ac pelagi* pondere gutta fluit

*Pelago comparat actus apostolorum propter profunditatem misteriorum sicut gutta de mari. ita hic liber de actibus apostolorum

hoc est cum profundissimos auctores
Inter grandiloquos per mille uolumina libros

Grandiloquos libros uocat carmina poetarum

.i.dificillima .i.intellegas uiliora nostra carmina
Maxima cum teneas hec breuiora lege

.i.ad similitudinem nature .i. secundum modum
Naturae quo modo quam rerum condidit auctor

-cordent .i.maiora .i. minora
Conueniant studiis celsa uel ima tuis.

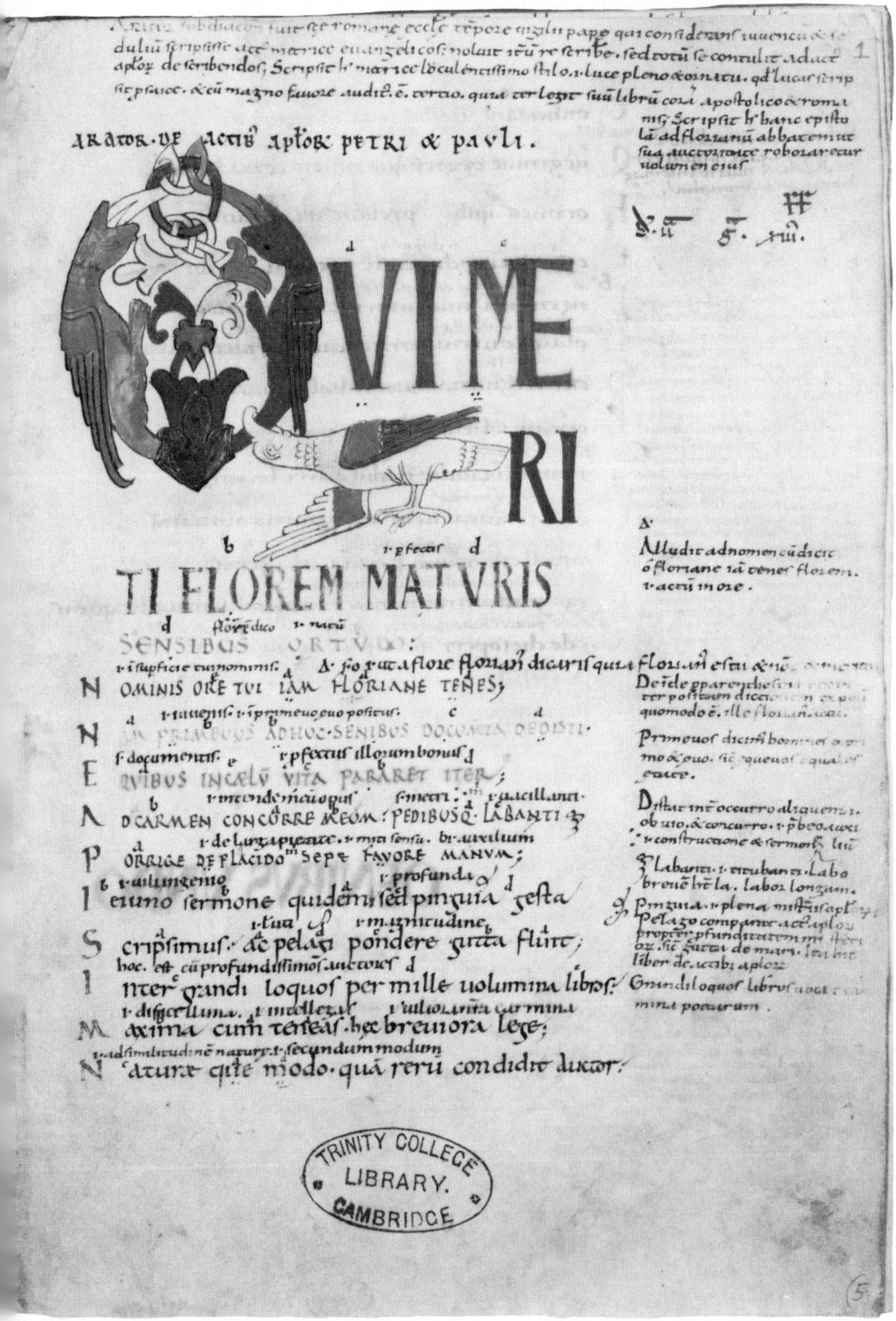

II. Cambridge, Trinity College, MS B.14.3 (289), f.5r: Arator, *De Actibus Apostolorum*, beginning of the prefatory *Epistola ad Florianum*.

That these interlinear glosses and marginal commentary are not unique to TCC B.14.3 (289) may be readily seen by comparing the interlinear glosses which occur in other Arator manuscripts of English origin. No other Anglo-Saxon manuscript is so extensively glossed, but others preserve enough glosses to enable us to identify a common core. For example, in Paris, BN lat. 8092, the following few interlinear glosses are found:

Paris, Bibliothèque Nationale, lat. 8092, f.45v

Qui meriti florem maturis sensibus ortum
s. o
Nominis ore tui iam floriane tenes
.i. iuuenis
Nam primaeuus adhuc senibus documenta dedisti
E quibus in caelum uita pararet iter
.i. titubanti
Ad carmen concurre meum pedibusque labanti
.i. miti sensu auxilium
Porrige de placido sepe fauore manum
Ieiuno sermone quidem sed pinguia gesta
Scripsimus ac pelagi pondere gutta fluit
Inter grandiloquos prae mille uolumina libros
minora
Maxima cum teneas et breuiora lege
Natureque modo quam rerum condidit auctor
.i.maiora uel minora
Concordent studiis celsa uel ima tuis.

There is only one interlinear gloss here which is not found in the previously mentioned manuscript from Christ Church, Canterbury (*breuiora*: *minora*). Each of the others, however, is found there as well, and this permits us to regard the few glosses in BN lat. 8092 as a sort of characteristic core of this set of Arator glosses. Thus vestiges of the same core may be recognized elsewhere, as for example in another tenth-century manuscript, possibly of English origin:

London, British Library, Add. 11034, f.3r

perfectis .i. natum
Qui meriti florem maturis sensibus ortum
Nominis ore tui iam floriane tenes
Nam primaeuus adhuc senibus documenta dedisti
E quibus in caelum uita pararet iter
.i. titubanti.nutanti
Ad carmen concurre meum pedibusque labanti
.i. miti sensu
Porrige de placido sepe fauore manum
Ieiuno sermone quidem sed pinguia gesta
Scripsimus ac pelagi pondere gutta fluit
Inter grandiloquos per mille uolumina libros
Maxima cum teneas et breuiora lege
Naturaeque modo quam rerum condidit auctor
.i. maiora l minora
Concordent studiis celsa uel ima tuis.

Once again, each of these glosses is found in the manuscript from Christ Church (TCC B.14.3). The glosses in this and Paris BN lat. 8092 cannot derive one from the other (both are only partial records of the hypothetical common core). Nor, given the dating of the manuscripts in question, can they have been copied from TCC B.14.3. We are dealing with a set of glosses which travelled (in varying measure) with the text of Arator. How widely they travelled may be estimated from the evidence of a continental manuscript, probably of the tenth century, which gives no indication of having been in England before the Norman Conquest: London, British Library, MS Harley 3072. The origin and provenance of this manuscript are unknown,[108] and its glosses (added by the main hand) are not for the most part identical to those in TCC B.14.3. Nevertheless, there are enough similarities once again to suggest that the glosses in this and in all the English manuscripts had a common origin.

London, British Library, MS Harley 3072, f.43r

tui .i.per meritum premium perfectis in florem dico
Qui meriti florem maturis sensibus ortum
.i. in pronunciacione
Nominis ore tui iam floriane tenes

parenthesis .i. prima etate positus
Nam primeuus adhuc senibus documenta dedisti

documentis s. illorum senium
E quibus in celum uita pararet iter

prebe assensum meo operi uacillanti.titibanti s.mihi
Ad carmen concurre meum pedibusque labanti

da tuo tuum adiutorium
Porridge de placido sepe fauore manum

.i. inornato.inculto .i.fecunda sanctitate
Ieiuno sermone quidem sed pinguia gesta

de .i.libellus hic decurrit
Scripsimus ac pelagi pondere gutta fluit

grande loquentes
Inter grandiloquos per mille uolumina libros meum scriptum est gutta aduersus illorum actus

carmina .i.quandoquidem mea
Maxima cum teneas hec breuiora lege

ad similitudinem s. naturam formauit
Naturaeque modo quam rerum condidit auctor

.i. fac concordare bassas
Concordent studiis celsa uel ima tuis.

These glosses are not an immediate relative of those in the Anglo-Saxon manuscripts: they lack, for example, what we have recognized as characteristic glosses (*miti sensu* for *fauore* in line 6, *maiora uel minora* for *celsa uel ima* in line 12, and so on). In lieu of such glosses, Harley 3072 has substituted glosses of its own. Nevertheless it is clear that Harley 3072 and the various Anglo-Saxon manuscripts all derive their glosses from a common ancestor. Without the assumption of such a common ancestor, it would be impossible to explain certain of the interlinear glosses in Harley 3072. For example, the (otherwise meaningless) gloss to line 3, *parenthesis .i. prima etate positus*, only acquires meaning through comparison with two adjacent glosses in TCC B.14.3: *primeuus .i. primeuo euo positus* (interlinear) and *deinde per parenthesim* (*interpositam dictionem*) *exponit* . . . (marginal). Striking, too, is the concurrence of glosses to *labanti* in line 5: *uacillanti*, *titubanti*; compare the two glosses in TCC B.14.3: *labanti .i. uacillanti* (interlinear) and *labanti .i. titubanti* (marginal). The glosses *perfectis* to *maturis* and *florem dico* occur in identical form in TCC B.14.3 In other words, these glosses in Harley 3072 must derive from the same ultimate sources as those in the Anglo-Saxon manuscripts. Furthermore, the fact that the glosses in the (somewhat earlier) continental manuscript have already been confused and conflated suggests that some time must have passed between the time when they were devised and when they were copied into Harley 3072 and later into the Anglo-Saxon manuscripts. This situation can best be explained by the assumption that the Arator glosses originated in a ninth-century continental school, and that they were in origin a commentary on Arator very similar in form to the commentaries by Remigius of Auxerre on the *Disticha Catonis* and Sedulius's *Carmen Paschale.*

No pre-Conquest English manuscript appears to preserve a commentary on Arator which might be considered as the source of the various Arator glosses. However, in a manuscript written shortly after the Conquest, probably in England – the aforementioned London, British Library, MS Royal 15.A.V, fos. 86–147 – there is found an anonymous commentary on Arator, which, on closer inspection, can be confidently identified as a late copy of that commentary from which the glosses in the above-mentioned manuscripts derive. As far as I am aware, this commentary has never been printed. I reproduce that part of it which deals with the first 12 lines of the prefatory *Epistola ad Florianum.*

London, British Library, MS Royal 15.A.V, f.86r

[*Floriane*] Alludit ad nomen cum dicit 'O Floriane, iam tenes florem', .i. actum in ore, .i. in superficie tui nominis, .i. in tuo nomine.

ortum: .i. natum.

maturis: .i. perfectis, quia Florianus es tu et nomine et merito. Deinde per parentesin (.i. per interpositam dictionem) exponit quomodo est ille florianus actu.

nam primeuus: .i. iuuenis, .i. in primo euo positus. Primeuos dicimus hormines ex primo et euo, sicut equeuos equales etate.

concurre: .i. auxilium presta. Distat inter occurro aliquem, .i. obuio, et concurro, .i. prebeo auxilium.

pedibus: .i. constructione et sermone.

labanti: .i. titubanti. labo breuem habet la-, labor longam.

fauore: .i. miti sensu.

inculto: .i. inornato, uili.

pinguia: .i. plena misteriis apostolorum

Pelago comparat actus apostolorum propter profunditatem misteriorum.
Sicut gutta de mari: ita hic liber de actibus apostolorum.
Grandiloquos libros uocat carmina poetarum.
nature modo: .i. ad similitudinem nature.
celsa uel ima: .i. maiora. Debes, inquit, considerare naturam, quia natura (terra uidelicet) nutrit in se magna et parua animalia.

So closely does this commentary correspond to the interlinear and marginal glossing in TCC B.14.3 that one might think *prima facie* – given the late date of Royal 15.A.V – that the scribe had simply copied out in long hand the glosses from the earlier manuscript. Such cannot be the case, however. The commentary in Royal 15.A.V has several explanations not found in TCC B.14.3; furthermore, the commentary was clearly based on a manuscript of Arator which had the reading *inculto* (in lieu of the far commoner reading *ieiuno*) in line 7. TCC B.14.3 and the other Anglo-Saxon manuscripts all read *ieiuno* at this point. The reading *inculto* appears to be attested only in two late ninth-century French manuscripts.[109] Once again, then, the trail leads back to the ninth-century French schools. Until the commentary has been printed, and surviving manuscripts of Arator containing glosses derived from it identified, it is not possible to know the author or the place of origin of the commentary.[110] For now, all that can be safely deduced from the widespread diffusion of Arator glosses in tenth-century manuscripts is that the commentary from which they derive was probably compiled in a ninth-century continental (possibly French) school.

What implications does this preliminary survey of Latin glossing in late Anglo-Saxon manuscripts have for our inquiry into the workings of Anglo-Saxon schools? Before drawing any conclusions I should wish to re-emphasize the severely restricted scope of my investigations: in the case of each text I have examined only a handful of manuscripts, for the most part in British libraries, and collated the Latin glosses to only a few lines. Yet for each of these texts dozens, sometimes hundreds, of manuscripts survive. It is quite fair to say that no final statement on the relationships between glosses in manuscripts may be made until all have been collated: fuller collation of any extent could easily invalidate my initial impressions. Bearing this *caveat* in mind, however, it will be seen that most of my evidence points in the one direction: that the Latin glosses to texts which we know from other sources to have been widely studied in Anglo-Saxon England cannot be the *ad hoc* annotations of

Anglo-Saxon masters expounding the texts nor of students attempting to comprehend them. For the most part, the Latin glosses appear to have travelled from the continent to tenth-century England in the company of the texts they were designed to explicate. In this respect, glosses accompanying the Christian-Latin poets resemble those which frequently accompany the Classical poets in Anglo-Saxon manuscripts. For example, T. A. M. Bishop, in discussing two Anglo-Caroline manuscripts of Statius's *Thebaid*,[111] has been able to demonstrate that the interlinear and marginal glosses in these manuscripts are also found in a tenth-century manuscript from Tours.[112] In other words, we are obliged to look to ninth-century Carolingian schools in order to understand the transmission of these Statius glosses, for it was in the ninth century that the great masters such as Remigius of Auxerre assembled their commentaries on classical texts with the aid of ancient *scholia*. Although there were no ancient *scholia* handed down with the texts of the Christian-Latin poets, it seems probable that the commentaries and glosses to these poets were first compiled in the ninth century. I have suggested that the manuscripts of Juvencus, Sedulius and Arator all point to a ninth-century origin for their accompanying glosses; and it will take no leap of imagination to think that the glosses to Prosper and the *Disticha Catonis* had a similar origin. In other words, we have here yet another example of Anglo-Saxon England's intellectual indebtedness to continental schools.

If the Latin glosses accompanying the texts of the Christian-Latin poets did not originate in England, then we must be scrupulously careful in drawing any conclusions about the way in which such texts were studied in Anglo-Saxon schools on the evidence of these glosses. Here I suspect a very considerable difference between Latin glosses and Old English glosses: there does not seem to be any consistent agreement between English glosses in various manuscripts, and dry-point glosses do indeed seem to reflect the *ad hoc* responses of individual readers to textual difficulties. But if Latin glosses were not the annotations of masters or students, did they have any vital function? Or were they simply the repositories of learning which was (in some cases at least) a century old? A salient feature of glossed Anglo-Saxon manuscripts comes to mind. In many cases – perhaps the majority – of the manuscripts I have discussed, the Latin glossing begins intensively on the first folio or two, peters out over the next few folios, and then usually ceases altogether.[113] Why? The only explanation I can offer is that the glossing was not felt by the scribe(s) to be an essential or important ingredient of the finished work. And if the Latin glossing had no essential function (in the classroom or elsewhere), it could be dispensed with. Thus many a well-intentioned scribe stopped reproducing the glosses of his exemplar after a few folios: they could be dispensed with, perhaps, because no one paid them serious attention.

That is why I am inclined to urge caution in the use of the term 'classbook'. Books containing poetic texts with Latin glosses such as those I have examined *may* have been read in classrooms. But there is no proof that they were; and their Latin glosses do not *per se* point in that direction. However, if these books were not copied and glossed with classroom use in view, what *was* their function? One possible answer lies in a consideration of monastic custom. It will be recalled that, according to the stipulations of the Benedictine Rule, private reading held a substantial place in the monastic life: three hours each morning in winter, two hours each afternoon in summer, nearly all day every Sunday throughout the year – an average of some 20 hours per week.[114] During Lent in particular, according to c.XLVIII of the Rule, each monk was to receive a single codex from the *bibliotheca* which he was obliged to read entire: 'in quibus diebus quadragesimae accipiant omnes singulos codices de bibliotheca, quos per ordinem ex integro legant'.[115] As A. Mundó has shown,[116] *bibliotheca* to the founder of the Rule meant 'Bible': each monk was to take away a book of the Bible and read it through during Lent. However, what is interesting is that Carolingian commentators came to understand *bibliotheca* in the more modern sense of 'library', and – since medieval monks appear to have read more slowly than modern scholars – reinterpreted the Rule as a requirement for each monk to read *one* book *in extenso* during the course of a year.[117] The procedures governing this form of private reading are specified in a number of medieval customaries. Most relevant to late Anglo-Saxon England are the procedures described in a customary from Fleury.[118] This customary is preserved in an early thirteenth-century manuscript from Fleury,[119] but commentators are in agreement that the customs it prescribes date from a much earlier period. The procedure concerning private reading is as follows:

> . . . a carpet is spread out on the floor of the chapter-house, on which all books brought from the *armarium* (='monastic bookcase' or even 'library') are placed. After a reading of the Rule, the librarian (*armarius*) recites from his tablets the names of all monks to whom on the very same day of the preceding year books had been given. When each monk is named, he gets up and places his book on the carpet. Afterwards the books are given out to the monks, each

> one seeking the book he wishes. The junior librarian writes down the names of the monks and the books they have taken . . . After the books have been handed out, the remainder are taken back in the book-case. When this had been done, if any monk had not read his book, he would seek forgiveness (from the abbot) . . .[120]

As far as I am aware, there is no surviving customary of the Anglo-Saxon period which stipulates such a procedure. However, it will be recalled that monks from Fleury had been invited to Winchester to help Æthelwold with the drafting of the *Regularis Concordia*,[121] the document which established the custom of reformed Benedictine monasticism in late Anglo-Saxon England. Furthermore, it has been recognized that the *Regularis Concordia* is indebted in many important ways to the customs of Fleury.[122] One may surmise, therefore, that the procedure outlined in the Fleury customary would have been familiar to Anglo-Saxon monks, even though no such stipulations are found in the *Regularis Concordia* itself.[123]

The Fleury customary gives us an unequivocal account of the use to which books in a monastic library were normally put. Each monk was responsible for reading one book *per annum*. I would suggest that many of the manuscripts discussed above were in fact written with this purpose in view: they were what we call 'library books' rather than 'classbooks'. One book a year may not seem like an intensive reading programme (unless the book in question should happen to be CUL Gg.5.35), but we should remember that not all Anglo-Saxon monks would have had the voracious appetite for reading possessed by an Aldhelm or a Bede. One book a year may have suited the majority of monks to a nicety. And perhaps this is why many of the manuscripts I have discussed show no signs of intensive use. In many of them, the parchment is as crisp and clean as on the day it was prepared. Compare the 'classbooks' from which all of us teach (Klaeber's *Beowulf*, Sweet's *Anglo-Saxon Reader*, Robinson's *Chaucer*, whatever): the spines are broken, every available space crammed with annotation, pages soiled and torn, students' telephone numbers spilling across the fly-leaves, and so on – a far cry from the pristine state in which most so-called Anglo-Saxon 'classbooks' survive. I would conclude, therefore, by stressing that the Anglo-Saxon manuscripts of Christian-Latin poets which survive did *not necessarily* see service in the Anglo-Saxon classroom, and that the glosses which they contain are *not necessarily* an index to the Anglo-Saxon master's teaching procedures. Yet – paradoxically – it is only by continuing to study these manuscripts that we can form any estimate of the way Latin culture was absorbed by the Anglo-Saxons.

NOTES

I should like to acknowledge the help of Professor Bernhard Bischoff, who generously gave me his opinion on the dates and origins of several of the manuscripts I discuss, and of Dr David Dumville, who criticized the article in typescript and saved me from a number of errors. I also owe a large and indefinable debt to Dr Raymond Page, with whom I have worked through some of the manuscripts mentioned above, and from conversations with whom I have been challenged to appreciate the function of glossing in Anglo-Saxon manuscripts.

1. R. W. Hunt, *St Dunstan's Classbook from Glastonbury: Cod. Bibl. Bodl. Auct. F. 4. 32* [*Umbrae Codicum Occidentalium*, 4], (Amsterdam, 1962).
2. A. G. Rigg and G. R. Wieland, 'A Canterbury classbook of the mid-eleventh century (the 'Cambridge Songs' manuscript)', *ASE*, IV (1975), 113–30. I should state at once that my remarks in the following discussion are in no way intended as a rebuttal of this earlier scholarship (indeed I have myself described the Canterbury manuscript in question as a 'classbook': *ASE*, IV (1975), 76), but simply as a plea for care in our assumptions about the way Anglo-Saxon manuscripts were read and used.
3. Old English glosses in manuscripts of the Anglo-Saxon period are discussed by R. I. Page, below, pp. 141–5.
4. P. Riché, *Éducation et culture dans l'Occident barbare VIe–VIIIe siècles* (3rd edn, Paris, 1962), 510. Riché has returned to these problems in his more recent book, *Les écoles et l'enseignement dans l'Occident chrétien* (Paris, 1979), 214–20 and 222–36.
5. Ed. W. H. Stevenson, *Early Scholastic Colloquies* (1929), 27–74. Bata has never received the scholarly attention he deserves, but it is interesting to note that Riché at various points cites him as witness to the procedure in a medieval schoolroom (*Les écoles et l'enseignement*, 205–9 *et passim*).
6. E.g. the passage beginning 'Tu sochors! Tu scibalum hedi! Tu scibalum ouis! Tu scibalum equi! Tu fimus bouis! Tu stercus porci! Tu hominis stercus!' etc. (ed. Stevenson, *Early Scholastic Colloquies*, 52).
7. E.g. the scene described in Stevenson, *Early Scholastic Colloquies*, 62.
8. The word is not listed in the new *Dictionary of Medieval Latin from British Sources*, fascicule I: A–B (1975), but its meaning is clear from the context.
9. Translated from Stevenson, *Early Scholastic Colloquies*, 28.
10. Translated from Stevenson, *loc. cit.*
11. Cf. the remarks by Riché, *Éducation et culture*, 521, and *idem*, *Les écoles et l'enseignement*, 219: 'les véritables cahiers d'écoliers sont presque inexistants et sont le plus souvent des exercises d'écriture'. A manuscript apparently containing the annotations of a schoolboy owner is discussed by R. McKitterick, 'A ninth-century schoolbook from the Loire Valley: Phillipps MS 16308', *Scriptorium*, XXX (1976), 225–31.
12. See Riché, *Éducation et culture*, 511–13, and *idem*, *Les écoles et l'enseignement*, 222–5. This technique was handed on to the middle ages by Roman schools; cf. S. F. Bonner, *Education in Ancient Rome* (1977), 126–30.
13. See E. C. R. Armstrong and R. A. S. Macalister, 'A wooden book with leaves intended and waxed found near Springmount Bog, Co. Antrim', *J. Roy. Soc. Antiquaries of Ireland*, L (1920), 160–6. The tablets are now preserved in Dublin,

National Museum, MS S.A. 1914:2; see *CLA Supplement*, no. 1684.

14. See R. Cramp in *The Archaeology of Anglo-Saxon England*, ed. D. M. Wilson (1976), 227–8.
15. It is hardly necessary to demonstrate a knowledge of Vergil on the part of the Anglo-Latin authors I have mentioned. Bede's knowledge of Vergil, however, has recently been cast in doubt by P. Hunter Blair (in *Famulus Christi*, ed. G. Bonner (1976), 243–53), who argued that all the quotations of Vergil in Bede's writings *could* have been derived at second hand from Latin grammarians. Curiously, Hunter Blair did not take Bede's metrical *Vita S. Cuthberti* – a poem which is redolent of Vergilian diction – into consideration. Hunter Blair's arguments have now been effectively disposed of by N. R. Wright, 'Bede and Vergil', *Romanobarbarica*, VI (1981), 145–62.
16. Rome, Biblioteca Apostolica Vaticana, MS Reginensis lat. 1671; see below, n. 18.
17. The manuscripts in question are: London, British Library, MS Royal 8.F.XIV, fos. 3–5 (s.x^{in}); London, College of Arms, MS Arundel 30, fos. 5–10 and 208 (s.x: the fragments of the *Aeneid* are the lower script of a palimpsest); Oxford, Bodleian Library, MS Lat. class. c.2, f.18 (s.x^{2}?); and Kettering (Northants.), Deene Park Library, s.n. (property of Edmund Brudenell, Esq.). It is possible that the last two items, which are scraps recovered from bindings, are from the same manuscript. I am extremely grateful to Dr Bruce Barker-Benfield for information on these two binding scraps, and for the suggestion that they are of English origin: a suggestion which merits further investigation.
18. See T. A. M. Bishop, *English Caroline Minuscule* (1971), 17 (=no.19), who attributes the manuscript to Worcester and dates it tentatively to the second half of the tenth century.
19. On the medieval curriculum in general, see E. R. Curtius, *European Literature and the Latin Middle Ages*, tr. W. R. Trask (New York, 1963), 48–54; R. B. C. Huygens, *Accessus ad Auctores: Bernard d'Utrecht, Conrad d'Hirsau, Dialogus super Auctores* (Leyden, 1970); J. Gessler, *Une bibliothèque scolaire du XIe siècle d'après le catalogue provenant de l'abbaye d'Anchin* (Brussels and Paris, 1935); P. Vossen, *Der Libellus Scolasticus des Walther von Speyer: Ein Schulbericht aus dem Jahr 984* (Berlin, 1962). A comprehensive treatment of the school curriculum in Anglo-Saxon England remains to be written.
20. The material is conveniently assembled by J. D. A. Ogilvy, *Books Known to the English, 597–1066* (Cambridge, Mass., 1967), a book which needs to be treated with extreme caution, particularly at points where the author refers to surviving manuscripts.
21. See E. M. Sanford, 'The use of Classical Latin authors in the Libri Manuales', *Trans. and Procs. American Philological Assoc.*, LV (1924), 190–248; J. de Ghellinck, 'En marge des catalogues des bibliothèques médiévales', in *Miscellanea Francesco Ehrle* V, Studi e Testi 41 (Rome, 1924), 331–63; J. Engels, 'Les noms de quelques manuels scolaires médiévaux', *Neophilologus*, L (1970), 105–12; G. Glauche, *Schullekture im Mittelalter: Entstehung und Wandlungen der Lekturekanons bis 1200* (Munich, 1970); *idem*, 'Die Rolle der Schulautoren im Unterricht von 800 bis 1100', *SSCI*, XIX (1972), 617–36; there are also several essential studies in *SSCI*, XXII (1975), by B. Bischoff (59–86), T. J. Brown (237–93), G. Billanovich and M. Ferrari (303–52), G. Cavallo (357–414), M. Diaz y Diaz (135–75), C. Leonardi (459–504), and A. Vernet (89–123).
22. The standard edition is that by M. Boas, *Disticha Catonis*, rev. H. J. Botschuyver

(Amsterdam, 1952). There is a translation of the *Disticha Catonis* by W. Chase, *The Distichs of Cato, A Famous Medieval Textbook* [University of Wisconsin Studies in the Social Sciences and History 7], (Madison, Wisconsin, 1922). On the transmission of the work in the early Middle Ages see M. Boas, 'De librorum Catonianorum Historia atque Compositione', *Mnemosyne*, n.s. XLII (1914), 17–46.

23. E. Voigt, 'Das erste Lesebuch des Triviums in der Kloster- und Stiftschuler des Mittelalters', *Mitteilungen der Gesellschaft für deutsche Erziehungs- und Schulgeschichte* (1891), 42–53.
24. See R. Hazelton, 'The Christianization of Cato: The *Disticha Catonis* in the Light of Late Medieval Commentaries', *Mediaeval Studies*, XIX (1957), 157–73.
25. See R. Hazelton, 'Chaucer and Cato', *Speculum*, XXXV (1960), 357–70.
26. Stevenson, *Early Scholastic Colloquies*, 29; the reference is to *Disticha Catonis*, epist. praef. (ed. Boas, 4).
27. *Byrhtferth's Manual*, ed. S. J. Crawford (EETS, 1929), 133.
28. The manuscripts in question are Cambridge, Trinity College, MS R.9.17 (819) (s.xi/xii), fos. 45r–48r; London, British Library, MS Cotton Julius A.ii (s.xii^{med}), fos. 141r–144r; and Cotton Vespasian D.xiv (s.xii^{med}), fos. 7r–11v. The text has been edited critically by R. S. Cox, 'The Old English Dicts of Cato', *Anglia*, XC (1972), 1–42.
29. See N. R. Ker, *Catalogue of Manuscripts containing Anglo-Saxon* (1957), 268–9 (=no. 207). Fos. 2–77 are one manuscript containing various sententiae and sayings, such as the *Parabolae Salamonis* and Alcuin's *De Virtutibus et Vitiis*. The *Disticha Catonis* are found on fos. 73v–76v. The text is incomplete, containing only Book I and the first 27 distichs of Book II; the remainder of f. 76v is blank. This incomplete text of the *Disticha Catonis*, therefore, cannot have been the exemplar of the full text which is found in the later St Augustine's manuscript, CUL Gg.5.35 – which supposes at the least a third manuscript of the *Disticha Catonis* at that monastery.
30. See Ker, *Catalogue*, 21–2 (=no. 16), and Rigg and Wieland, *op. cit.* in n. 2, 126. The *Disticha Catonis* are found on fos. 407r–412v, and are lightly glossed (in Latin) by the main scribe (Rigg's scribe A).
31. See Ker, *Catalogue*, 137–8 (=no. 95), and T. A. M. Bishop, 'Notes on Cambridge Manuscripts, Part VII: the early minuscule of Christ Church, Canterbury', *TCBS*, III. 5 (1963), 413–23, esp. 413–14. The *Disticha Catonis* are found on fos. 34r–40v. They are glossed by several hands (at least three); note that Books I and II are fairly heavily glossed, Book III lightly, and Book IV scarcely at all. It is interesting that the manuscript contains both the *Disticha Catonis* and Prosper's *Epigrammata* (see n. 44), the two most elementary texts of the schoolbooks I discuss.
32. See Ker, *Catalogue*, 427–8 (=no. 350). The *Disticha Catonis* are found on fos. 1r–5v; they begin acephalously with I.35; the first 34 distichs were presumably contained on the folio which has been torn out before the present f.1 and whose stub remains. The work is glossed in Latin and Old English; on the Latin glosses, see n.34 below, and on the Old English, see the remarks of R. I. Page, below pp. 146–7. The Old English glosses prove that the manuscript was in England before the Conquest, but it is difficult to affirm that the manuscript was written in England (there is need for caution on this point). Note that Rawlinson G.57 was formerly part of the manuscript which is now Rawlinson G.111 (SC 14836).

33. Only a full collation of the texts of the *Disticha Catonis* in all these Anglo-Saxon manuscripts could determine whether they derive from one or several exemplars. Such collation is fundamental if – as I shall argue – the glosses frequently travelled with the texts they were designed to explicate. In the case of the *Disticha Catonis* it is nearly impossible to determine exact manuscript affiliations because there are so many surviving manuscripts and Boas's apparatus is necessarily restricted to readings deemed to be significant.
34. This commentary has never been printed in its entirety, although excerpts have been printed in various places: see A. Mancini, 'Un commento ignoto di Remy d'Auxerre ai *Disticha Catonis*', *Rendiconti della reale Accademia dei Lincei*, 5th ser., XI (1902), 175–198 and 369–82 (from Lucca, Biblioteca Governativa, MS 1433) and M. Manitius, 'Remigiusscholien', *Münchener Museum*, II (1913–14), 79–113, at 109–13 (from Rouen, Bibl. munic. MS 1470). Both Mancini and Manitius were solely interested in Remigius's classical learning, and accordingly only printed those glosses which contained some classical reference. In his edition of the *Disticha Catonis* Boas (as cited in n. 22) printed various excerpts from the same commentary (from Paris, BN lat. 2773 and Rome, Bibl.Apost.Vaticana, Reginensis lat. 1560) following individual distichs; but he only printed an excerpt from Remigius when it cast light on a textual problem. Remigius's commentary on the *Disticha Catonis* deserves to be printed entire from all surviving manuscripts (including Gonville and Caius 144/194) for what it would tell us of the way an elementary text was handled in a Carolingian school, and also of the way Remigius's commentaries were disseminated throughout Europe, both in the form of a long-hand commentary (see, for example, M. de Marco, 'Una nuova redazione del commento di Remigio d'Auxerre ai *Disticha Catonis*', *Aevum*, XXVI (1952), 466–7) and in the form of interlinear glosses. It is interesting to note that, of the several Anglo-Saxon manuscripts of the *Disticha Catonis*, only one appears to contain interlinear glosses derived directly from Remigius's commentary: Rawlinson G.57.
35. London, British Library, MS Cotton Domitian i, f.55v: *glossam super Catonem*. See Ker, *Catalogue*, 185–6 (=no. 146), and T. A. M. Bishop, 'Notes on Cambridge Manuscripts, Part IV: manuscripts connected with St Augustine's, Canterbury', *TCBS*, II. 4 (1957), 334–6; a facsimile of the book-list is found in Plate XIV (b). The book-list has been printed by A. J. Robertson, *Anglo-Saxon Charters* (1939), 251.
36. Excerpts from Remigius's commentary are found on fos. 74v–75r. At least one bifolium has fallen out between fos. 74 and 75, since 74v ends with glosses to the prefatory apophthegms ('*parrentes ama*: parentibus amor debetur (est antiquum prouerbium maioribus . . .)' = Boas, *Disticha Catonis*, 11) and 75r recommences with glosses to IV.32. The date and origin of this manuscript has been much debated. N. R. Ker suggested a date of s.ix^{ex} (*Medieval Libraries of Great Britain* (2nd edn, 1964), 41), and Bishop argued that it was written in a continental scriptorium, in spite of its many Insular features ('Notes on Cambridge Manuscripts, Part II', *TCBS*, II. 2 (1955), 187–9). More recently, he suggested that it was written at Auxerre but was at St Augustine's by s.x/xi (*English Caroline Minuscule*, 19). As far as I am aware, there is no evidence to connect the manuscript with Auxerre except that it contains two commentaries by Remigius of Auxerre. Bernhard Bischoff has suggested to me (pers.comm.) that it may be of tenth-century *English* origin – a theory which would account for

the many Insular features in its preparation and abbreviations, even though one does not usually associate such slovenly examples of book production as is Gonville and Caius 144/194 with tenth-century English scriptoria. The manuscript merits further study.

37. The *Epigrammata* are printed in Migne, *Patrologia Latina* 51, cols. 497–531, from an early eighteenth-century edition of LeBrun and Mangeaut. This edition is simply inadequate for scholarly purposes, and it is welcome news that a new edition is being prepared by M. Gastoldo for *CCSL*.
38. See *Aldhelmi Opera*, ed. R. Ehwald [MGH *Auctores Antiquissimi*, 15], (Berlin, 1919), 318–19; Prosper is also quoted frequently by Aldhelm in the *Epistola ad Acircium*, ed. Ehwald, 79, 93, 95, etc.
39. Ed. C. B. Kendall in *Bedae Opera Pars I: Opera Didascalica*, ed. C. W. Jones [*CCSL* 123A], (Turnhout, 1975), 91, 92, 94, 111, 115, etc.
40. *Versus de Sanctis Euboricensis Ecclesiae*, 1551, ed. E. Dümmler [MGH, *Poetae Aevi Carolini Latini*, I], (Berlin, 1881), 204.
41. Byrhtferth quotes Prosper in his historical miscellany which is embedded in the *Historia Regum* attributed to Symeon of Durham (ed. T. Arnold, *Symeonis Monachi Opera Omnia*, II (RS, 1885), 61); the epigram in question is no. CIV, ed. *Patrologia Latina* 51, col. 531 (not identified by Arnold). On Byrhtferth's authorship of this work, see my article, 'Byrhtferth of Ramsey and the early sections of the *Historia Regum* attributed to Symeon of Durham', *ASE*, X (1981), 97–122.
42. See n.37 above.
43. There are other manuscripts of Prosper's *Epigrammata* now in British libraries (e.g. London, British Library, MS Harley 3093, fos. 26r–34r), but since these show no signs of having been in England before 1066, I do not consider them here.
44. On this manuscript, see above p. 103 and n.31; the text of Prosper is found on fos. 1r–33v.
45. See Ker, *Catalogue*, 304 (=no. 228) and Bishop, 'Notes on Cambridge Manuscripts, Part VII: the early minuscule of Christ Church, Canterbury', *TCBS*, III. 5 (1963), 421–2, and *English Caroline Minuscule*, xxvi; according to Bishop the scribe who wrote Harley 110 was also responsible for a manuscript of Sedulius's *Carmen Paschale* (BL Royal 15.B.XIX, pt I) discussed below, p. 113. The text of Prosper is found on fos. 3r–24v; it is lightly glossed by the main hand throughout, except for an inexplicable burst of intensive interlinear glossing on fos. 4v–5r (to *Epigr.* VI–IX). It is also interesting that the Prosper text in Harley 110 is followed immediately by Isidore's *Synonyma* (fos. 25r–53r), an identical collocation of texts to that found in Cambridge, Corpus Christi College, MS 448 (discussed below, n. 47); but until a critical edition of the *Epigrammata* is available, it is impossible to speculate on the relationship of these two manuscripts.
46. See Rigg and Wieland, *op. cit.* in n. 2, 121. Prosper is found on fos. 126v–146r, and is very lightly glossed by the main scribe (Rigg's Scribe B).
47. The text of Prosper is found on fos. 1r–36r and is lightly glossed in a (?later) Anglo-Caroline hand. The Winchester provenance is known from a note on f.103v concerning one 'Henricus Dei gratia Wintoniensis ecclesie minister . . .' The text of Prosper is followed immediately by Isidore's *Synonyma*, as in Harley 110.

48. See Ker, *Catalogue*, 250 (=no. 189); the text of Prosper's *Epigrammata* XC–XCIV is found on fos. 165–6, which have been mounted (in reverse order). There are a very few Latin glosses, which appear to have been added before the numerous glosses in Old English (which have been printed, somewhat inaccurately, by T. Wright and R. P. Wülcker, *Anglo-Saxon and Old English Vocabularies* (2nd edn, 1884), I, cols. 248–57). Ker rightly expresses doubt about the English origin of the manuscript. It is perhaps worth noting that, like Harley 110, Tiberius A.vii omits the prose preface to *Epigr.* XCI, and that the titles given to the various epigrams correspond exactly to those in Harley 110; but again, without a full collation, it is impossible to say what relationship if any exists between the two manuscripts.
49. Printed by A. Riese, *Anthologia Latina I: Carmina in codicibus scripta*, II (Leipzig, 1894), 50–51 (=no. 493a). Although this prefatory poem occurs in most manuscripts of Prosper's *Epigrammata*, it is not printed with them in Migne, *Patrologia Latina*, LI.
50. I omit Tiberius A.vii from consideration since it does not preserve the text of *Epigr.* II.
51. Such speculation must properly wait until all manuscripts of Prosper's *Epigrammata* have been collated with respect to both text and glosses. My statement implies – perhaps misleadingly – that the common source of Prosper glosses was English, which in turn might imply a centre of diffusion in Anglo-Saxon England and hence a programmatic approach to the renewal of Latin learning. I am inclined to suspect, on the contrary, that the Prosper glosses originated on the continent in a ninth-century Carolingian school (as I believe to be the case with glosses to Sedulius and Arator: see below), but this suspicion needs very careful examination in the light of fuller manuscript evidence.
52. The exception is Cambridge, Corpus Christi College 448, where the glosses were added by a (?later) Anglo-Caroline hand.
53. There are two usable editions of Juvencus: by C. Marold (Leipzig, 1886), and by J. Huemer [*CSEL*, 24], (Vienna, 1891).
54. Aldhelm quotes Juvencus at several places in his *Epistola ad Acircium* (ed. Ehwald, 85, 154, 156, 186, etc.), and Bede in his *De Arte Metrica* (ed. Kendall, 92, 93, 116, 117, 120, etc.).
55. *Versus de Sanctis Euboricensis Ecclesiae*, 1550 (ed. Dümmler, 204).
56. In his edition of Frithegod and Wulfstan of Winchester, Alistair Campbell adduced a number of parallels to Juvencus (*Frithegodi Monachi Breuiloquium Vitae Beati Wilfredi et Wulfstani Cantoris Narratio Metrica de Sancto Swithuno* [*Thesaurus Mundi*, 1] (Zürich, 1950)); e.g. Frithegod, *Breuiloquium*, 304, 900, 1006; Wulfstan, *Narratio*, Praef. 495; I.521 and II.655. These parallels merit re-examination, since Campbell was extremely uncritical in his citation of such parallels.
57. See Lowe, *CLA*, VII, no. 1172.
58. *Ibid.*, II, no. 127. The manuscript contains only Juvencus. A number of glosses to the first part of Book I are added by a small Anglo-Caroline glossing hand (fos. 5r–6v), but thereafter they cease abruptly, and make only one further fleeting appearance on f.18v. Another scribe writing a very crude Insular minuscule makes several marginal annotations at various points in the manuscript, usually for the purpose of copying out passages from the Vulgate to correspond with certain biblical episodes in Juvencus (e.g. on fos. 29v–30r).

59. See M. R. James, *The Ancient Libraries of Canterbury and Dover* (1903), xxviii and 11.
60. See H. Bradshaw, *Collected Papers* (1889), 455 and 484; W. M. Lindsay, *Early Welsh Script* (1912), 16–18 and plates VI–VII; and T. A. M. Bishop, 'The Corpus Martianus Capella', *TCBS*, IV. 4 (1967), 257–75, esp. 258–9, and plate XX.
61. See Bishop, *ibid.*, 258, who identifies the scribe of the Anglo-Caroline glosses (s.x/xi) on fos. 2r–5v of CUL Ff.4.42 as the scribe who wrote London, British Library, MSS Cotton Vespasian D.xv, fos. 102–21 (Amalarius) and Harley 3376 (glossary). It is not known where in England the manuscript was in the eleventh century; Bishop draws attention to some Middle English marginalia of the thirteenth century in Harley 3376 whose dialect suggests that its provenance is western; see also Ker, *Catalogue*, 312–3 (=no. 240).
62. Juvencus is found on fos. 2r–59r; there are some accompanying Latin glosses, mostly on the first few folios. On the manuscript see E. M. Thompson, *Catalogue of Ancient Manuscripts of the British Museum, Part II: Latin* (1884), 74 and plate 50 (which is a facsimile of f.2r containing the opening of Juvencus's poem and shows some of the glosses I discuss); Ker, *Catalogue*, 334 (=no. 267); Bishop, 'Notes on Cambridge Manuscripts, Part IV', *TCBS*, ii. 4 (1957), 329; E. Temple, *Anglo-Saxon Manuscripts 900–1066* (1976), 102; and L. L. Brownrigg, 'Manuscripts containing English Decoration 871–1066, catalogued and illustrated: a review', *ASE*, VII (1978), 239–66, at 256 (Brownrigg observes that the manuscript contains 'an excellent text of the Latin poem' by Juvencus – on what grounds I do not know, for my trial collations suggest otherwise). The St Augustine's provenance of the manuscript is certain (Bishop identified several English scribes in the manuscript who are known from other St Augustine's manuscripts), but its date and origin are unknown. Professor Bischoff suggests to me (pers. comm.) that it is s.ix$^{4/4}$ or ix/x and that it is from the 'Kanalküste – oder sogar schon auf englischen Boden entstanden', a fascinating suggestion which deserves careful consideration.
63. Juvencus is found on fos. 1r–53r; see Rigg and Wieland, *op. cit* in n. 2, 120. The text is fairly consistently glossed in Latin and Old English (see Ker, *Catalogue*, 21) by the main text hand (Rigg's Scribe A).
64. The manuscript contains only Juvencus (fos. 2r–61v) and is not glossed. It bears no indication of provenance. It is written in Caroline minuscule by a careful but inexpert scribe whose writing has a deliberate, angular aspect. The minims are finished with clean serifs and the ink is very dark, features which may be suggestive of an English origin. Quires are regular eights, usually arranged HFHF. Professor Bischoff concurs in my suspicion that the manuscript might be of English origin (pers. comm.), but the matter requires further investigation.
65. Juvencus is found on fos. 1r–70v; it contains no glosses except for a few jottings on fos. 1r and 2r. This important manuscript has hitherto been neglected by students of Anglo-Saxon culture. Since the description of it given by C. Kohler (*Catalogue des manuscrits de la Bibliothèque Sainte-Geneviève*, II (Paris, 1896), 340–3) is unfortunately inadequate for modern scholarly purposes, a few remarks may be useful. As it was donated to the Bibliothèque Sainte-Geneviève in the eighteenth century, the manuscript consisted in two volumes, now bearing the shelfmarks 2409 and 2410. However, the manuscript is composite and is made up of at least five originally separate parts; each of these five parts appears

(from palaeographical considerations) to have been written in England at various times in the late tenth and early eleventh centuries. Part I is the manuscript now numbered 2409, consisting in 245 folios and containing Flodoard's *De Triumphis Christi* (see P. C. Jacobsen, *Flodoard von Reims: Sein Leben und seine Dichtung De Triumphis Christi* [Mittellateinische Studien und Texte, 10], (Leyden, 1978)). Part II is represented by MS 2410, fos. 1–117, containing Juvencus and a commentary on the gospel of St Matthew. Part III (MS 2410, fos. 118–21) consists in two bifolia which appear to have been written later (s.xi[1]) than the other parts; it contains a number of prayers in Greek and the Hisperic poem *Rubisca*. Part IV (MS 2410, fos. 122–173) contains Sedulius's *Carmen Paschale* (see below, p. 114) and an excerpt from Aldhelm's *Epistola ad Acircium*; this part of the manuscript is an excellent example of Anglo-Caroline calligraphy (s.x[2]), and the splendid initial on f.126r deserves attention by art historians. Part V (MS 2410, fos. 174–229) contains an incomplete text of Odo of Cluny's *Occupatio*, and is to be completed by Paris, Bibliothèque de l'Arsénal, MS 903.

66. Ogilvy, *op. cit.* in n. 20, 190, claims to know of 'at least ten MSS of Juvencus with English associations', but I have been unable to discover what these are.
67. Juvencus is found on fos. 1r–19v. There is a large amount of Latin glossing on fos. 1v and 2r, but thereafter it ceases entirely. The manuscript also contains Prosper's *Epigrammata* (see above, n. 43), as well as Sedulius's *Carmen Paschale*, Arator's *De Actibus Apostolorum*, Prudentius's *Psychomachia* and the *Ecloga* of Theodulus, and hence might be thought *a priori* a classbook; but none of the texts are glossed and it shows little sign of extended use.
68. Juvencus is found on fos. 2r–54v; it contains no interlinear glossing, though there are occasional marginal glosses in Old High German (see H. Thoma, 'Altdeutsches aus Londoner Handschriften', *Beiträge zur Geschichte der deutschen Sprache und Literatur*, LXXIII (1951), 197–271, at 228–30. The tenth-century dating was suggested to me by Professor Bischoff (pers.comm.).
69. The glosses in CCCC 304 were evidently copied from a manuscript which read *uisus* not *uidit* in line 11 (note the gloss *scilicet -sus* above *uidit* in that line).
70. A photograph of f. 2v is found as Plate I below. It will be seen that I have simplified somewhat the scheme of glosses.
71. Bradshaw, *op. cit.* in n. 60, 484, followed by Lindsay, *op. cit.* in n. 60, 16, identified some seven scribes in this manuscript, but there are certainly more. Bradshaw's Scribe E is probably the same as my first scribe (the vagueness of his descriptions leaves room for doubt); my second and third scribes are not accounted for by Bradshaw.
72. The source of the Hebrew meanings was probably Isidore, *Etymologiae*. Thus Isidore glosses *Herodes* as *pellicius* (*Etym.* VII.x.6), and *Zacharias* as *memoria Domini* (*Etym.* VII.viii.30). The source of the first scribe's gloss *Zacharias. benedictus* probably derives through error from Isidore's explanation a line or so earlier of *Barachia. benedictus* (*Etym.* VII. viii. 29). When the third (Anglo-Caroline) glossator added the further explanation *uel memor domini*, he appears to be deriving his information not from Isidore but from Jerome's *Liber Interpretationis Hebraicorum Nominum*, ed. P. de Lagarde, *CCSL* 72 (Turnhout, 1959), 122 and 138). It may be that the first scribe, working while the manuscript was still in Wales, had access only to Isidore's *Etymologiae* (it was probably the same scribe who copied part of *Etym.* I. xxxv. 2–3 on to f. 1r), whereas the later scribe, working in England, had access to Jerome's treatise. In any case, the

glosses in this manuscript are a rich source of information about Welsh and Anglo-Saxon scholarly method, and are deserving of detailed study.

73. Ed. J. Huemer, *CSEL*, x (Vienna, 1885).
74. Aldhelm quotes Sedulius both in the prose *De Virginitate* (ed. Ehwald, 232, 249, 250 etc.) and in the *Epistola ad Acircium* (ed. Ehwald, 85, 89, 153, 154, 156, 157, etc.).
75. E.g. in the *De Arte Metrica*, ed. Kendall, 105, 110, 112–14, 117, etc.
76. *Versus de Sanctis Euboricensis Ecclesiae*, 1550 (ed. Dümmler), 204.
77. E.g. *Narratio Metrica de S. Swithuno* (ed. Campbell), II. 411–12 are from the *Carmen Paschale*, I. 85–6.
78. See *CLA*, II, no. 123. The *Carmen Paschale* is found on fos. 57–83 of this composite manuscript; on the origin and composition of the manuscript see M. B. Parkes, 'The palaeography of the Parker Manuscript of the *Chronicle*, Laws and Sedulius, and historiography at Winchester in the late ninth and tenth centuries', *ASE*, v (1976), 149–71.
79. The glossing in CCCC 173 is discussed in detail by R. I. Page, below, pp. 154–9, and will not be discussed further here, save to mention that its Latin glosses do not appear to derive from the same continental sources as those which I discuss below.
80. Part I of the manuscript (fos. 1–36: quires I^8–IV^8, V^4) contains only Sedulius, *Carmen Paschale*, which ends on f.35r; 35v is blank, 36r contains various jottings, and 36v is badly worn, suggesting that the present Part I once circulated as a book on its own. The text is glossed sporadically on the first few folios, and not thereafter. On the scribe of Royal 15.B.XIX, part I (who was also the scribe of the aforementioned Harley 110), see Bishop, 'Notes on Cambridge Manuscripts, Part VII', *TCBS*, iii. 5 (1963), 421–3.
81. Sedulius's *Carmen Paschale* is found on fos. 53r–81v; see Rigg and Wieland, *op. cit.* in n.2, 120. The text is consistently glossed by the two main scribes who cooperated in copying this section of the manuscript (Rigg's Scribes A and B). On the source of the glosses, see below, p. 115.
82. See Bishop, *English Caroline Minuscule*, 19 and plate XIX, and Ker, *Catalogue*, 418 (=no. 340). The manuscript is a fragment consisting in four leaves only. Note that, in Bishop's opinion, the hand of one of the glossators in this manuscript (of possible Worcester origin) resembles that of a glossator in the above-mentioned manuscript of Juvencus, CUL Ff.4. 42.
83. Sedulius is found on fos. 1r–40v. The provenance of the manuscript is Thorney, but its origin is unknown. It is glossed intensively in both Latin and Old English. The Latin glosses for the most part are in a minute glossing hand, though occasional glosses have been added by various larger, cruder hands. On the manuscript, see I. Cunningham in *Scriptorium*, XXVII (1973), 87–8.
84. Sedulius is found on fos. 1r–36v; the manuscript also contains a text of Arator, on which see below p. 117 and n. 104. The prose preface to the *Carmen Paschale* contains a number of glosses in Old English (fos. 1r–4r), which have not been printed hitherto (see now my 'Some OE Sedulius glosses from BN lat. 8092' *Anglia*, C (1982)), and indeed Ker's *Catalogue of Manuscripts Containing Anglo-Saxon* has no notice of BN lat. 8092. With the beginning of the poem itself, however, the interlinear glossing ceases. The margins have been ruled wide to take a commentary, but except for a few brief marginal annotations (e.g. on fos. 5r, 8v, 23v, 24v, 27v, etc.) none has been added. On the manuscript in general

and the characteristics of its Anglo-Caroline script, see J. Vezin, 'Manuscrits des dixième et onzième siècles copiés en Angleterre en minuscule caroline et conservés à la Bibliothèque nationale de Paris', in *Humanisme Actif: Mélanges d'art et de littérature offerts à Julien Cain*, II (Paris, 1968), 294–5.

85. On this manuscript, see above, n. 65; Sedulius is found on fos. 122r–70r. Unlike the text of Juvencus in this manuscript, the text of Sedulius is provided with abundant interlinear Latin glosses.
86. Remigius's commentary on the *Carmen Paschale* has never been printed in its entirety, though it is a cardinal text for the study both of Remigius and of the reception of Sedulius in the early middle ages. It was partially printed by Huemer in his edition of Sedulius (as cited in n. 73 above), 316–59. Huemer was particularly interested in the transmission of classical (especially Greek) learning, and accordingly he prints only those glosses which contain some vestige of that learning. See also his discussion 'Über ein Glossenwerk zum Dichter Sedulius', *Sitzungsberichte der kaiserlichen Akademie der Wissenschaften zu Wien*, phil.-hist. Kl., XCVI (Vienna, 1880), 505–51.
87. See above, n. 36, and Bishop, *English Caroline Minuscule*, 19.
88. See N. R. Ker, 'Salisbury Cathedral manuscripts and Patrick Young's Catalogue', *Wilts. Arch. and Nat. Hist. Mag.*, LIII (1949–50) 167, n. 1.
89. H. M. Bannister, 'Bishop Roger of Worcester and the church of Keynsham, with a list of vestments and books possibly belonging to Worcester', *EHR*, XXXII (1917), 387–83, at 389.
90. See above, n. 81.
91. Even in the brief passage I have quoted, one may note the erroneous gloss *uigili* (to *tragicoque* in line 2) for *uili*, and *ridiculo uegete* for *ridiculoue Gete* in line 3.
92. *English Caroline Minuscule*, 19.
93. Nevertheless, in most of the manuscripts of Sedulius which I have examined, there are so many cases where glosses agree exactly with those in Remigius's commentary that one must suppose some sort of indirect influence, perhaps *via* other glossed manuscripts of Sedulius. For example, in Harley 3072, a tenth-century continental manuscript of unknown origin, one notes the glosses *pompare .i. dealbare uel ornare* in line 2 and *monimenta .i. recordationes* in line 5, where the coincidence with Remigius is striking, even though other glosses in this passage do not appear to derive from him. Similarly, in Paris, Bibliothèque Sainte-Geneviève 2410, a heavily glossed manuscript of Sedulius, there are several glosses to the passage in question (on f.126v) which apparently derive from Remigius: *figmenta .i. mendacia* in line 1, *pompare .i. exaltare uel ornare* in line 2, *tragicoque boatu .i. hircyno sono* also in line 2, and so on. In Edinburgh, UL Adv. 18.7.7, we likewise find the gloss *hircino sono* to *tragicoque boatu*, which implies some sort of connection with Sainte-Geneviève 2410 and some indirect debt to Remigius; the crude Anglo-Saxon minuscule hand which has written *ornare* over *pompare* (f.4r) in this manuscript also appears to have been working from Remigius. But without a full collation, it is impossible to state what exactly the relationship between these various manuscripts and Remigius's commentary may have been.
94. Ed. A. P. McKinlay, *CSEL*, LXXII (Vienna, 1951).
95. Arator is frequently quoted by Aldhelm in the *Epistola ad Acircium*, e.g. Ehwald, 80, 92–93, 153, etc.
96. See *De Arte Metrica*, ed. Kendall, pp. 86, 92, 112, and 140–1. For Bede's debt to

Arator in the *Expositio Actuum Apostolorum*, see his remarks in the preface to that work: 'in quo me opusculo, cum alii plurimi fidei catholicae scriptores, tum maxime iuuauit Arator, sanctae romanae ecclesiae subdiaconus, qui ipsum ex ordine librum heroico carmine percurrens nonnullos in eodem metro allegoriae flores admiscuit, occasionem mihi tribuens uel alia ex his colligendi uel eadem planius exponendi' [ed. M. L. W. Laistner, *Expositio Actuum Apostolorum et Retractatio* (Cambridge, Mass., 1939), 3].

97. *Versus de Sanctis Euboricensis Ecclesiae*, 1551 (ed. Dümmler), 204.
98. *Byrhtferth's Manual*, ed. Crawford, 150, where Byrhtferth quotes Arator I. 226–7 ('Spiritus alme ueni, sine te non diceris umquam/Munera da lingue qui das in munere linguas') and describes it as *oratio patris Byrhtferði*; he thereupon translates it into Old English hexameters.
99. The surviving manuscripts of Arator are surveyed by A. P. McKinlay, *Arator: The Codices* (Cambridge, Mass., 1942).
100. E.g. Eton, College Library, MS 150 (Monte Cassino, s.x/xi); London, British Library, MSS Harley 3072 (continental, s.x), Harley 3093 (France (?), s.xi), Harley 3121 (Germany, s.xi/xii), Add. 11034 (see below, p. 121), and Add. 18363 (which is completed by the now destroyed Dresden, kgl. Bibl. A.199: Germany, s.x); and Oxford, Bodleian Library, MS e Mus. 66 (SC 3655) (N. Italy, s.vi/vii). On the latter, see *CLA*, *Supp.*, no. 1740.
101. Arator is found on fos. 5r–65r. The text is very heavily glossed. The manuscript was ruled with wide margins to take a continuous gloss; glosses are written in both margins as well as between lines (see plate II). On the manuscript, see F. Wormald, 'Decorated initials in English manuscripts from A.D. 900 to 1100', *Archaeologia*, XCI (1945), 135; Ker, *Catalogue*, 129–30 (=no. 85); Bishop, 'Notes on Cambridge Manuscripts, Part VII', *TCBS*, III. 5 (1963), 414–5, 418, and 421–2, and *English Caroline Minuscule*, 7.
102. The manuscript contains only Arator (fos. 1v–45r). The text is incomplete (it breaks off at I.650 and recommences at I.1022), and it appears that a single quire of eight has been lost between fos. 16 and 17 (note that McKinlay's statement on p. xvi of his edition, to the effect that all of Book II is missing, is false). The manuscript contains virtually no glosses. The text was collated by McKinlay; on the manuscript affiliations of Rawlinson C.570, see A. P. McKinlay, 'Studies in Arator II: the classification of the manuscripts of Arator', *Harvard Studies in Classical Philology*, LIV (1943) 105. The manuscript is an excellent example of Anglo-Caroline calligraphy, and contains one fine decorated initial; see F. Wormald, *English Drawings of the Tenth and Eleventh Centuries* (1952), 135, and Bishop, 'Notes on Cambridge Manuscripts, Part IV', *TCBS*, II.4 (1957), 329.
103. Arator is found on fos. 84v–126r; see Rigg and Wieland, *op. cit.* in n. 2, 121. The text and multifarious glosses were copied by the two main scribes (Rigg's Scribes A and B). Although there were at least two other manuscripts of Arator in Canterbury at the time Gg.5.35 was copied, its text of Arator does not appear to derive from either: it does not have the reading *conueniant* peculiar to TCC B.14.3 in line 12 of the *Epistola ad Florianum* (Gg.5.35 reads *concordent*) nor the reading *inmundo* peculiar to Rawlinson C.570 (Gg.5.35 has the usual *ieiuno*).
104. Arator is found on fos. 45v–84v; the text is lightly glossed throughout. On the manuscript, see above, n.84.
105. Professor Bischoff has suggested to me that the manuscript is of English origin, 'wohl saec. x' (pers. comm.). It does not exhibit many of the characteristics

usually associated with Anglo-Saxon manuscripts of the period, nor does its script have any of the features of Anglo-Caroline minuscule which would decisively suggest an English origin. But our knowledge of Anglo-Saxon manuscripts of this period is far from complete, and Add. 11034 requires further attention.

106. Royal 15.A.V is a miscellaneous codex consisting in three parts which were apparently combined during the early twelfth century. The parts are as follows: Part I (fos. 1–29), the Vulgate Acts of the Apostles (Norman or International script, s.xii^{1}); Part II (fos. 30–85), Arator (late Anglo-Caroline script, s.xi^{ex}); Part III (fos. 86–147), a commentary on Arator (Norman or International script, s.xii^{1}). It is difficult to say whether Parts I and III were written by the same scribe; they were quite possibly written in England. Part II (Arator) consists in seven regular quires of eight; it was apparently in origin a separate book which was subsequently bound up with the other two parts by a librarian who was attempting to assemble in one codex all the material necessary for serious study of Arator. Part II (Arator) contains very few glosses, which is possibly one reason why it was necessary to add the commentary (on which see M. Esposito, 'A Commentary on Arator', *JTS*, XXX (1928–9), 288–9, and discussion below).

107. Several independent sets of glosses are identified and discussed by A. P. McKinlay, 'Latin Commentaries on Arator', *Scriptorium*, VI (1952), 151–6, repr. in *Catalogus Translationum et Commentariorum I*, ed. P. O. Kristeller (Washington, 1960), 241–7. The set of glosses which I discuss here is that described by McKinlay as 'Anonymous X', and is preserved variously in some 23 manuscripts.

108. From McKinlay's collation of Arator manuscripts, it appears that the text of Harley 3072 is closely related to a small subgroup of manuscripts of French origin, including Paris, BN lat. 17905 (s.ix/x) and the aforementioned BL Harley 3093 (s.xi); see McKinlay, *op. cit.* in n. 102, 108–9, and his edition of Arator, xii–xiii. The script of the Arator section of Harley 3072 is difficult to localize (there is a facsimile in McKinlay's *Arator: The Codices*, plate XXVII).

109. Paris, Bibliothèque Nationale, MSS lat. 17905 (s.ix/x) and 18555 (s.ix^{ex}); see McKinlay, apparatus *ad loc.*

110. Of the 23 manuscripts listed by McKinlay (*op. cit.* in n. 107) as containing all or part of this set of glosses ('Anonymous X'), the earliest dates from the first quarter of the ninth century (now Paris, BN lat. 12284), and at least ten others are of ninth-century date. Most of these manuscripts have their origins in Francia.

111. *English Caroline Minuscule*, XXV and 18.

112. The manuscript of Tours provenance, Paris, BN nouv.acq.lat. 1627 (s.x) was copied from the same exemplar as an Anglo-Caroline manuscript of Statius, London, BL, Royal 15.C.X; the second Anglo-Caroline manuscript, Worcester, Cathedral Library, Q.8, part II, was copied directly from the Tours manuscript. Bishop observes: 'A comparison of the three MSS shows the interlined and marginal gloss of the common ancestor disposed and rendered with a fidelity extending to the forms of the syntax marks and *signes de renvoi*' (*English Caroline Minuscule*, 18). The common ancestor in question must be somewhat earlier than the three surviving tenth-century manuscripts.

113. That is why, among other things, I have been obliged to take my trial collations from the first few lines of each poem in question. There are of course exceptions:

notably CUL Ff.4.42 (Juvencus), where layer upon layer of glosses was added at various times and places.

114. The calculations have been done by P. Riché, *Education et culture*, 159.
115. Ed. R. Hanslik, *CSEL*, LXXV (Vienna, 1960), 117.
116. '"Bibliotheca": Bible et lecture du Carême d'après Saint Benoît', *Revue Bénédictine*, LX (1950), 65–92.
117. *Ibid.*, 66–7. Mundó attributes the Carolingian interpretation to the circles of Paulus Diaconus and Benedict of Aniane.
118. Ed. B. Albers, *Consuetudines Monasticae*, V (Monte Cassino, 1912), 137–51.
119. The text was first printed in the seventeenth century from an unspecified manuscript by Jean Dubois (Ioannes de Bosco), whence it was reprinted by Albers in 1912. The manuscript in question has recently been identified as Orléans, Bibliothèque munic. 129 (107), of Fleury origin and datable to the first third of the thirteenth century. It is now clear that Dubois printed only short excerpts from the customary. A new edition is in preparation by A. Davril for the series *Corpus Consuetudinum Monasticarum*, edited by K. Hallinger.
120. Translated from Albers, *Consuetudines Monasticae*, V, 139–40.
121. Ed. T. Symons (1953), 3.
122. See T. Symons, '*Regularis Concordia*: history and derivation', in *Tenth-Century Studies*, ed. D. Parsons (1975), 37–59, and the important article by L. Donnat, 'Recherches sur l'influence de Fleury au Xe siècle', in *Etudes Ligériennes d'histoire et d'archéologie médiévales*, ed. R. Louis (Auxerre, 1975), 165–74, who demonstrates that a previously unknown account of monastic customs at Fleury by the monk Thierry (Theodoricus), who was at Fleury until 1002, which is preserved in a manuscript from Wolfenbüttel, has some extremely striking parallels with the slightly earlier English *Regularis Concordia*.
123. Cf., however, the stipulations concerning reading in the *Regularis Concordia*, ed. Symons, 54.

Postscript: Since this article was written (May 1979), the study of texts and glosses in manuscripts of the Anglo-Saxon period has been greatly advanced by the publication of H. Gneuss, 'A preliminary list of manuscripts written or owned in England up to 1100', *ASE*, IX (1980), 1–60.

The Study of Latin Texts in late Anglo-Saxon England [2] *The Evidence of English Glosses*

R. I. PAGE

In this paper I shall concentrate on a single type of glossing. I am not here concerned with Old English (and Latin) glossaries though they can have important links with glossed texts. Nor shall I discuss the (more or less) continuous glosses like those of the Lindisfarne Gospels and the Vespasian Psalter. Both these are proper fields of study, and neither can be divorced completely from the present subject. Here, however, I am concerned more with establishing some principles for the study of the casual interlinear glosses in the vernacular that Angus Cameron lists under the general heading 'Occasional glosses'.[1]

Two scholars in this century have been particularly industrious in publishing this type of material. The first is A. S. Napier, whose splendid *Old English Glosses chiefly Unpublished* (1900) made much of the evidence available for the first time. Anyone who has worked in detail through any of the sections of this volume will have marvelled at the high standard of accuracy and knowledge it shows. It stands as a monument of exact scholarship. The second worker in the field is H. D. Meritt, whose life has been devoted to probing the detail of the Old English vocabulary. Over the decades he has published freely on it (as well as supervising research dissertations on related topics). His work is scattered generously through the learned journals and recorded in his books. It is appropriate here to point to a few of the more important publications: his edition of *Old English Glosses (a Collection)* (New York, 1945) supplemented Napier with 73 glossed texts, many of them printed for the first time; a later article, 'Old English glosses, mostly dry point', *J. English and Germanic Philology*, LX (1961), 441–50, added 18 more; and in *The Old English Prudentius Glosses at Boulogne-sur-Mer* (Stanford, 1959), Meritt re-edited the material of a single manuscript, experimenting with a new type of layout. Meritt's work is, perhaps, somewhat less accurate than Napier's; but then Napier had the first choice of texts, and his great edition often used easily readable glosses. In the main he avoided such troublesome subjects as scratched or dry-point glosses which Meritt valiantly attempted, and which are hard to see, difficult to interpret, and very wearing on the eyes.

Fundamentally both Napier and Meritt were interested in publishing the material of the Old English vocabulary. Napier (1900) came in very useful for the Supplement to Bosworth-Toller, and his own *Contributions to Old English Lexicography* (1906) shows him using gloss evidence for dictionary purposes. Meritt, of course, used much gloss material in his supplement to the fourth edition of Clark Hall's dictionary, while many of his articles are demonstrations of how to tussle away at meanings of words recorded in glosses. In essence, then, neither of these scholars was concerned with glossing as such; both were interested in what glossing could tell us of the lexis and semantics of Old English. Of course, they did not stop there, and much of Meritt's work in particular depends on examining gloss contexts to see why a particular word appears, to find out if it could properly be emended, or assigned to a new lemma, or explained by some transference of meaning. In his fascinating book *Fact and Lore about Old English Words* (Stanford, 1954) he discusses some of the principles of gloss scholarship: the importance of context; the use of Old High German glosses for comparison; the ways a gloss may interpret a lemma; the possibilities of mistranslation; glosses that comment on rather than translate; and so on. However, I think that the primary interest of both scholars was in forms and meanings of Old English words, and this led them to present their data in the glossary form which is in any case the most convenient for reference: they give lemma + variants, Old English gloss, manuscript folio reference, and a cross-reference to a printed version of the base text so that the reader can find out the context for himself. There is nothing particularly wicked about this mode of presentation, and indeed it has been generally used in publishing the Old English gloss material. I have used it myself in younger and more carefree days, and Helmut Gneuss, in commenting on the principles of preparing this sort of text for edition, says, 'If a number of OE glosses are found scattered in a Latin text, it seems best to print them in the form of a glossary', but that again was with dictionary-making in mind.[2]

For other purposes this method is quite inadequate, as I have tried to show in a recent article.[3] Presumably Meritt found it so, since when he published the Boulogne-sur-Mer glosses he tried a new technique, giving not only the Latin-Old English equivalents, but also the full context together with a commentary on the relationship between lemma and gloss. Helpful though this is, it is only part of the answer, since a scholar who wants to know why a particular word is glossed in a particular way may want more than this. The Boulogne-sur-Mer manuscript also has Latin glosses. According to Ker they precede the vernacular ones.[4] Meritt gives no information on the relationship between the two languages of glossing, nor on whether the limited distribution of the Old English ones coincides with or differs from that of the Latin glosses. Sometimes too he gives us tantalisingly too little information about the manuscript forms. For instance, his gloss 263 reads *tumidis, horridis, ontoblawenum*. His note points out that *BTS* interprets this as a form of *toblawan* with the preposition *on*. Meritt argues that this is inappropriate to the context, and moreover in the manuscript the group is written as a single word; so he takes it as a compound *ontoblawenum*. This is fine as far as it goes, but we need more facts. Obviously we would want to know what this scribe's common practice is in writing the preposition *on* + following word. Does he keep the two separate, or does he, as some scribes do, append the preposition to the word that follows? A brief look at the select facsimiles that accompany Meritt's edition shows that the editor does not reproduce precisely the manuscript's word division throughout. The gloss he prints *sordibus ac luto. of fylþum 7 of fenne* (8, visible on the reproduction of f.4r) reads in fact *offylþum 7 offenne*, with the prepositions appended to their governed nouns. It seems then that the manuscript evidence for a single word *ontoblawenum* is inconclusive. Accepting Meritt's argument from sense, *on* seems unlikely to be a preposition, but there might be a case for regarding it as an adverb. The matter may seem trivial, but its implications are quite important since it raises one of the troubled points of Old English lexicography: how to treat what Campbell has called 'adverbs of full meaning plus verb'.[5]

The Boulogne-sur-Mer example is only one case of a general condition. When I compare other gloss editions with the glosses as they appear in their manuscripts, I am intensely aware of their inadequacies. A few examples follow:

1. MS CAMBRIDGE UNIVERSITY LIBRARY GG.5.35

A. G. Rigg and G. R. Wieland have made a detailed study of this manuscript.[6] They conclude that its major part consists of three classbooks that form a collection of educational texts. The first has straightforward material in increasing order of difficulty, Juvencus, Sedulius, Arator, Prosper, Prudentius, Lactantius, Boethius; the second in order of composition (part III as the manuscript stands) is a riddle collection with some difficult poems; the third (part II) is a less clearly organized group of difficult texts. Wieland promises a full study of the glosses, so my comments are only introductory. Napier published the Old English glosses of this manuscript: Juvencus (*Old English Glosses* no. 43), Sedulius (no. 51), Prudentius (no. 49) in part I; Aldhelm, *de laudibus virginum* (no. 16), Milo (no. 44) in part II; and Aldhelm, *Aenigmata* (no. 23) in part III. He used his customary glossary form, with footnotes giving additional details. His work shows its usual precision, but the form of presentation entails the omission of details that may be significant and are certainly suggestive. For instance:

A. *Juvencus glosses*

1. Napier 1 reads *statuit, firmauit ł prædestinauit, fore*, and he suggests that the latter represents the OE verb *foresette*. The arrangement is misleading; the text reads *statuit genitor* over which is written 'firmauit ł forepr*æ*destinauit'. I have suggested elsewhere that 'fore' is intended to gloss *genitor* (? =*foregenga*) and that *firmauit ł prædestinauit* glossing *statuit* was added round it.[7] The glosses seem to be all in the same hand, but there are some differences which may be important, though they are certainly not conclusive. The reasons for my interpretation are: 1. the curious word order (which Napier disguises); 2. 'fore' looks slightly different from other words in this group: its letter forms are slimmer and taller than those that surround it; 3. the words are not in line: *prædestinauit* is noticeably, and the other words slightly, out of line with 'fore'; 4. the initial letter of 'fore' is exactly above that of *genitor*, suggesting that the two words go together.

2. Napier 5 is *auricolor, gyldenhiwe*. Here the word division may be relevant, though it is hard to be sure since as yet there is inadequate study of manuscript word division, and I have not checked whether the various scribes of Gg.5.35 have a consistent policy about compound words. At any rate the manuscript here reads 'gylden hiwe', with a small but distinct gap between the two. The point is worth probing because this is the only

example of *gyldenhiwe* in *BT*, its Supplement and Addenda, nor do those works list any *-hiwe* compounds that have a colour word as first element, nor do Ball and Cameron in their specimen entry for *hiw* for the Toronto Old English Dictionary.[8] The manuscript's division may imply that the writer here is producing, not a genuine Old English equivalent of *auricolor*, but a loan-translation (*Lehnübersetzung*) translating each half in turn. There is the alternative possibility that here we have two words, *gylden hiwe*, 'golden as to hue'. Or the division may have no significance at all, but the editor ought to give us the information to judge by.

3. Napier 11 is *pupim, steorsetl*, followed closely by *proram, anker* which Napier expands by analogy to *ankersetl*. In fact *steorsetl* seems to have been written at two attempts: first *steor* and then (perhaps by a different writer since the form of *s* is somewhat different) *setl* with the *s* encroaching upon the serif of the preceding *r*. Perhaps the first writer meant to gloss *pupim* by the simplex *steor*, 'helm, rudder'; *anker* glossing *proram*, is then a parallel. On the other hand *steor* may have been a partial or abbreviated gloss, standing for *steorsetl* (as a later glossator assumed); but it might have been intended for *steorstefn* which glosses *puppis* elsewhere. In that case *anker* might also have to be expanded, but its second element must remain uncertain. Napier's conjecture is probably right, since *steorsetl, ancersetl* are a recorded pair glossing *puppis* and *prora*,[9] but there is residual doubt.

B. *Aldhelm's* Aenigmata *gloss*

Napier 55 reads *caumate, wallendre hæte ł swoloðan*, and the reading is accurate save that there is a stop after *hæte*. The full line glossed is *siccior estiuo torrentis caumate solis*, with 'wallendre' written above the second part of *torrentis* which it would seem to gloss admirably, having the senses of 'bubbling out' and of 'heat' that the Latin contains. Why then did Napier omit *torrentis* from his quoted lemma? Presumably on grammatical grounds. *Torrentis* is masculine genitive, agreeing with *solis*. Since *wallendre* is feminine (formally it could be either genitive or dative) it cannot render *torrentis* directly. Apparently Napier preferred to take it as a dative modifying *hæte* which he identified with the feminine noun *hæto* (even though on this reading there is no lemma for *wallendre*). If this was Napier's argument it is hardly conclusive. The form of *torrentis* is not unambiguously masculine, while *wallendre* could be thought to agree with an unspecified feminine *sunnan* translating *solis*. Or perhaps a careless scribe read the following *hæte* and unthinkingly made *wallendre* agree with it. Personally I would take the manuscript form as supporting a pair *torrentis, wallendre* here, particularly as, between *wallendre* and *hæte*, there is a gap rather wider than is usual between successive words.

2. MS BODLEIAN, RAWLINSON G.57

This manuscript has the Cato and Ilias glosses published by Förster and Napier.[10] The texts have both Latin and English glosses, each in more than one hand. There are several anomalies in the pattern of Old English glossing that a knowledge of the manuscript explains. For instance, Förster and Napier record a number of abbreviated glosses, those that give only part of the glossing word. In the printed text these look like what L. Goossens called 'merographs', that is glosses deliberately abbreviated since the shortened form gives the reader as much information as he needs.[11] Normally a merograph would not inform the reader of the meaning of the lemma, but remind him of a meaning that he already knew was attached to the lemma. In Rawlinson G.57, however, there is often good practical reason why an Old English word is abbreviated. For instance, Förster and Napier 9 reads *sumptus i. substantia, spen*, the last word for *spendig*. At this point the text reads *cum sumptus habundat* and the line above has *uexat*, with the tail of one stroke of *x* descending into the space above *sumptus*. The English glossator wrote 'spen' and was then stopped by this descender so he did not complete the word. The Latin gloss *i.substancia* follows the descender, above the opening of *habundat*, and it is tempting to think that this left no space for the completion though in fact we do not know the order of writing of the glosses. The glossator may have been satisfied with the incomplete *spen* since the full word *spendig* already appeared glossing *sumptum* earlier in the text. Again, Förster and Napier 18 reads *in aduersis i. in contrariis, widerw*, the last word expanded as *wiðerward*. When the glossator reached the second *w* he came up against the descender of the first letter of *quicquid* in the line above, and did not bother to complete the word after it. Cases like these are different from those abbreviated glosses elsewhere where there is no purely practical reason for the abbreviation; where, say, the first two letters of the gloss are put in and thought adequate to act as an *aide-mémoire*.

I do not claim that there is anything revolutionary in what I have said here about these manuscripts. I simply point out how deficient are transcripts in glossary form, even good transcripts like those printed by Napier and Meritt. They certainly cannot give the gloss scholar all he needs. Indeed, I have suggested that they cannot give even the lexicographer all he needs, whereas the student who is interested, not just in Latin-Old English equivalents, but in the nature of glossing, the reasons it took the forms it did and the audience the glosses appealed to, will find many of the existing editions of limited use. There is no substitute for the manuscript, but there may be better ways of publishing the gloss material, of defining it more precisely, and it is time these were explored.

It is worth looking at some of the things that the gloss scholar wants to know about the manuscripts I have been speaking of. In his introduction to the Gg.5.35 glosses Napier noted that, though the manuscript is from Canterbury, the dialect of its English glosses is West Saxon, not Kentish.[12] The implication is that the glosses record a single dialect, and this evades the point that they are not all in the one hand. Rigg and Wieland distinguish two hands supplying the original three classbooks, and think these also responsible, each within its own section, for most of the glossing.[13] In so far as this applies to the Old English glosses we should perhaps be looking for two idiolects rather than one dialect, and so it is important to have the glosses attributed to their particular hands. Moreover, to one with no special expertise in paleography it seems that occasional Old English glosses are not by the main scribes. A clear example is Napier no. 43, 3, *regio*, *kynedome* which looks in a different, less professional, hand from the text hereabouts, and is probably in the same that wrote occasional Latin glosses nearby, as *longinqua* over *ulterior* a few lines above. Of course, even the distinction of hands made here is naive. If Rigg and Wieland are right, it seems likely that the two main scribes of Gg.5.35 were copying a text already glossed, indeed were copying the glosses alongside the text. In the archetype, however, such glosses may have been in several hands, added at different times. In that case the two main hands of the manuscript would give a misleading impression of homogeneity and coherence.[14]

Gg.5.35 should give educational information whether, as Rigg and Wieland think, the manuscript was compiled 'for classroom use' or whether it should rather be understood as the library copy of a school collection of texts. It is then interesting to examine the scatter of both Latin and Old English glossing throughout the texts. In Aldhelm's riddle collection, for instance, the distribution is irregular. In the preface and first 40-odd riddles (up to and including *de hirundine*) there are quite a lot of Latin glosses but only one English one, *swa* for *sic*, Napier 1. It does not seem a word hard enough to need glossing, but presumably here the glossator is guiding the reader through the massed columns of the entry on *sic* in Lewis and Short. After *de hirundine* there is little or no Latin glossing and no English until the final great riddle *de natura*, which is highly annotated. Here the Old English glosses are equivalents of their Latin lemmas, except in the case of Napier 53 where, as he points out, *mǽl scaua*, 'caterpillar', renders the whole line *centenis pedibus gradior per gramina ruris*. The Latin glosses and notes are of various kinds. Some are simple equivalents, as *mouentur* for *uertuntur*, *sopore* for *somno*. Others add words that the glossator thought would help the reader gain the sense. *Setigero rursus constans audacior apro* has, over *rursus*, the words *s.sum*; over *uellera* in the line *candidior niuibus dum ningit uellera nimbus* is *s.sua* in case anyone has not followed the image. Sometimes the Latin adds detail: to the phrase *flagrantior halans* the glossator has added *ut cinamomum & balsamum*. Sometimes the Latin divides the complex riddle into its various meanings. For instance, over the two lines

> Peruigil excubiis numquam dormire iuuabit
> Sed tamen extemplo clauduntur lumina somno

are the comments *Animal quoddam est quod nunquam dormit ut mfqxt* (the last a code form of *lepus*) and *Alia loquitur creatura econtra*. Finally there are marginal comments on the content of the riddle: *Sententia hec uaria & multiplę quia loquitur de uisibili & inuisibili. de mortali & inmortali. de honesto & inhonesto*, opposite the opening lines. The implication is that Latin glosses served the needs of more advanced readers than Old English. English was used to give definitions or equivalents of hard words; the Latin also to expound the content and technique of the poem.

If the glossing of this schoolbook tells us what was read – or expected to be read – from it, it seems there was little or no interest in many of Aldhelm's riddles. The early ones may have been studied, but it is the last that attracted most attention, apparently from beginners and advanced alike since its glosses show a range of approaches. Ker and Cameron list three other substantial glossed manuscripts of these riddles, British Library Royal 12 C xxiii (Napier no. 26), British Library Royal 15 A xvi (Napier no. 25) and Bodleian, Rawlinson C. 697 (Napier no. 24). The two last have few English glosses, only one coinciding with those of Gg.5.35. Napier's text of the Royal 12 C xxiii glosses has 75 entries spread much more evenly throughout the riddle corpus, and its glosses to the *de natura* riddle show little similarity to those of Gg.5.35 as I shall show later. To get a real impression of the importance of our manuscript in the schools we need an account of the Latin glossing in other Aldhelm riddle manuscripts to give a standard of comparison.

The scribe of the base text of Gg.5.35 was not always accurate or sensible. For instance, in the phrase *necnon accipitre properantior* he has misread the second word and divided it *accipit re* which looks Latin but is not. Despite this the correct gloss 'musħ' for *mushafoc*, 'mouse-hawk', is put in over *accipit* without any indication that the lemma needs emendation. It looks as though the English was copied mechanically from an exemplar without any understanding of the Latin.

Finally, if this is a schoolbook, one might expect to see signs of handling and perhaps casual annotation, as on that typical schoolbook, the Sedulius section of MS Corpus Christi College, Cambridge, 173. In fact there is comparatively little sign of use, and perhaps this was a schoolbook more in theory than in practice.

In the case of Rawlinson G.57 the arrangement of the glossing, Latin and English, can sometimes give information on priority. Sometimes Latin precedes Old English, sometimes Old English precedes Latin, and in particular there is a Latin hand that adds explanatory and detailed comment on meaning which certainly is later than the laconic Old English translation glosses. For instance, in the phrase *prospice qui ueniunt* the first word has over it a Latin gloss *i.alonge aspice* (Förster and Napier 15); there follows in the base text *qui* written with a superscript *i*, and the Old English gloss to *prospice* then has to follow the superscript and to stand above the following word *ueniunt*. Here it is fairly clear that the space above *prospice* was already filled when the later English glossator came to write *forsceaƿ þu*. On the other hand Förster and Napier point to a couple of cases (21, 36) where there is a Latin gloss that postdates the English one. The Old English is in several hands, and if my interpretation is right, three closely following English glosses, *se idele*, *ƿeregat* and *spen* (7–9) could well be in three different hands. The implication of all this is that the text was being continuous glossed, some scribes using Latin, some English.

Anyone reading through Förster and Napier's text of this manuscript's Cato glosses will be struck by how often OE *gelimp* and related words occur as translations: 16 *hos casus, þas limpes*; 22 *occasio, gelimp*; 75 *si forte, gif þu mid gelimpe*; 83 *fati, limpes*; 92 *forsan, mid gelimpe*; 94 *cui sis discrimine, þam þu on ungelimpe*; 96 *si contingat, gif gelimpat*; 99 *fortunę limpe*. A conclusion from this might be that the glossator was trying to show the reader how different Latin words could be rendered by the same (or a related) Old English word. Alternatively, of course, he may just have been an unimaginative commentator whose range of English words was small – there are other, less striking, repetitions within these glosses.

Before we could conclude either of these, however, we should have to be sure that all these glosses were entered by the same hand, and on this Förster and Napier give no information.

My experience hitherto is that practically any glossed manuscript, if looked at in detail, will yield information on glossing that is hidden in the existing editions. For instance, British Library MS. Harley 110 is a late tenth-century English manuscript with texts of Prosper's *Epigrammata* and Isidore's *Synonyma*. They have a few, mainly interlinear, Old English glosses, published as Meritt (1945) nos. 23 and 21, but are much more heavily glossed and annotated, in several hands, in Latin. Ker judged that the Old English was nearly contemporary with the texts and their Latin glosses. Of Meritt's three examples from Prosper, two give evidence of the relationship between the English and the Latin. The first, Meritt 1, is *penetralibus.i.secretis, incofun*. This is in a well-annotated line that runs

i.secretis

i.mansitat i.potens *.i.$\overline{xps}$*

incofun

Inque illis habitat diues penetralibus hospes

All four Latin glosses are in the same hand. Three, *mansitat*, *potens* and *cristus* are roughly in line midway betwen the two text lines; but *secretis* is higher up, raised to avoid *incofun* which is written low down just above its lemma. Had the Latin glosses preceded the Old English, *secretis* would presumably have been on a line with the others, and *incofun* squeezed in as best may be. Thus either *incofun* preceded the Latin glosses or all the glosses were written at the same time, which is unlikely unless the Latin and English are in the same hand, which seems not to be the case. The second gloss shows that Old English had clear priority over the Latin. The word *exilio* is glossed *wræcsið*, Meritt 2, the Old English not attempting the Latin case ending. The Latin *i.peregrinatione* is then added above and to the right of the lemma, and indeed after the descender of *proximus* in the line above. The third gloss is *.i.brædas* above *figmenta*, Meritt 3. Here there is no parallel Latin, but I would not be surprised if the English is in the same hand as neighbouring Latin glosses, for instance *.i.liberiora* over *absolutiora*. If so, the two languages were recorded here at about the same time.

The Old English glosses of this manuscript are so scanty that it is worth asking why these particular words were glossed at all, and to this I can give no reply. Two may have been common equivalents for Latin words. Certainly *incofu* glosses *penetralia* in an Aldhelm passage,[15] while *exilium* is commonly rendered *wræcið* in the glossaries.[16] I know of no other case of the pair *figmenta, brædas*. There are in any case plenty of other words in this text which have common Old English glosses, nor are the specific words glossed in this manuscript especially hard ones. I can only assume that the English glossing is sporadic and haphazard.

There is a contrast with the extensive and more purposeful Latin glossing of this manuscript. This is obviously originally intended to help the reader get a grasp on the meaning of the text by giving:

1. Synonyms, as *bona* for *pia*.
2. Correlations between different parts of speech, a modifier and its noun, a relative and its correlative, etc.; as *omne operum meritum transit amore dei/quo (s.amore)*.
3. Explication of meaning, when a noun or adjective refers indirectly to someone, as *cristus* for *hospes*, *marię* for *matris*.
4. Explication when the text gives a metaphor; as *puluis* glossed *nihilum, sapientia* glossed *cristus dominus noster*.
5. Addition of a preposition to explain the use of an oblique case; *hoc* with *ex* added, *pro* put in above *amore*.
6. The name of the case given when the form is ambiguous; as *abl.* added above *domino*.
7. A difficult abbreviation explained, as *etiam* over 7 *m*.
8. Elaborate comment on the meaning of the text.

Yet the contrast between Old English and Latin suggests that the Latin glosses are not intended simply to illuminate the text. They are also part of a scheme to teach Latin vocabulary. In the case of *incofun* glossing *penetralibus*, for instance, the Old English would be enough to give the reader the meaning of the word, and it would be unnecessary to add *i.secretis* if the Latin glossator were concerned only with meaning. The same applies to the group *exilio, wræcsið i.peregrinatione*. In these cases it looks as though the Latin glossator is giving the reader a set of further Latin equivalents so as to increase his stock of vocabulary, rather than to help him follow the text. In turn this throws light on the Latin-Latin, where there is no English equivalent. It could explain, for example, why the glossator put *mansitat* (which I suppose is a rarish word) above *habitat* (which must have been common enough). It was not to explain *habitat* but to introduce the reader to a new Latin word.

Finally, a brief comment on the glosses to Aldhelm's riddles in British Library Royal 12 C xxiii (Napier no. 26), which has already been mentioned. Of the 75 English ones that Napier gives, three coincide with those in Gg.5.35. Only one of these is a complete correspondence, *Sic, swa* (26, 6; 23, 1) and this is the one Old English gloss of Gg.5.35 that falls outside the last riddle. The 59 glosses of the final riddle in Gg.5.35 compare with only ten to this riddle in Royal 12 C xxiii. Of that ten there are two that have part equivalents in Gg.5.35: *ceu serica pensa, swaseolcenðræd* (26, 73), *seoloken toppa* (23, 44–5); *atomo, mote* (26, 74), *dust swerme.oððmote* (23, 52). There are three cases where a common lemma has a different gloss: *zephiri, suðernes*, wrongly (26, 67), *westernes windes* (23, 17); *calamistro, of wolcspinle* (26, 70), *þrewel spinle* (23, 26); *Pallida, æ* (26, 71), *wann* (23, 34). The other five lemmas of Royal 12 C xxiii are not thought to require an English equivalent in Gg.5.35. The two gloss groups show little similarity. They are clearly independent, representing the reactions of two different (sets of) readers to the text. A fairly cursory examination of Royal 12 C xxiii gives something of the principle on which the lemmas were chosen. A glance at Napier's edition shows many of the glosses signalled as marginal. In fact, Napier's practice in this respect is misleading. If the first word of a line is glossed in the left-hand margin, or the last word glossed in the right-hand one, Napier does not always signal it. So, for instance, the glosses to *Pallida*, *Sperula*, first words of their lines, are in the left-hand margin (gutter) of the manuscript alongside their lemmas; those to *halans*, *ceu serica pensa* and *atomo* are in the right-hand margins, since these are final words, and the gloss to *calamistro*, also a final word, begins above its lemma and spreads into the margin. Only four words out of the ten in the final riddle are other than first or last words; one of these has a marginal gloss, the other interlinear. This concentration on first or final words in a line hardly looks chance. The riddle averages almost exactly six words to the line, so with random distribution there is a one in six chance of any gloss being on the first or on the last word, and a one in three chance of it being one or the other. Six out of ten glosses on first or last words looks well above random and suggests that the distribution of glossing over the whole riddle collection needs looking at. Napier's 75 examples include two from the prefatory letter, which is not in verse. Of the remaining 73, six are to riddle titles (for it is obviously important to understand the solution to a riddle) and one is a long marginal descriptive gloss that I will deal with later. That leaves 66 within the body of the riddles and their prefatory poem. Nine of these glosses are on the first word of a line, which is non-significant. Twenty-six are on the last word of a line, and this is clearly significant. Striking is Napier 4, from the introductory poem. The last letters of the lines of this poem form the telestich ALDHELMVSCE-

CINITMILLENISVERSIBVSODAS, and are in capitals separated from the body of the text by a gap. It is in this gap that Napier 4 is written: thus, 'menti ḡþoht S'. It seems a bizarre conclusion, but a practical one, that a lot of the riddle lemmas were chosen, not primarily because they were important or hard words, but because they were final words with plenty of space to accommodate a gloss. Indeed in some cases the glosses look like casual later additions in an available gap. If this summary of the evidence is correct, there is no educational reason for choosing many of the lemmas of this text, only one of convenience or layout, and again the traditional method of printing these glosses hides the significant detail.

Before leaving this point I must look briefly at another aspect: the possibility that Napier's presentation of the material is inaccurate. The difficulty of marginal glosses is that, unless the scribe makes special provision for cross-referencing, there is no certain way of attributing a gloss to the right lemma. Napier points to this problem in his note on gloss 17 of this text. Another example may be Napier 3, *erroR*, *hi*. Presumably Napier takes the gloss *hi* as referring to *error* because it is in close proximity to that word; indeed it is written in the gap before the last letter in his prefatory poem, 'erro hi R'. However, Napier does not explain what *hi* means here. In fact the sentence contains the phrase *uana specie* (in the following verse line), and OE *hiw* is a common gloss for *species*. Whether *hiw* could be a gloss for *error* I doubt, and certainly Ball and Cameron give no example. Did Napier get the right lemma for this gloss, then? Removing from Napier's list a number of doubtful examples (3, 17, 25, 28, 30, 59) still leaves 20 cases of glosses on final words, which remains a significant number. But I am left feeling that, before we can reach a conclusion, we need a closer examination of this manuscript's glosses than Napier's edition allows.

Before leaving Royal 12 C xxiii I would like to make one further comparison with Gg.5.35. Royal 12 C xxiii also has Latin glosses as well as Old English. Simple Latin glosses to words are invariably interlinear, and the only marginal Latin glosses are the extended commentaries on difficult words or the comments on the structure of the text, as in Gg.5.35. As in Gg.5.35 extended marginal glosses are in Latin but there is one exception, a detailed Old English description, now damaged and only partly read, DE SCILLA (Napier 26, 61).[17] Some of the English glosses of this manuscript are grammatical rather than lexical. For instance, the prepositional glosses, *Sole*, *of* (5), *fronde*, *on* (58), *aruis*, *on* (60) and *certamine*, *on* (68), all interlinear, show the glossator(s) using English prepositions to indicate the meanings of the Latin ablative as the

Gg.5.35 glossators used Latin prepositions. It seems then that in Royal 12 C xxiii there is a more extended use of the vernacular for glossing.

Of course, we need here too a more detailed examination of the hands responsible for the Royal 12 C xxiii glossing to see if different glossators showed different practices. Ker distinguishes two hands[18] but I do not think – I speak with great hesitation here – that his account of this manuscript is one of the best entries in his catalogue, and I would hope for a more detailed investigation linked to the principles of glossing shown in the text.

It is easy enough to criticize existing publications of the Anglo-Saxon glosses, but hard to suggest improvements that can be put into practice. As an example of some of the problems I take a difficult and complex glossed text (plate III), the schoolbook that has as its main item Sedulius's *Carmen Paschale*, Corpus Christi College, Cambridge, MS 173 part 2.[19] Lowe dates the manuscript to the eighth century and places it 'in England, probably in a Kentish centre'. It was at Winchester c. 900, for scribe 1 of the Parker Chronicle (part 1 of this manuscript) filled lacunae in the Sedulius text about then. The Chronicle text went to Canterbury c. 1000, and the Sedulius section probably, but not certainly, went with it. There are Old English glosses in Caroline minuscule which Ker attributed to several scribes of the tenth and eleventh centuries; Parkes, however, has suggested that the Caroline forms are 'not inconsistent with a mid-tenth-century date'.[20] There are also scratched Old English glosses, and Latin glosses both inked and dry-point. I give here the opening of Sedulius's prologue to his *Carmen* (f.59r, col.1).

1 INC[IP]IT
2 PAS
3 CHALES QUI
4 cumque dapes
5 conuiuaj^{e}rquiris; Digna
6 tus nostris Accubi
7 taretoris; Pone
8 super cilium Site cog
9 noscis amicum. Necquę
10 ras opus hic codicis
11 artificis . Sedmodicae
12 contentus . adi sollemnia
13 mensae . Plusque libens animo
14 quam sati a-re, cibo;
15 A t si magnarum caperis

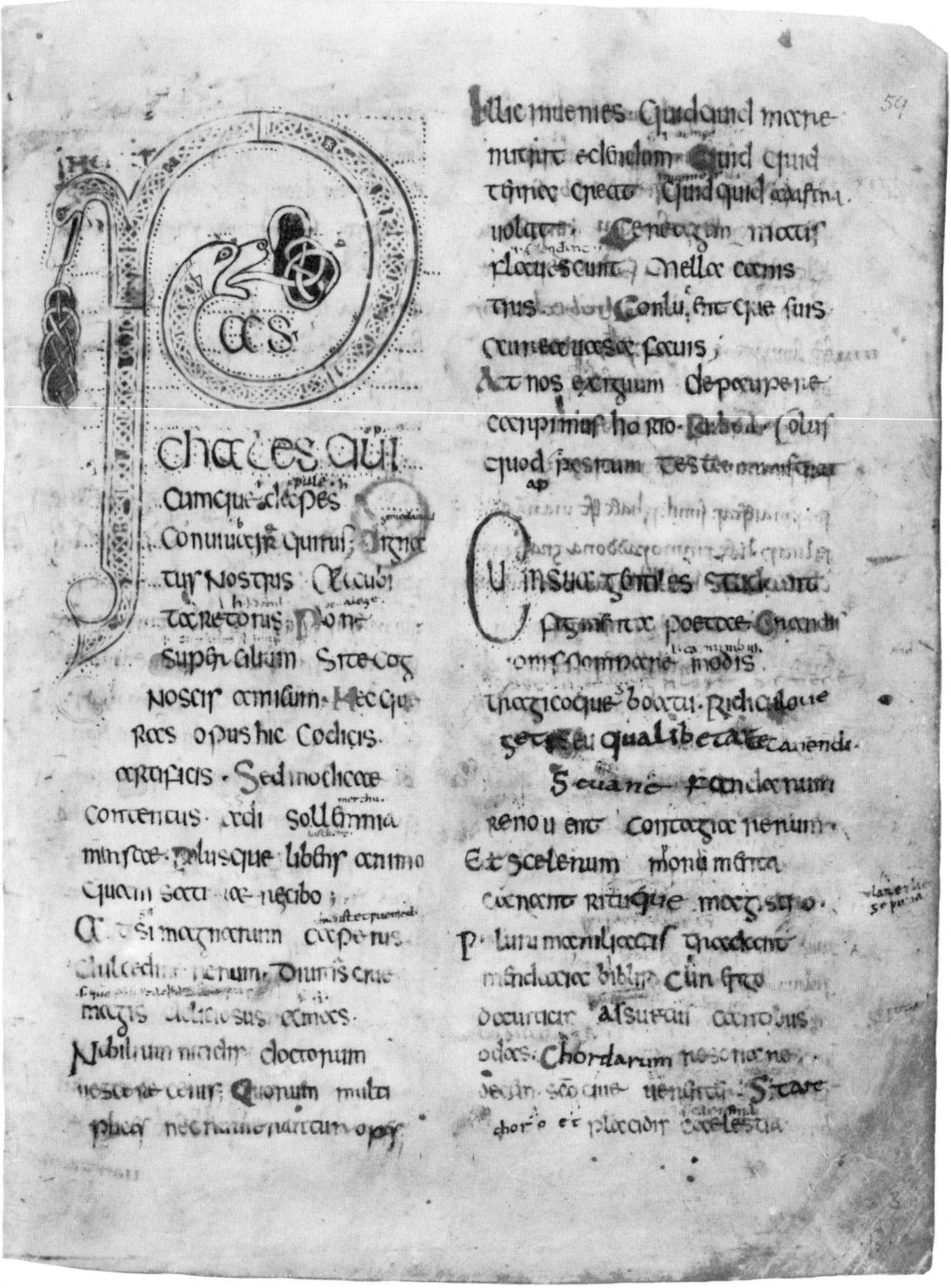

III. Cambridge, Corpus Christi College, MS 173 pt 2, f.59r: Sedulius, beginning of the Prologue to *Carmen Paschale*.

16 dulcedine rerum . diuit^{a}is que
17 magis deliciosus amas.
18 Nobilium nitidis doctorum
19 uescere cenis; Quorum multi
20 plices necnumerantur opes;

Of course it is impossible to reproduce in type the exact form of the original (see plate III). Some things are uncertain – spacing between words or the distinction between capital and lower case, while punctuation is also a problem. Hence the above is only an approximation. Even then, however, it is some distance from the scribe's original since the manuscript underwent some alteration at an early date, and the question must arise whether the alteration preceded or postdated the glossing. Either the ink must have become damaged or was liable to fade unevenly; at any rate, a later writer (perhaps the scribe 1 who touched up parts of the text elsewhere) inked over some parts: probably bits of line 2 (the ornamental initial and its two inset letters) and odd letters elsewhere in the column. Some capitals were certainly rewritten in a red ink that has remained fairly bright. There are a few substantial textual alterations. On line 5 the prefix *re* seems to have been put in afterwards (though perhaps by the original scribe). Line 14 had some sort of error or alternative reading that cannot now be recovered. Though it now has *satiare* there is a gap between *i* and *a* where a letter has been removed; *a* has been joined by a hyphen to the following *re* which is now divided from the following word *cibo* by a comma. The first word of line 15 has been also amended, apparently from *Aut* to *At*, while on line 16 *a* was inserted to turn *diuitis* into *diuitias*. There may be alterations and additions to the punctuation.

Both Meritt and I printed glosses from this *Carmen Paschale*, but our publications are incomplete.[21] There are several Latin glosses in these lines that we both ignored, as well as a number of single-letter glosses or annotations. Further examination reveals a few Old English glosses that we missed too. I give below, as far as I can, the full glossing of this column, using the following conventions: inked glosses between single inverted commas, scratched glosses between round brackets (); glosses above their lemmas unless otherwise stated; line numbering as in my text above; * indicates that this is not the original reading of the lemma; two glosses to the same lemma where I cannot determine the priority are separated by commas; where I can suggest priority this is indicated by numbers; / gives the line end of a word on more than one line.

3 *qui/*: 'p.'
qui/cumque: (swa hwe/lc swa/þv) 'a' in three lines in the

inner margin,

4 *dapes*: 1, '.i.epule.h'; 2, (symblv)

5 *conuiua*: 'b', (ḡbr̄)

digna/tus: 'gemedamad'

6 *accubi/tare*: (hlinian/ł sit/tan) on three lines, partly in the centre margin.

7 *toris*: 1, 'h.i.domibz'; 2, (ræstv̄)

pone: 1, 'de, alege.'; 2, (onhłd)

8 *super cilium*: a long inked gloss partly erased along with the *P* on the preceding line; begins *.i.superbiam* but the continuation is illegible.

9 *quę/ras*: (r) if that is not an accidental mark on the parchment.

10 *hic*: (hr̄)

12 *contentus*: a lightly scratched English gloss of which little is legible: (e[. . . . .]). The second letter may be intended as majuscule *a* and the final one as *g*; perhaps some compound of *eaþ-*.

adi: (þa, ḡs ec)

sollemnia: 'merthu.'

13 *libens*: 'lustbere.'

14 **satiare*: a scratched Latin gloss, imperfectly legible, but which seems to be (imp̄[.]tiare)

15 *si*: 'gif'

caperis: 1, 'th[u]bistetwuemed.'; 2, (ḡfange)

16 **diuitias*: (s̄files), apparently, though the line over *s* could perhaps be a continuation of the top stroke of that letter. Could this be a form of *(ge)sundfules*, 'prosperous', in which case it presumably glosses the original reading *diuitis?*

17 *magis deliciosus*: a Latin inked gloss, only partly legible, beginning '.s.quō'

deliciosus amas: (þv bleofvl b̄liofest)

amas: 's.si.', (si)

18 *nitidis*: (h̄.s̄.)

19 *uescere cenis*: (greordan ḡreordv̄), with two words, (? beo, þv) in the inner margin

I have here corrected a couple of details in the existing editions of these glosses. On line 15 Meritt 44 read *thu bist etwuenied*. The past participle *etwuenied* worried him since 'the verb *ætwenian* means "to wean from" but the context here requires something like "to attract"'. It is equally possible to read here *ætweman* which would give better sense. It is not recorded elsewhere, but there are several examples of *(ge)weman*, 'attract, allure', and a compound with *æt-* in the sense of 'to, towards' is plausible enough. Campbell took up this gloss as a quotation to illustrate *ætwenian*, and this needs removing from the corpus, and the Toronto Old English Dictionary editors need alerting to a new word *ætweman*. I would also make a change to my reading of the gloss to *deliciosus amas* in line 17. Previously I took this to be (b̄ldofvl) or perhaps (b̄lædofvl). Now I am inclined to think that the stroke that I read as the ascender of *d* is in fact accidental, and that the correct interpretation is (bleoful). Again no such word is recorded, but I would liken it to *bleofæstnes*, 'pleasure, delight', and *bleomete*, 'a delicacy', both of which gloss, in different senses, *deliciae*.

There are quite a lot of things about the glosses printed here that I do not understand. There are, for instance, the single letter annotations. These are not, as far as I can see, syntax markers. In two cases they may be notes for the capitalization: *p* on line 3 and *a* in the inner margin of line 6 indicating that these two letters should be supplied, one in elaborate decorative form and the other in red, to the text. If so, there is no consistent annotation of this sort. The two separate letters over *nitidis* may be intended as single-letter glosses, standing for forms of *hador* and *scir*, but there is no way of proving it. Other glosses in this group show an interesting interaction between different types. *Pone*, for instance, has the Latin *de* added to tell the reader that this verb is to be taken in the sense *depone*, 'lay aside'. The Old English inked gloss *alege* translates this accurately. A second and later Anglo-Saxon has put in the scratched gloss (onhłd) which Meritt expands as *onhild*, not a very good equivalent of *depone*. I wonder why a second gloss (and a scratched one at that) was thought necessary when the reader had so much accurate help already. Some glosses guide the reader to the shape of the sentence. The two forms of *si* (why two?) over *amas* tell him that the conjunction is to govern that verb too. The added *þa* over *adi* shows him that this begins a new clause (If you are content with moderate fare, *then* approach the feast).[22] The two glosses to *caperis* are instructive. The inked one is correct. The later scratched one is wrong. Apparently its scribe took *caperis* as *caperes*, translating it with the singular past subjunctive active of *gefon* in disregard of sense. Interesting too are the glosses to *uescere cenis*. It rather looks as though the glossator took *uescere* to be an infinitive, for he translated it by one. Then perhaps the words *?beo þu* in the margin were added to show the reader that this should be taken as an imperative.

Clearly quite a lot can still be got from a small portion of a glossed text that has already been scrutinized very carefully. Of course, this still only skims the surface of the subject. We need to distinguish between the different hands that produced these glosses, which is hard enough for the inked ones and very difficult indeed for the dry-point. I think, for instance, but I am not sure, that over *adi* there are two hands at work, for the glossator who translated the verb as *gesec* was probably not the same man who put in *þa*. On the other hand, it is likely but not certain that the scholar who put in the Latin gloss over *satiare* also added some of the Old English dry-point glosses. Later it will be important to look at the linguistic characteristics of the separate glossators; and also to see how these glosses, in their various layers, fit in with Sedulius glosses elsewhere. Ker lists three other Sedulius manuscripts with Old English glosses, not to mention the small fragment Bodleian, Lat.Th.C.4. They are MSS Cambridge University Library Gg.5.35 (Napier no. 51), National Library of Scotland, Advocates' 18.7.7 (Meritt no. 30) and British Library Royal 15 B xix (Meritt no. 29). In the same ten verse lines as I have quoted from CCCC 173:

1. Gg.5.35 has no vernacular glosses (and indeed only one Old English gloss in the whole text). The Latin glosses are of two elementary sorts, and all in the one hand. Most are straight translations: *desideras* for *requiris*; *intellegis* for *cognoscis*: *ueni* for *adi*: *replere* for *satiare*: *delectaris* for *caperis*: *utere* for *uescere*. A few are simple interpretations: *paschales . . . dapes* is given as *sollempnes*, *celestia . . . misteria*; *thoris* as *carminalibus*; *diuitiasque* as *honores*; and *cęnis* as *carminibus*.
2. Advocates' 18.7.7 has two Old English glosses: *cræftboce* for *codicis artificis* and *estfulra* for *magis deliciosus*. Both are entered, in a distinctive hand, in the right-hand margin, and, as Ker notes, are comparatively late additions.[23] The Latin glossing is of a rather different sort from those mentioned hitherto. There are a few simple translation glosses, as *pone supercilium* given as *dimitte superbiam*, and perhaps *euangł* for *paschales* and *?pascuaria quasi habundantia* for *sollempnia*. There are explanations and additional comments – *adomnes* over *conuiua*, *tuo* above *animo*, and *in libro inuenies* above *quam satiare cibo*. But there are also etymological glosses derived from Isidore. Above *thoris* is written *torus dicitur ab tortis herbis*; linked to *supercilium* is *supercilia dicta sunt ex quo superposita sunt ciliis i.oculorum tegminibus*.
3. Royal 15 B xix has hardly any annotations. There is the marginal note METAFORA, opposite the opening line, and two additions to the text to clarify the wording; *Site* has an accent over the last vowel, presumably to show this syllable has some stress and so that there are two words involved; *Atsimagnarum* was run together, and an added vertical stroke

divides it into two groups, *Atsi magnarum*. Otherwise there is only one gloss, *depone* written over *Pone*, corresponding here with CCCC 173.[24]

Obviously no conclusion can be drawn from a check so slight, but a first glance might suggest that there was no strong tradition of Sedulius glossing in Anglo-Saxon England. The various Old English glosses may be individual attempts to clarify the text.[25] Glossing, however, may vary from page to page as individual readers got to work on the book, so at the least a carefully planned sample check of the whole work is needed; at best an edition of the whole gloss material. Ideally we should then be prepared to look at other glossed manuscripts that may have been in the same library (?Winchester, Canterbury) as CCCC 173, to try to trace the practices of an individual scriptorium. I do not know of any similar study of a group of glossed manuscripts from a single Anglo-Saxon house (and indeed there may be too few such manuscripts that can be certainly provenanced and dated), though some German scholars have approached vernacular glosses in this way. Classic, for instance, is J. Hofmann's examination and enumeration of those from the old library at Würzburg and from the Anglo-Saxon missionary field in Francia in general.[26] There are other Germans working on the glosses from individual houses, and it seems time for Englishmen to follow suit.

This paper, then, is a plea for a more varied approach to Old English glossing which will link it to the peculiarities of the base text and to the other glossing of the manuscript. There are, of course, practical problems, since it is difficult to know (a) how to set out the results so as to make them easily available, and (b) whether the results would justify the amount of work put in. At the least the study of Latin and vernacular glossing together should do something to clarify the glossators' purpose, and this may even be a help to the lexicographer, even if it only confirms his 'healthy suspicion of glosses as indicators of normal usage'.[27]

APPENDIX: THE GLOSS *de Scilla*

The set of glosses connected with Aldhelm's riddle *de Scilla* in British Library MS Royal 12 C xxiii shows the importance of studying Latin and English glossing together. Napier printed the vernacular material alone, prefacing it with the title of the riddle;[28] but there are at this point three long glosses, two in Latin and one in Old English, and only the first is clearly linked by name forms to *Scilla*. This, the more important Latin gloss, is in the top margin of f.100v, a couple of lines above the beginning of the riddle (plate IV). A second Latin gloss is in the outer margin alongside the riddle. Below that is the Old English published by Napier as a single gloss, though probably it should be thought of as two. All these seem to be in the one hand. The top corner of this folio is badly damaged, apparently by damp, and the opening letters of most lines of each gloss are lost. The following are now visible; conjectural additions are in square brackets.

1. [Scilla] filia porci & cretidis nimphę pulcherrimę aglauco deo maris adamata est.
   [Circe] filia solis quę glaucu*m* amauerat cu*m* uiderit scilla*m* frequentare ad aliu*m* fontem
   ad[. . . . . n]du*m* iecit ueneficia infonte*m*. et in belua*m* marina*m* transfigurata est. et fretum siculu*m* (MS. silicu*m*)
   obsedit. ibiq*ue* p*rae*tereuntes naufragio afficiebat. ea*m* neptun*us* p*er*cussit tridenti. & inscopulu*m*
   mutauit. & sonos undaru*m* scopuli putant. Vnde uirg*ilius*. canes ininguine scillae;;
2. [. . . . .] filia
   [. . . . .] carmi
   [. . . . .] mersit clas
   [. . . .]cis;
3. [. . . . . .]e for^{s} ceop
   [. . . .] þet hi of þem
   [. . .] rigum gewiton
   [on] sæ 7 wurdon to hun
   [d] um./gecweden;
4. Scilla ðet is sǽhund

Napier read *wurdon to hundum* though I am less certain of the first letter of the last line. On the evidence of Napier's text *BTS* entered the occasional definition of the word *hund*, 'some sea-beast, a seal (?), a dog-fish (?)'. Meritt, however, noted that a link between Scilla and dogs is pointed in the first line of Aldhelm's riddle (*Ecce molosorum nomen mihi fata dederunt*), suggesting that the writer may have linked *Scilla* with Greek σκύλαξ, 'puppy', perhaps influenced by such a gloss as *Sculles: canes marini*. He concludes that the Old English gloss 3 'is merely a variation on the lore to the effect that sailors were thrown to the dogs with which the waist of Scilla was girdled', and the word *hund* used there simply means 'dog'.[29]

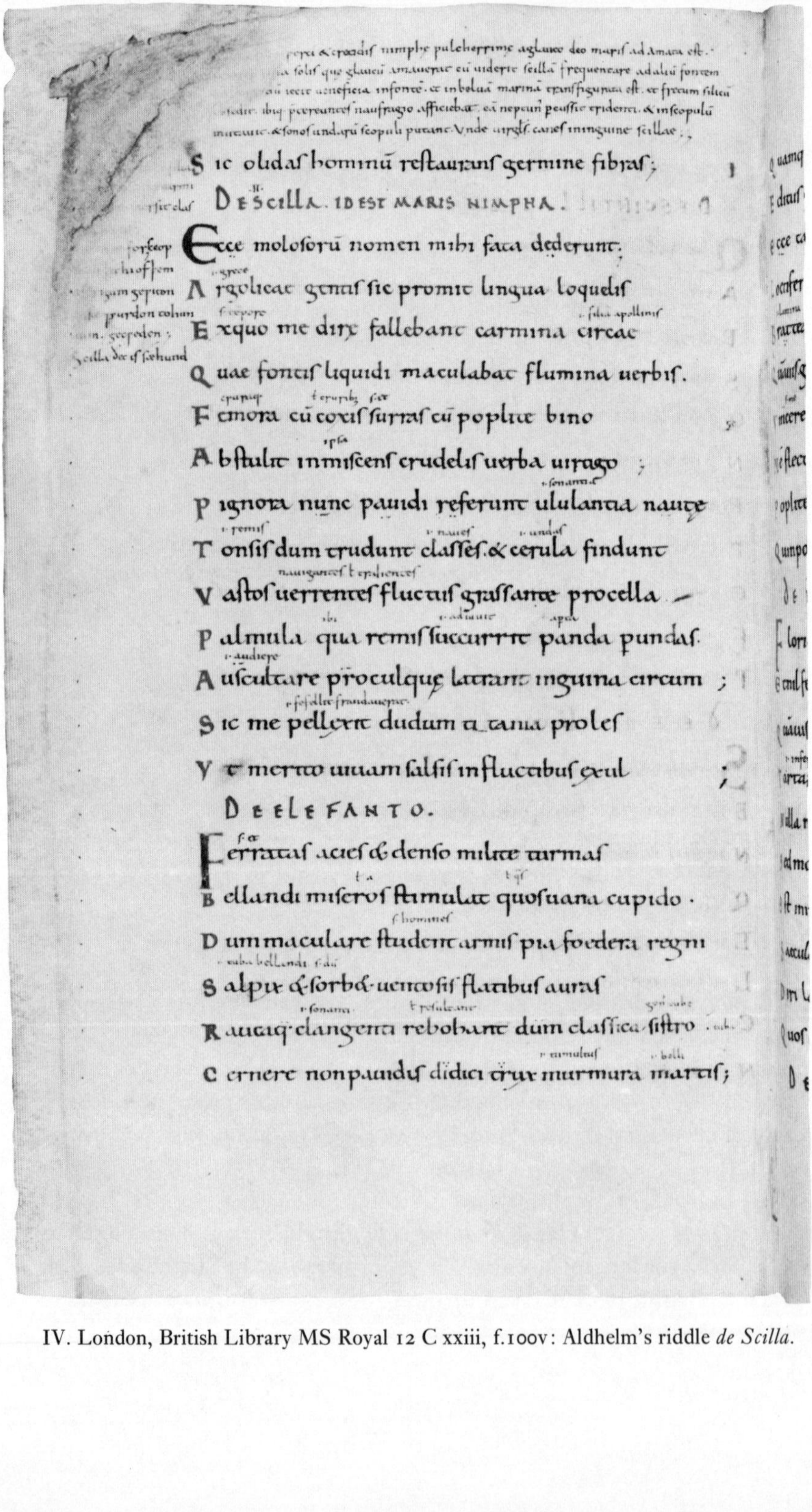
Sic olidas hominū restaurans germine fibras;
DE SCILLA. ID EST MARIS NIMPHA.
Ecce molosorū nomen mihi fata dederunt.
Argolicae gentis sic promit lingua loquelis
Ex quo me dirae fallebant carmina circae
Quae fontis liquidi maculabat flumina uerbis.
Femora cū coxis surras cū poplite bino
Abstulit inmiscens crudelis uerba uirago
Pignora nunc pauidi referunt ululantia nautae
Tonsis dum trudunt classes. & cerula findunt
Vastos uerrentes fluctus grassante procella
Palmula qua remis succurrit panda pundas.
Auscultare proculque latrant inguina circum
Sic me pellexit dudum titania proles
Ut merito uiuam salsis in fluctibus exul
DE ELEFANTO.
Ferratas acies & denso milite turmas
Bellandi miseros stimulat quos uana cupido.
Dum maculare student armis pia foedera regni
Salpix & sorbet uentosis flatibus auras
Rauciq; clangenti reboant dum classica sistro
Cernere non pauidus didici crux murmura martis;

IV. London, British Library MS Royal 12 C xxiii, f.100v: Aldhelm's riddle *de Scilla*.

The weakness of Meritt's position is disguised by the general way it is worded. The English is defective and the story it tells is therefore confused, but as far as I can make out it means '[. . . . . .] (sg.) transformed [. . . .] (pl.) so that they went from [. . . . . . .] (? *-igum*, 'islands') into the sea and turned into (?) dogs'. Whatever this is it is hardly a simple variant on the story about throwing sailors to Scilla's dogs. I suspect that Meritt was misled by the form of Napier's publication. The lemma *de Scilla* was Napier's choice, simply the title of the riddle near which the gloss was written.[30] Gloss 1 is clearly connected with Scilla by the name forms and the story. Gloss 4 names Scilla, but Napier's layout hides the fact that the glossator deliberately began a new line for it, leaving the previous line half-empty, to be filled with *gecweden* later. Glosses 2 and 3 have nothing obviously to do with Scilla.

Gloss 4 represents the etymology that links *Scilla* to σκύλαξ; perhaps *sæhund* is the equivalent of one of the related words for a sea-creature, σκύλιον or σκύλλα.[31] I have not traced where the glossator got the text of gloss 1 from if he did not compose it himself. The material is common enough in the early Middle Ages. Isidore, of course, has a couple of good accounts of Scilla,[32] and there are more detailed versions in Servius's commentary on Virgil (particularly on *Aeneid* III, 420) and in the Vatican glossators' collections on mythological themes.[33] From these can be parallelled most of the material in gloss 1 (though there is nothing quite so specific as Neptune's turning Scilla into a rock), as well as some of the wording, though none are the direct exemplars of our gloss. Gloss 1 is not explicit about the link between Scilla and the dogs – that Circe's poison so deformed her that she turned into a monster round whose loins dogs and wolves were girdled – nor does it make clearly the point that the sound of the waves about the rock Scilla resembled the barking of dogs, but all this is implied in the glossator's shorthand account.

The material of glosses 2 and 3 is baffling. Gloss 2 obviously began with a new character with a new patronymic. With conjectural material supplied to the third and fourth lines, this seems to say, '[. . . . .], daughter of [. . . . .], by her songs (? spells) sank the fleet of [. . . . . . .]'. I do not know who this could have been. There may be a connection with Scilla in the second Vatican mythographer's sentence *Haec* (i.e. Scilla now turned by Glaucus into a sea-goddess) *classem Ulixis cum sociis ejus evertisse narratur*. The subject of gloss 3 could not have been Scilla either if, as I read it, the first name ended with *-e*, and in any case there seems to be no story about Scilla that fits this wording. Just below the second Vatican mythographer's account of Scilla is the story of

Liber seized by Tyrrhenian pirates. Its climax is: *Quamobrem iratum numen tigrides sibi sacratas visibus eorum objecit: quo terrore se illi in fluctus dedere praecipites, et facti sunt delphini.*[34] Something like this may be the origin of gloss 3. At least, since that gloss is no longer connected to Scilla, there is no reason to translate *hundum* (if that is the correct reading) as 'dogs', which are hardly beasts you would expect to find in the sea. The *BTS* 'sea-beasts' or 'dog-fish' may not be a red herring after all.[35]

NOTES

1. R. Frank and A. Cameron, *A Plan for the Dictionary of Old English* (Toronto, 1973), 230–47.
2. *Ibid.*, 20.
3. R. I. Page, 'More Old English scratched glosses', *Anglia*, XCVII (1979), 27–45.
4. N. R. Ker, *Catalogue of Manuscripts containing Anglo-Saxon* (1957), 5.
5. A. Campbell, *Enlarged Addenda and Corrigenda* to *BTS* (1972), v. On this point B. Mitchell has recently written: 'Prepositions, adverbs, prepositional adverbs, post-positions, separable prefixes, or inseparable prefixes, in Old English?', *Neuphilologische Mitteilungen*, LXXIX (1978), 240–57. I am not even sure that Meritt's argument from sense is sound. He says, '*BTS* lists this gloss with the following one as *on toblawenum dracum*, but the context does not call for 'on swelling dragons'; rather it calls for 'with blown-on, windblown, dragons'.' The context is *signaque bellica praetendunt tumidis clara draconibus. Tumidis* certainly means 'swelling, swollen, puffed-up', but I do not know that it can mean 'blown-on' unless you think of the dragons being on some sort of banner, swollen because the wind blows it out. *Toblawan* is recorded (though rare) in the sense 'inflate, swell', and I am not clear that *ontoblawen* could have the sense 'blown-on', or what the particle *-to-* would be doing in such a meaning. As to the context, much depends on what an Anglo-Saxon reader would have made of it. Could he have taken the phrase *tumidis clara draconibus* as meaning 'bright (or famous) by virtue of their swelling dragons'? If so, *on toblawenum dracum* would be an acceptable Old English equivalent.
6. A. G. Rigg and G. R. Wieland, 'A Canterbury classbook of the mid-eleventh century (the 'Cambridge Songs' manuscript)', *ASE*, IV (1975), 113–30. But see Michael Lapidge's comments on this manuscript, p. 127 above.
7. R. I. Page, '"The proper toil of artless industry"; Toronto's plan for an Old English dictionary', *Notes and Queries*, n.s. XXII (1975), 151.
8. *Op. cit.* in n. 1, 338.
9. T. Wright, *Anglo-Saxon and Old English Vocabularies* (2nd edn, rev. R. P. Wülcker, 1884), I, 166, 12–14; 182, 19–21; 289, 18–19. *Steorstefn* for *puppi* is *ibid.*, I, 482, 15.
10. M. Förster and A. Napier, 'Englische Cato- und Ilias-Glossen des 12. Jahrhunderts', *Archiv*, CXVII (1906), 17–28.
11. L. Goossens, *The Old English Glosses of MS. Brussels, Royal Library, 1650 (Aldhelm's De Laudibus Virginitatis)* (Brussels, 1974), 29.

12. Napier, *Old English Glosses*, xvii.
13. *Op. cit.* in n. 6, 115.
14. Cf. the case of a large number of the glosses in MS Bodleian, Digby 146. These, Ker's group iii (*Catalogue*, 382), are in a single hand, but copied from glosses in a variety of hands in MS Brussels, Bibliothèque royale 1650.
15. Goossens, *op. cit.* in n. 11, 5282; Napier, *Old English Glosses*, 5407.
16. Wright-Wülcker, 116, 16; 172, 36; 397, 8.
17. See the Appendix to the present article.
18. Ker, *Catalogue*, 332.
19. *Ibid.*, 59; Lowe, *CLA*, II, *Great Britain and Ireland* (2nd edn, 1972), 3. M. B. Parkes has made a detailed study of the make-up and contents of this manuscript in 'The palaeography of the Parker manuscript of the *Chronicle*, laws and Sedulius, and historiography at Winchester in the late ninth and tenth centuries', *Anglo-Saxon England*, V (1976), 149–71.
20. *Op. cit.* in n. 19, 168.
21. Meritt, *Old English Glosses*, no. 28; R. I. Page, 'Anglo-Saxon scratched glosses in a Corpus Christi College, Cambridge, manuscript', in *Otium et Negotium: studies . . . presented to Olof von Feilitzen*, ed. F. Sandgren (Stockholm, 1973), 209–15.
22. The reading is not very clear, and Michael Lapidge has suggested that it should perhaps be (þv), showing that the following verb is to be taken as an imperative.
23. Ker, *Catalogue*, 150.
24. *Depone* is the reading in the corresponding passage of the prose *Opus Paschale* (Migne, *Pat. Lat.*, XIX, 549).
25. But see Michael Lapidge's remarks, pp. 113–16 above.
26. J. Hofmann, 'Altenglische und althochdeutsche Glossen aus Würzburg und dem weiteren angelsächsischen Missionsgebiet', *BGDSL* (Halle), LXXXV (1963), 27–131.
27. *Op. cit.* in n. 1, 6.
28. *Old English Glosses*, no. 26, 61.
29. H. D. Meritt, *Fact and Lore about Old English Words* (Stanford, 1954), 138–9.
30. The full title is *De scilla. id est maris nimpha.* Above *Scilla* is the symbol .π. to connect it with the appropriate gloss, but the openings of all the glosses are lost, so that this is now no help. In the practice of this scribe the appropriate gloss could be either in the margin or at the head of the page.
31. H. Fisch, *Griechisches Etymologisches Wörterbuch* (Heidelberg, 1960–70), s.v.
32. W. M. Lindsay, *Isidori . . . Etymologiarum sive Originum Libri XX* (1911), XI, 3, 32; XIII, 18, 4.
33. G. Thilo and H. Hagen, *Servii Grammatici. . . in Vergilii Carmina Commentarii* (Leipzig, 1881–1902), I, 417; III, 79; G. H. Bode, *Scriptores Rerum Mythicarum Latini Tres* (Cellis, 1834), particularly Myth. II, ch.169.
34. Myth. II, ch.171.
35. I would like to thank Geoffrey Woodhead and Michael Lapidge for guiding me through these Classical mysteries. Since this paper was written Michael Lapidge has pointed out to me a text that bears closely on the *de Scilla* gloss 1 of MS Royal 12 C xxiii. This is printed in H. Hagen, 'Scholia Bernensia ad Vergili Bucolica atque Georgica', *Jahrbücher für classische Philologie*, Supplementband IV (Leipzig, 1861–7), 803–4. The text obviously needs closer examination in an attempt to trace its relationship to the various glosses that I print in the Appendix to my paper, and Dr Lapidge hopes to return to it at a later date.

INDEX